1,001
WAYS TO
INSPIRE

Your Organization,
Your Team and
Yourself

1,001

WAYS TO

INSPIRE

Your Organization, Your Team and Yourself

By
David E. Rye

CAREER PRESS
3 Tice Road, P.O. Box 687
Franklin Lakes, NJ 07417
1-800-CAREER-1
201-848-0310 (NJ and outside U.S.)
Fax: 201-848-1727

1,001 Ways to Inspire Your Organization, Your Team and Yourself

Cover design by Jim Fanzone
Printed in the U.S.A. by Book-mart Press

To order this title, please call toll-free 1-800-CAREER-1 (NJ and Canada: 201-848-0310) to order using VISA or MasterCard, or for further information on books from Career Press.

Library of Congress Cataloging-in-Publication Data

Rye, David E.
    1,001 ways to inspire : your organization, your team, and yourself
/ by David E. Rye.
    p. cm.
    Includes index.
    ISBN 1-56414-348-1 (paperback)
    1. Employee motivation.   2. Teams in the workplace--Psychological
aspects.   3. Personality.   I. Title.
    HF5549.5.M63R935   1998
    658.3'14--dc21
                                                                    97-46188
                                                                        CIP

Acknowledgments

Without the help of my literary agent, Michael Snell, this book never would have been written. He worked with the publisher, prompted me, and most important, inspired me to push for the assignment. Through all of the challenges associated with this project, he never lost his patience or sense of humor. For all of his help I am extremely grateful.

A special thanks goes to Kristi and Kori, my daughters, who helped me with this project from its inception. They took care of the many details of the manuscript preparation and the research. Thanks also goes to my wife, Cheri, who put up with me and my grouchy, unmotivated moods after numerous late nights of working on the final manuscript. If it had not been for her inspiration, I never would have completed the project.

Contents

Introduction

It happens to all of us in business, social, and even family encounters. We meet people with common interests and instantly establish a rapport. We may laugh at the same things, or discover perhaps that we've had very similar life experiences. Then we meet others and it is a challenge just to hold a conversation. We're on guard, uncomfortable, and sometimes, inexplicably hostile. Why? We would probably shrug off the encounter as nothing more than a "personality conflict." And we would be right! Noted psychologists, such as the famous Meyers-Briggs team, group various aspects of personality and behavior into four different categories. For our purposes, we will name those categories as follows: Power Players (Type 1), Team Players (Type 2), Diplomatic Players (Type 3), and Party Players (Type 4). Each of these personality types will be described in Chapter 1.

Personality has always been a mystery to many people. They become frustrated when they do not understand the basis of their actions and reactions. Understanding your personality and the personalities of others is the only way to grow. *1001 Ways to Inspire Your Organization, Your Team and Yourself* shows you how to gather enough knowledge about yourself and others to begin controlling positive and negative personality attributes to achieve higher levels of motivation throughout your organization, and in your personal life as well. You'll learn how to apply the best elements of your own personality to motivate yourself and others. Knowing what your personality type is and how to apply its strengths to motivate others is an essential step if you want to climb the corporate ladder. You'll also learn how to bolster the weaker sides of your personality, how to accept others for what they are, how to establish working relationships with greater ease, and how to motivate others to do what you need to get done. The knowledge you gain from this book will give you the power to change your behavior when appropriate in order to influence and motivate others.

Your Personality Traits

Every child is born with a unique set of personality traits, which are often different from those of their brothers and sisters. Any parent will attest to the fact that, in most cases, their children show marked differences in their behavior. One may be very demanding while the other is content to quietly grow up. Everyone knows that no two sets of fingerprints are alike. How could we possibly believe that human personalities are any less unique than fingerprints? Some people see the world through rose-colored glasses while others see it through dark glasses. Unfortunately, we can't switch personalities in the same way we try on glasses. Personality is not black or white, but rather like a kaleidoscope, composed of many twists and preferences. We can only understand our own personality by opening our eyes to a whole new kind of understanding of ourselves and others. Personality is a solid core of traits reflecting the unique essence of a particular human being.

Your personality traits determine whether you are easily depressed, casual, formal, cautious, or carefree. They determine whether you are passive or assertive. Do you dash off at the last minute for an appointment or always arrive at a meeting with time to spare? Do you prefer to play a quiet game of chess on your personal computer or would you rather dance the night away with your friends? Your personality is key to how you react to these and other situations. It's what causes you to act and react the way you do.

In many respects, your personality watches over you and is what makes you different from everyone else. It tends to be rigid, resistant to change, and is very protective of itself and you. Your personality accepts you as its sole commander and does not like to venture out to experience or understand other types of personalities. Although it will accept criticism from you, your personality will not readily accept unsolicited criticism from others. In fact, it will often lash out if it feels threatened by an intruder.

Your Behavior Code

Your personality includes a behavior code, a core of thoughts and feelings that tells you how to conduct yourself in different situations. It's a checklist of responses that are based on your innate values and strongly held beliefs. Your behavior code directs your emotional and rational reactions to every life experience you encounter and even determines if you are more likely to use an emotional or rational reaction when confronted by an adverse situation. It is the active, ongoing process in your heart and mind that dictates how you think, feel, and behave.

Behavior codes point each of us in a particular direction. When we deviate from what these codes tell us, we feel uncomfortable. Without clear-cut personality traits to mark our paths through life, we will become lost, which is what a personality fears most. If you branch out from your personality's comfort zone, you'll feel disoriented and uncomfortable and become mentally exhausted when you try to deny or explain away thought processes that are unusual for you. You'll become confused and overwhelmed if your thoughts and feelings have led you to seemingly irrational behavior as you desperately try to right yourself and turn over a new leaf.

Understanding your personality traits and behavior code is vitally important to understanding yourself. If you don't understand yourself, it will be difficult for you to change bad personality traits. If you do not learn how to control your own personality, you can never hope to effectively motivate others.

How to Use This Book

1,001 Ways to Inspire Your Organization, Your Team and Yourself covers management techniques you can apply to motivate people—your employees, peers, senior management, friends, and even yourself. The proven method of teaching motivation by example is applied here. You'll be introduced to real business situations in a format that is as engaging as an action novel and as instructive as the best MBA programs.

Here's how to use this book. First, take the personality test in Chapter 1 to determine your personality type. Read Chapter 2 to learn the basics of how to motivate yourself. Then, read those sections that present problems similar to yours. A brief description of each problem is followed by a vignette in which the problem is played out. Then, motivation tips are broken down into each of the four personality types. For example, if you believe that you're dealing with a Type 1 personality, then zone in on the recommended motivation techniques that work best to solve Type 1 problems. These obviously will be different than the solutions for Type 2, 3, or 4 personalities. Certain paragraphs that provide additional help, warnings, or ideas are marked with icons. They are summarized as follows:

The **Help** icon flags handy information that will help you further understand the problem and solutions covered in a section. It may refer you to other chapters in the book, offer helpful tips, or, for complex problems, point you toward outside reading material.

The **Warning** icon cautions you to pay extra attention to key issues presented in a chapter. Warnings tip you off to potential career pitfalls if certain critical situations are ignored or improperly handled.

The **Idea** icon alerts you to solutions to problems covered in a section.

Because many outcomes in *1,001 Ways to Inspire Your Organization, Your Team and Yourself* can be applied to a wide variety of management situations, you will find yourself constantly referring to this book to find motivational strategies that best fit your situation. Good luck!

Chapter 1

Taking the Personality Test

This chapter will help you identify your personality and its primary attributes. By taking the personality test that follows, you will discover what type of personality you have (Type 1, 2, 3, or 4). You'll learn things about yourself that you were not aware of, such as why you have certain tendencies and reactions. You will also learn to identify the personality types of others, allowing you to understand them better and develop more meaningful relationships.

What is Your Personality Type?

When you take the multiple choice personality test, mark the answers that most readily come to you. Skip the more difficult questions and return to them later. If you need help, ask your friends and associates how they would answer a difficult question on your behalf. Strive to choose answers that are most often typical of your thoughts and actions.

After you take the personality test, you'll most likely find that your personality will not prove to be 100 percent any one type. A majority of individuals who fall primarily into one particular type will find it tinged with influences from the other types. If your test results reflect high scores in more than one personality type, you may at first find it difficult to identify your true personality. Don't worry. In Chapter 2 we'll help guide you in the right direction to determine your primary personality type and its attributes and drawbacks.

When you discover your personality type, you will see yourself more accurately and become more aware of your many strengths and weaknesses and the balance that exists in any personality type. But don't be discouraged by any of your weaknesses. In the next chapter, you'll learn how to overcome your limitations.

The Personality Test

On page 17, you will find the personality test. Choose the one word in each of the 40 word categories that best describes you most of the time. When you complete the test, add the total number of *a, b, c,* and *d* answers that you recorded. The letter with the greatest total reflects your natural personality type.

The Personality Types

Congratulations! As a result of taking the personality test, you have discovered the first important truth about yourself. If you recorded more responses in any one letter, or personality-type category, then you are predominantly that personality type [i.e., Type 1 (a), Type 2 (b), etc.]. You have a mixed personality if you recorded an equal number of responses in any two or more letters, or personality-type categories.

When you took the test, you were asked to select from many behavioral words because of the dominant role that behavior plays in shaping personalities. Behavior is determined by a person's needs and wants. For example, if you have a dominant need to always be right, you will likely display opinionated behavior, typical of the Type 1 personality. In Chapter 2, the behavior traits of each of the four personality types will be examined. A summary of each of the four personality types follows.

Type 1s are the *power players*. They like to have things done their own way and can have problems with authoritarian figures who may not allow them to do everything they want to do. Type 1s like to work, and if given the proper motivation, are highly productive individuals. They want to be knowledgeable in everything they do and actively seek out respect and recognition. They like to be in the driver's seat and will aggressively pursue any management position that will allow them to climb the ladder.

The Personality Test

a. Intimidating b. Careful c. Unproductive d. Afraid	a. Powerful b. Deliberate c. Gentle d. Optimistic	a. Determined b. Detail- oriented c. Good listener d. Social person	a. Direct b. Creative c. Adaptable d. Performer	a. Decisive b. Loyal c. Content d. Playful

a. Impatient
b. Moody
c. Passive
d. Impulsive
	a. Power
	b. Perfectionist
	c. Indecisive
	d. Self-
	   oriented
		a. Opinionated
		b. Nurturing
		c. Inventive
		d. Outgoing
			a. Calculating
			b. Self-
			   righteous
			c. Self-critical
			d. Disorganized
				a. Arrogant
				b. Concerned
				c. Stubborn
				d. Flighty

a. Task-driven b. Sincere c. Diplomatic d. Lively	a. Insensitive b. Judgmental c. Boring d. Undisciplined	a. Action b. Analytical c. Easygoing d. Carefree	a. Demanding b. Unforgiving c. Unmotivated d. Vain	a. Independent b. Dependable c. Even- tempered d. Trusting
a. Always right b. Guilt-prone c. Unenthusiastic d. Uncommitted	a. Critical b. Sensitive c. Shy d. Obnoxious	a. Dominant b. Sympathetic c. Tolerant d. Enthusiastic	a. Confident b. Disciplined c. Pleasant d. Charismatic	a. Logical b. Emotional c. Agreeable d. Popular
a. Assertive b. Reliable c. Kind d. Sociable	a. Responsible b. Idealistic c. Considerate d. Happy	a. Strong-willed b. Respectful c. Patient d. Fun-loving	a. Aggressive b. Depressed c. Ambivalent d. Forgetful	a. Self-serving b. Suspicious c. Unsure d. Naive

a. Argumentative
b. Unrealistic
c. Lack
   direction
d. No direction
	a. Tactless
	b. Hard to
	   please
	c. Lazy
	d. Loud
		a. Merciless
		b. Thoughtful
		c. Uninvolved
		d. Show-off
			a. Pragmatic
			b. Well-behaved
			c. Accepting
			d. Spontaneous
				a. Bossy
				b. Self-critical
				c. Reluctant
				d. Teaser

a. Protective b. Concerned c. Supportive d. Optimistic	a. Aggressive b. Caring c Easy-going d. Playful	a. Recognition b. Appreciation c. Respect d. Praise	a. Adventure b. Security c. Safety d. Excitement	a. Driven b. Deliberate c. Patient d. Spirited

a. Openly angry
b. Quiet
   revenge
c. Control anger
d. Avoid
   conflict
	a. Opinionated
	b. Responsible
	c. Accepting
	d. Positive
		a. Determined
		b. Honest
		c. Content
		d. Charismatic
			a. Productive
			b. Right
			c. Positive
			d. Easy
				a. Task-
				   oriented
				b. People-
				   oriented
				c. Free of
				   pressure
				d. Lighthearted

Total Scores

Type 1 (a) _____ Type 2 (b) _____ Type 3 (c)_____ Type 4 (d)_____

Type 2s are the *team players*. They look for opportunities to bring happiness to others. They'll hold doors open for others, offer rides when someone's car breaks down, and volunteer for company charity functions. More than anything else, they want others to like and respect them. Type 2s are in their best element when people listen to them and appreciate them. They'll readily admit to any mistakes they make and will seek out corrective advice in their search to be understood. Type 2s need to be constantly thanked for any good work that they do and come equipped with a strong sense of integrity.

Type 3s are the *diplomatic players* who will do almost anything to avoid confrontations. They like to work on teams where confrontations are neutralized with team consensus. Type 3s have a dominant need to always feel good about themselves. Although they are amiable people, they exhibit silent stubbornness when they are treated unkindly. They will open up instantly to people who are kind and will recoil like snakes to people who are hostile. They will seldom render an opinion unless it is solicited.

Type 4s are the *party players*. They are the happiest of all the personality types and consider life to be one big party at which they are the hosts. Type 4s need to be noticed and are in constant search for praise. As perpetual optimists, they believe they have the world by the tail and will only confide their fears and frustrations to people they trust. Looking good socially is very important to Type 4s. Friendships command a high priority in their lives because popularity answers one of their basic needs. Easily bored, they actively seek adventure and can never sit still for long periods of time.

Motivating Basics

Even the newest and least experienced manager realizes that employees who want to do good jobs usually produce more than those who don't. When people are genuinely committed to accomplishing organizational objectives, there is almost always a corresponding low rate of absenteeism, turnover, and all the other familiar drains on productivity. That is why employee motivation should be the number one concern of any organization. If you're looking for greater productivity in your work force, and you want your employees and co-workers to spend more time and energy on assigned tasks, then you need to figure out a way to motivate them to become more enthusiastic about their work and more committed to achieving goals that are important to you.

Independent of their personalities, all people possess a common set of needs and wants that, when triggered, activate their respective levels of motivation. There are five motivational premises that underlie the concepts in this book. Although the approaches applied in the examples may be different for each personality type, all personality types share common interests. Think about them and apply them when you attempt to motivate people in and outside of your organization.

People have reasons for what they do. Everybody has goals and objectives that they are constantly sorting through and choosing from to make everyday decisions. People do not act blindly when selecting goals. The selection process has direction for each individual, and others will not always agree with the goals that that individual selects. Your challenge as a manager is to influence individual members of your team, and ultimately your organization, to select and pursue goals that coincide with where you want them to go.

People act to gain something they believe is good for them. People's behavior is directed toward goals that they believe will be good for them. Their goals must, therefore, have perceived values to them before they will pursue them. For example, one of your best friends just inherited a fortune. You wonder why he doesn't take the opportunity to retire and do all the things he's always wanted to do. However, the gratification that this person is enjoying from his job overshadows his goal to achieve wealth.

People have to believe their goals are attainable. Most people, no matter how valuable a goal might be to them, won't make the effort to go after it unless they believe they have a good chance of attaining it. For example, an employee may fantasize about becoming the company's president, but won't do anything about it if she believes that her education is inadequate to reach the goal.

The value of a goal can change when unknown benefits are undesirable. A goal's value can change if its attainment comes with factors not desired—such as work environment or location. For example, your boss tells you that if you meet your sales quota for the quarter, you'll be promoted to branch manager. Your desire to become a branch manager has been one of your most important career goals. Your supporting goal of meeting your quarterly sales objectives is met, and in keeping with his promise, your boss promotes you to branch manager. When you learn that you will be branch manager in a remote location, the goal loses its value to you. Had your manager told you the location of the branch you would be managing before you started pursuing the goal, you would have sought another goal.

Managers play a major role. This is the essence of what this book is all about. Managers are an integral part of the goal-attainment process. People will only pursue goals if they are motivated. Likewise, if they do not have goals to pursue, they won't be motivated. As a manager, you need to know what actions to take in order to influence their choices of behavior. What you say and do can increase the expectations needed to motivate people to achieve common goals. And as a manager, you have a number of resources at your disposal to favorably influence people's motivation. Arranging special training, acquiring needed equipment, or rewarding behavior that moves the group closer to goal attainment can all play a major role in motivating people.

Although the emphasis of this book is on the behavior of others, we should first focus on you. An important consideration is how you look at people. If you convey the message, "I'm okay, you're okay," your chances of influencing the behavior of others will be improved substantially. If you show suspicion, flaunt your superiority, or reflect self-doubt, your chances of motivating anyone, including yourself, will be diminished greatly. Managers who convey the message that they are committed to the job and are winners are the ones who are moving their careers onto the fast track.

Chapter 2

Understanding
Your Personality

In Chapter 1, you took a personality test to determine your dominant personality type. It's important that you read and understand the material in this chapter before you begin to apply the motivational techniques and strategies covered in the remainder of the book. You'll learn how to quickly recognize the four personality types, what turns them on and off, and most important, how to motivate them to do what you want them to do. Also included is an in-depth discussion about the strengths and weaknesses of each personality type. This will show you how you can leverage the strengths and overcome the weaknesses of your own personality as well.

Type 1: Power Players

People with Type 1 personalities, often referred to as power players, are independent and want things done their own way. If they were raised in an environment where they were allowed to manipulate their parents, brothers, and sisters, they became more difficult to manage as they got older. If the situation was allowed to persist, it will be almost impossible for Type 1s to relinquish the power that they established from early childhood.

Type 1s like to work, are very career-oriented and are subsequently prone to becoming workaholics. If they are properly motivated, they'll always get the job done for you. However, they'll resist doing anything that doesn't interest them or that they don't believe in. Type 1s crave approval from others for their intelligence, want to be respected for their logical and practical minds, will debate any issue about which they feel strongly, and like to be knowledgeable about anything that interests them. They will argue the facts as they see them, but will seldom get emotionally involved in the discussion and are unmoved by emotional outburst—what they consider a display of weakness. Type 1s like facts and consider their own opinion simply to be a statement of the facts. When you deal with a Type 1, you must be precise and factual.

Type 1s love daring and bold sports, such as mountain climbing, skiing, and flying. They can often be found involved in major projects, such as building their own home or restoring a vintage sports car. If you can channel their energy into a work-related project that motivates them, they'll get the job done in record time. However, they can wear you down with their tenacious and bossy personalities. They're hard to work with because they like to order people around and display little regard for other people's feelings. If they are challenged, they can become very aggressive, and they are not afraid to vent their feelings in public without much tact.

The greatest weakness of Type 1 personalities is their inability to be intimate. They are so determined to be productive that they often ignore human relations. If this trait is not corrected, extreme Type 1s will ultimately aspire to the position of corporate hatchet man or woman, or be unemployable. Type 1s will be the first to tell you that they were out on their own at an early age with no help from anyone, and they are not about to help anyone else do it either. Most extreme Type 1s are either divorced, in the process of getting a divorce, or have no intention of ever getting married.

Type 1 Strengths

Known for their dominant nature and powerful leadership capabilities, Type 1s are the movers and shakers in any organization. They value productivity, love to set goals with precise completion dates, and like being in leadership positions. They become frustrated if they cannot control a given situation. They'll actively seek challenging assignments and, as a result of their tenacious nature, are often successful at whatever they commit to doing. Because of their productive natures, Type 1s are highly committed to causes and will work diligently to accomplish whatever life places in front of them. They crave productivity and measure their success in terms of how much they accomplish, and, quite often, in monetary terms.

Type 1s are not afraid to challenge those in authority and can become very resourceful at protecting themselves from unsolicited challenges. Because they are action-oriented, they're determined that no situation will get the best of them until they have exhausted every possible option. They are rarely intimidated by upper management or highly competitive situations. They will relentlessly pursue objectives in which they believe. If you need a team leader to tackle what may appear to be an impossible task, select a Type 1. He will throw himself into the project if he feels you have something to offer.

If asked for their advice, Type 1s will express themselves in a logical manner that few people can refute, and they always consider themselves to be right. Many Type 1s are notably intelligent and good decision-makers. Their desire to lead drives them to seek opportunities for advancement to the top of the organization.

To summarize their strengths, Type 1s:

- Excel with logical and creative thinking.
- Thrive on independence and in competitive situations.
- Are natural leaders who are committed to productivity.
- Verbally communicate their thoughts well.
- Set goals comfortably and with confidence.
- Are highly disciplined and make decisions quickly.
- Thrive in leadership and power positions.
- Are direct and quick with suggestions.
- Operate well under extreme pressure.
- Maintain high self-esteem.
- Are very dependable.
- Give work a high priority and take commitments seriously.

Type 1 Weaknesses

In spite of their self-confidence, arrogant Type 1s often suffer from insecurity complexes. To compensate for their insecurity, they'll seek acceptance and understanding from others. Type 1s can become so sensitive to their own insecurity that they will go to great lengths to hide it from others. Don't be surprised to see Type 1s abruptly leave a stressful meeting if they feel their security is threatened. If you confront them as to why they left the meeting, they'll refuse to acknowledge any emotional vulnerability and will tell you they left because they were bored or for some other nebulous reason.

Type 1s tend to be insensitive to other people's problems. For example, a Type 1 manager, after learning that the father of one of his key employees had died earlier that morning, calls the employee at home and asks him if he would be able to come into the office to complete a proposal he had been working on. Type 1s can be very insensitive to the feelings of others, a weakness that explains why they are more successful developing business ventures than maintaining personal relationships. Over time, strong Type 1s convince themselves that they have no need for emotion.

Type 1s are highly critical of others and can become very impatient with what they perceive as human inadequacy, believing that nothing short of absolute efficiency should be tolerated. Although Type 1s do not place quality as high as they do productivity, they still want the job done right. They have no tolerance for people who they believe get in the way of productivity. They expect results and waste little time reminding others of their expectations. If they are in positions of power, they'll fire on the spot people who, in their judgment, are not productive. The rigidity that permeates their thinking and behavior is also used to bury their own insecurities. They'll walk over anyone who is vulnerable, and they have little sympathy for anyone who is impeding progress, be they employees, peers, upper management, friends, spouses, or even their own children.

Driven by the need to hide their emotional insecurities, Type 1s believe they are right all of the time. They'll never ask if others perceive them to be right because they already believe they are right. If they're presented with evidence that shows they are wrong, they'll brush their error aside as someone else's misunderstanding.

Type 1s are comfortable with most verbal arguments as long as the confrontation does not threaten their inner ego. Most Type 1s are very opinionated and will spend the same amount of energy arguing about how a bill should be paid (i.e., cash, check, or credit card) as they would arguing about how a key project should be funded. Even though they love to argue, they are not good conversationalists. You will seldom find them talking about trivia at the company picnic. Most likely, the conversation will be business related.

Extreme Type 1s find it difficult to be intimate or to even like other people, which is one of their greatest weaknesses. They can become so determined in their quest for higher productivity that all personal relationships become meaningless to them. If they reach this extreme stage, they are often left alone by others who do not want to have anything to do with them. Their role in the organization gets relegated to some function where they must work by themselves.

To summarize their weaknesses, Type 1s:

- ◆ Are self-serving and consider themselves always right, even when they are wrong.

- ◆ Are inconsiderate and insensitive to the feelings of others.

- ◆ Promote turmoil and conflict if it suits their needs.

- ◆ Are quick to be adversely judgmental of others rather than themselves.

- ◆ Blame others for their misfortunes rather than taking personal responsibility.

- ◆ Dislike being told what to do and will challenge upper management.

- ◆ Are highly competitive, sometimes preventing them from seeing the big picture.

- ◆ Consider work more important than personal relationships.

- ◆ Can be very intimidating and arrogant if they are in their self-righteous mode.

Motivating Type 1s

In many respects, Type 1s are the easiest of the four personality types to motivate. They are direct, decisive, and determined, a combination that can be highly productive. They are task-oriented and find little need to waste time on intimacy or compassion toward others. If you can offer them any kind of leadership role, you will immediately trigger their hot motivation button. At a minimum, you'll get their attention. If you are in a subordinate role attempting to motivate a manager, show him how the new assignment you want will help get him promoted or recognized. But make sure you're the one who gets the position.

Establishing mutual respect is another way to motivate a Type 1. You must earn his or her respect if you want to establish lasting relationships. This issue is very important, particularly if you have a Type 1 personality and you're trying to motivate another Type 1. How do two Type 1 personalities get anywhere when both are absolutely certain their way is the best way and neither can agree? If you have the other's respect, he or she is more likely to accept your point of view, and as a result, alter the behavior that has been adversely affecting you.

Type 1s have a relatively short attention span that demands special treatment when you are attempting to motivate them. You should always be direct, brief, and specific when you have a conversation with a Type 1. Present your issues in a logical order, and if appropriate, offer the Type 1 you are dealing with leadership opportunities if it will help you solve specific problems. If you need his or her undying support, cater to the Type 1's decisive nature and intelligent reasoning, and be prepared to back up anything you say with facts and figures. Also keep in mind that Type 1s are not good listeners. When they do hear you, they'll selectively hear only the parts of the conversation with which they agree. If criticism is called for in your motivation strategy, make it short and to the point. Otherwise, they'll stop listening once they know you're trying to force them to admit to a mistake or trying to change their behavior.

Avoid embarrassing Type 1s in front of others, attacking them personally, or arguing with them from an emotional perspective. If you do, you'll quickly lose their respect for you and they will not be willing to work with you. Always use an authoritative approach when dealing with subordinate Type 1s and never be indecisive in a confrontation. Listen to what they have to say before you render an opinion. Whenever possible, get them to solicit your opinion before you present alternative courses of action to them.

Type 1s demand the right to control their own lives and they do not like or value anyone who tries to dictate their destiny. If you're trying to motivate a Type 1 to take on a particular project, offer the assignment as an option, even if you are the manager. In a manager-subordinate relationship, you might say, "Susan, I need someone like you with your qualifications to take on a critical assignment for me. Do you have any suggestion or recommendations?" The alternative, "Susan, I have an assignment for you. Come to my office and I'll give you the specifics," will irritate and annoy Type 1s. They'll probably take twice as long to complete the assignment and will bad-mouth you every chance they get. The use of power tactics and argumentative confrontations are a waste of time when trying to motivate a Type 1 personality.

Type 1s benefit from the fact that they limit the amount of emotional garbage they'll allow in their lives. Once they're motivated, they don't require a great deal of emotional support to perform well. They love to set goals and in a teaming situation, will push everyone on the team to be productive. The only detail you need to give a Type 1 is when you want the job done and they'll figure out all of the tasks that need to be completed to make everything come together on time. Just remember to compliment them on their ingenuity along the way.

Motivational techniques for Type 1 personalities are summarized as follows:

♦ Offer them challenges that include things they like to do.

♦ Type 1s are basically selfish. Offer them rewards and bonuses for good work.

♦ Type 1s hide their insecurities, so avoid talking about their personal failures.

♦ Appeal to their desire to be highly productive at whatever they do.

♦ Always explain to Type 1s, in a logical order, what you want them to do.

♦ If you are trying to motivate Type 1s to resolve personal conflicts, remember that they tend to be insensitive people. Appeal to them on logical, rather than emotional, terms.

♦ Type 1s are impatient, so always make sure you address the main subject first to capture their attention.

♦ Be careful not to cross Type 1s. They can become very unforgiving and impossible to motivate.

Type 2: Team Players

Of all the personality types, Type 2s are the easiest to work with. They like to do nice things for others and actively look for opportunities to give up something in order to bring happiness to others. They're likely the ones you'll see holding doors open for people, offering rides, and volunteering for company charity functions. More than anything, Type 2s want to be appreciated and will sacrifice career objectives to improve an important personal relationship.

Type 2s appreciate creativity, committed relationships, disciplined achievements, and are fiercely loyal to people they trust. They want others to listen to them and understand them, and they will often reveal their own inadequacies because of the value they place on being understood. As a result, they're easily upset when confronted with any kind of personal ridicule. Type 2s allow their behavior code to guide them to make the right moral decision—on and off the job. They have a strong sense of integrity and would rather lose than win by cheating. They're highly opinionated because they generally base their opinions on emotion and moral principle rather than on logic. Although they are logical when making strategic decisions, they can be heavily influenced by the emotional side of their personality.

Type 2s consider life to be a double-edged sword. On the positive side, they are sensitive to other people; on the negative side, they can become so emotionally involved in personal situations that the emotions overpower their judgment in business affairs. As a result, Type 2s are subject to emotional trauma and depression both on and off the job. For example, an extreme Type 2 could react to the announcement of a sudden corporate layoff with an immediate outburst such as, "I hate this company and everybody responsible for this layoff. I resent the fact that they didn't lay me off. How am I going to explain this to my friends who were terminated?" Shortly after making that statement, a smart Type 2 will quickly come to his senses and realize that he may have sealed his own fate. The Type 2 will quickly deploy damage control measures to neutralize what he has said and apologize for the outburst and redeclare his loyalty to the firm.

In their personal relationships, Type 2s like to be loved and subsequently love those who love them. If they trust you and consider you a friend, they'll do anything for you. They'll seldom miss an important birthday, wedding anniversary, or any other special event that means something to anyone they care about, which is one of their greatest strengths. They enjoy companionship and are willing to sacrifice personal gain to save a personal relationship. As a result, they tend to develop lifelong relationships, remaining loyal to their friends through good times and bad.

Type 2 Strengths

If you walk into a Type 2's office, you may find a sign neatly framed on the wall that says in big bold letters, "If a job is worth doing, then it's worth doing right." Self-discipline is an important component of the Type 2 personality. Type 2s become highly motivated when they are rewarded, and they like to cover their walls with award plaques. They'll constantly seek opportunities to refine their many talents and have no problem being thrown into complex projects where they can exploit their talents. Their self-confidence brings stability and order to their lives, and their steady, predictable nature is the reason why managers can depend on them. They thrive in environments where there is job security, and with proper motivation, they will give their all to accomplish any task you ask of them.

Type 2s like human relationships and, with rare exception, will think of others before themselves just as Jimmy Stewart did in his classic Type 2 role in the movie *It's a Wonderful Life*. Most Type 2s have a strong sense of moral behavior. They love to help friends because of their innate need to live life focusing on more than money or productivity. They readily accept corporate policies, procedures, and authority because they believe that any organization (corporate or social) requires structure and discipline in order to function properly. As a result, they have a strong work ethic and seldom waste time around the water cooler or engage in frivolous, unproductive activities. If they see their co-workers engaged in superficial activities, they won't openly ridicule them, but will tell them to get back to work.

Type 2 personalities are driven to participate in life in a steady, orderly fashion. They appreciate the finer things in life such as intimate relationships and their own creative accomplishments rather than material things. When they are working in creative organizations, Type 2s like to be involved in uplifting experiences, such as team assignments to solve serious problems, and feel comfortable in situations where they can apply their creative talents. They are motivated when they believe they have a purpose in life and will sacrifice personal short-term goals, such as money, to get there.

Type 2s, who are highly committed individuals, have a trademark loyalty and a corresponding sincerity. Likewise, they'll work for any cause that they believe will enhance their relationships. Type 2s will listen to others before rendering their own opinions on how to find the best way meet mutual goals and objectives. As a result, they expect the same from others. They accept the need for authority, even if it deviates from the way they think things should be done. In conclusion, Type 2s are often the peace-keepers in an organization or personal relationship, thanks to their inherent tendency to focus on such personal relationships.

To summarize their strengths, Type 2s are:

♦ High achievers with a deep sense of purpose.
♦ Highly disciplined with a strong goal orientation backed by superb follow-through.
♦ Stable, dependable, and emotionally solid.
♦ Analytically oriented and receptive to others' ideas and suggestions.
♦ Respectful of authority, and work well behind the scenes to support their boss.
♦ Loyal forever to friends and people they trust.
♦ Self-sacrificing, impressionable, and sensitive.

Type 2 Weaknesses

Type 2s are perfectionists who can become highly critical of themselves and others. This feature often forces Type 2s to hide their skills and talents because of a fear of inadequacy. As a result, they'll often struggle to communicate effectively with others and may confuse priorities. The difficulty for you, as a manager, then becomes determining what expectations they have and how they can be motivated. Even if you discover what the expectations are, they may be at such an unrealistic level that they are impossible to meet. Quite often, Type 2s will be very vague and won't tell you what they want. They assume everyone thinks the way they do and, thus, already knows what they want. It is, therefore, not uncommon for a manager, after talking to a Type 2, to walk away scratching his head, asking, "What does she want?"

Type 2s have a "mother hen" quality that impels them to watch over others, ensuring they don't make any mistakes. Type 2s assume this nurturing behavior is welcomed by everyone with whom they come in contact. But, in fact, many people resent it. It's difficult to convince Type 2s that their good intentions may not be accepted, or even understood, by others. This barrier must be broken down if they're to be properly motivated. Because they can become overly sensitive and can react irrationally, you have to take care not to offend mother hen Type 2s.

Type 2s are also very unforgiving if they are crossed. As a result, it is relatively easy to identify a Type 2 by asking, "Have you ever worked for someone whom you didn't like?" Although all of us have worked for bosses we probably didn't like, a Type 2 will describe their negative relationship in minute detail and tell you what she did to get even. Resentment is one of Type 2s' greatest personality weaknesses. This goes hand-in-hand with their excellent memory of bad situations.

Type 2s worry about everything, making it difficult for them to function in highly stressful work environments. Their worrying complex can lead them to feel guilty about almost anything, even if the problem or situation was not their fault. They'll chastise themselves to the detriment of getting their job done because they focus on emotional rather than rational issues. They tend to get stuck in ruts where they lose their perspective and often find themselves misunderstood.

To compensate for this weakness, Type 2s will pump more energy into a frustrating business or personal relationship, often at the expense of their careers, because of their need to develop relationships.

To summarize their weaknesses, Type 2s:

- ◆ Can become highly emotional, smug, and self-righteous in confrontations.

- ◆ Are rigid in their principles and unwilling to negotiate with people they don't like or don't respect.

- ◆ Expect others to understand them and to be sensitive toward their feelings.

- ◆ Can become easily discouraged if they fail to meet their goals.

- ◆ Crave job security and become highly emotional if job insecurity develops.

- ◆ Tend to downplay the capabilities of others relative to their own capabilities.

- ◆ Will avoid public exposure in adverse situations.

Motivating Type 2s

Type 2s are highly complex individuals who are, at best, difficult to understand. They have powerful personality strengths on the one side, debilitating weaknesses on the other, and are comprised of many personality extremes. They can be sensitive, tense, caring, critical, giving, and unforgiving. They are torn between feelings of guilt resulting from unrealistic expectations that are caused by their perfectionist attitude and their high-productivity expectations. Type 2s are often caught between wanting to be involved and their fear of failure once they are involved. One effective way to motivate Type 2s is to convince them that failure is not necessarily bad if used to learn from and improve performance. Remind them that Thomas Edison's experiment with the light bulb failed more than 2,000 times before he finally succeeded.

Type 2s counter their insecurities with self-righteous attitudes. Unlike their vocal Type 1 counterparts, Type 2s remain relatively quiet as they view the world through suspicious eyes, a practice that encourages their pessimistic attitude. Type 2s are their own worst enemy since their self-righteous attitude hides their insecurities. If this attitude continues, they'll depress themselves and others with unrealistic expectations of perfection. Unrealistic expectations must be recognized and eliminated before you can successfully motivate a Type 2.

Type 2s become resentful and are unforgiving of anyone who crosses them, in a business or personal relationship, even though they'll sometimes blame themselves for having caused the bad relationship. If they are in leadership positions, they'll often blame themselves rather than others for their irrational and emotional behavior. To help solve this motivational problem, convince them that they can't be responsible for everybody's problems in the world.

Motivational techniques for Type 2s are summarized as follows:

- Reward Type 2s. They like to cover their walls with award plaques.

- Reinforce their need for security whenever the opportunity presents itself.

- Limit the risk level of whatever assignment you delegate to them.

- Be sensitive and sincere when conversing with Type 2s.

- Promote creativity and allow them ample time to collect their thoughts on creative ideas.

- Avoid demanding immediate action unless you have their full cooperation.

- Earn their trust and respect before you place demands on them.

Type 3: Diplomatic Players

Type 3 personalities will do anything they can to avoid confrontation. They like work environments that are free of any hassles and discomforts because feeling good all the time is very important to them. They become highly motivated when they are treated with thoughtfulness, and conversely, will display a silent stubbornness when they are treated unkindly.

Type 3s are quiet, independent individuals who can become bull-headed when things are not going their way. Managers who try to take advantage of an apparently peace-loving Type 3 by being too demanding will soon be confronted with a wall of passive resistance.

Type 3s will avoid being controlled and will openly fight any manager who they believe does not respect them. They're also tougher than people think they are. Although they value the respect of others, they seldom go out of their way to earn it. In meetings, they will say little and seldom offer an opinion unless they are asked for one.

Type 3s like doing things their own way. They will not place demands on others to help them because they resent people who place demands on them. However, they'll often comply with unreasonable or impossible demands just to keep the peace.

Anger and frustration will be displayed when they can no longer stand being bossed around. Yet they respond well to suggestions and are open to work-related recommendations that will resolve problems or improve an overall situation. They make excellent team members providing they are encouraged to communicate their ideas.

Type 3s are difficult to get to know because they operate on a self-serving power base so subtle it can leave you wondering if they are the manipulated or the manipulators. They approach life with an easy, self-controlled manner that leads one to believe they're at peace with themselves, while their hidden feeling may be heavily influenced by fear, timidity, laziness, or personal inadequacy. For this reason, it's easy to underestimate their limitations, making Type 3s more difficult to motivate than the other personality types.

If left alone, Type 3s will proceed through life never assuming any independence or leadership on their own. Type 3s often make others the core of their existence so they do not have to develop their own sense of purpose or direction. They can become so attached to one person that they avoid developing outside interests or making any commitments that would separate them from that relationship. Transferring a close associate of a Type 3 to another location can have a devastating effect on him. You'll probably find the Type 3's transfer request to the other location on your desk the next day.

Type 3 Strengths

Type 3s are highly agreeable and content people who easily accommodate others. Their gentle nature and superb use of diplomacy wins them many loyal friends and business associates. They are a blend of the best qualities from all of the personality types. They have the ability to move with ease around business problems and stumbling blocks that get in their way. The path of least resistance is the course they'll take if they can find it, and they will seldom demand that obstacles be removed. They are fully capable of accepting other people's opinions, are more than willing to learn from others, and encourage teamwork. Like chameleons, they can adapt and blend in with everyone, and subsequently, they enjoy their enviable position of a balanced personality. They know how to keep the problems of life in the right perspective, are patient, tolerant, and have much to give if they are properly motivated.

The gentle nature of Type 3s typically shines through regardless of their level of trust or feelings of insecurity. They are blendable individuals who are agreeable with almost everyone they meet, including people they don't like. They're fully capable of adopting positive traits from the other personalities once they are convinced that those traits can better serve their purpose. Type 3s like to pay attention to the needs of others and strive at all cost to please the people whom they respect. Accepting others for what they are is a relatively simple task for them. Because of their tolerant expectations, people from other personality types will actively seek them out for advice.

To summarize their strengths, Type 3s:

♦ Are quiet, reflective, peaceful, and blendable in all situations.

♦ Accept whatever life dishes out.

♦ Are comfortable with others and receptive to their ideas because they are superb listeners.

♦ Recognize the values of setting goals and objectives.

♦ Receptive to suggestions and appreciate exposure to many possibilities.

♦ Are calm under pressure and can function well in crisis situations.

♦ Work well in bureaucratic environments and respect leadership qualities in others.

Type 3 Weaknesses

Type 3s are dominated by self-doubt and must constantly be stroked to reinforce their need to be accepted. Because of their insecurity, they don't trust others freely and will subsequently hold their true feelings close to their vest until they trust you. They love to dream and you'll often find them staring off into space thinking about being on a beautiful tropical island or doing something other than what is required. This unproductive personality trait can cause them to miss timely assignments and produce a minimum amount of work. They don't like change because they always perceive change as another word for work. These flaws make Type 3s a challenge to manage and motivate.

Because of their daydreaming tendencies, they lack real-world direction and are the least motivated of all the personality types. In fact, they'll remain completely unmotivated until they establish goals they can believe in and commit to. However, they're often unwilling to set goals, afraid that if they are not met, they'll have to face rejection. If they do find a goal they want to achieve, they'll tell you, "I've finally seen the light at the end of the tunnel. I now know what I want to do!" They'll remain committed to their goals until they see a better light, a pattern that has driven many managers crazy. However, establishing goals is the only way to motivate Type 3s.

Type 3s can be lazy and, as a result, are the first to miss out on opportunities. They'll move sluggishly throughout their job assignments with no desire to set any records. "Everything comes to he who waits" is one of their favorite mottoes. However, the effective use of emotional threats can frighten them into short-term bursts of productivity. They rely on others for opportunities, are prone to wasting time, and are reluctant to change.

Type 3s are not natural leaders and rarely seek leadership positions. They are more comfortable in subordinate roles, and, thus, leave the decision-making to others. They don't like to take risks that could have negative results, nor do they want to be responsible for making decisions. They will, therefore, avoid decision-making assignments at all costs.

To summarize their weaknesses, Type 3s:

- Are bored and often detached from their job.

- Are unsure of themselves, resist making commitments, and take the passive approach to anything they do.

- Are ambivalent about setting goals that require real commitment.

- Fear confrontation and can be easily manipulated.

- Are dishonest with their feelings, which can be misleading.

- Will not openly contribute to a conversation unless coaxed.

- Take a wait-and-see attitude rather than making a decision now.

- Lack consistency in setting goals and measuring accomplishments.

- Respect leadership but resent harsh leaders.

- Are not high producers, fear change, and are difficult to motivate.

Motivating Type 3s

Type 3s are easily overwhelmed by the variety of problems that are presented in everyday life. A sudden international conflict can cause them to lose their focus on what needs to be done now. One of the best ways to motivate Type 3s is to patiently listen to their concerns and then firmly remind them about what needs to get done today, regardless what is happening, either real or imagined. You'll be successful at motivating Type 3s if you can earn their trust and get them to honestly express themselves to you.

Because of their personal insecurities, Type 3s are reluctant to set and pursue goals. In many cases, if they have goals, they simply don't know which one to pursue first. In a management-subordinate relationship, you may have to set and prioritize goals for your Type 3 employees. The key to your successfully motivating Type 3s is to solicit their commitment to the goals you've set. Without firmly established goals, Type 3s are next to impossible to motivate.

Motivational techniques for Type 3s are summarized as follows:

- Be sensitive but firm when communicating with Type 3s.
- Listen carefully to what they have to say and look for nonverbal clues of expression.
- Accept their individuality and provide a work structure that's comfortable for them.
- Constantly offer them ideas for goals and present them with opportunities for involvement.
- Constantly monitor their progress toward completing assigned goals, and be prepared to initiate corrective action whenever appropriate.

Type 4: Party Players

Type 4s consider life to be one big party at which they are the center of attraction. Friendship commands a high priority in their lives because popularity and approval answers one of their basic needs. They must be constantly noticed and are highly motivated by praise. Type 4s need to know that they are appreciated and must have full management approval on anything they do. They'll often act as though they have the world by the tail and that nothing bothers them. Because of their nonchalant attitude, managers may think they don't care about anything. However, nothing could be further from the truth because of Type 4s' fear that they will lose their perceived popularity. For this reason, they need a great deal of management attention and stroking. In meetings, Type 4s like to be center stage, and if given the chance, will offer whatever they think anyone wants to hear. They love to talk and to look good in front of their peers.

Type 4 Strengths

Type 4s are impetuous by nature and love adventure. They're not afraid to make tough management decisions and are constantly looking for exciting opportunities that support their belief that life itself is exciting. They're great conceptionists who rarely become bogged down with details or emotional problems. Although they are as vulnerable to negative experiences as any of the personality types, they have a strong yearning for freedom and will quickly move away from any uncomfortable emotional event. They'll avoid listening to adverse gossip. But if it involves them, they will challenge the person responsible for the gossip to present proof.

Because of Type 4s' inherent enthusiasm for life, people like to be around them. They enjoy life even when they are working under pressure. They always believe that the best is yet to come, which reinforces their self-confidence. Type 4s find it easy to relate to people of all ages and walks of life. They have the most engaging style of all the personality types and attract others to them like magnets. You'll always find people gathered around Type 4s at the company Christmas party or social gatherings. They like to conduct business charismatically, and in the process, are good motivators themselves.

Type 4s actively promote the good in others and are willing to ignore their own limitations. They are the people-connectors and the social glue that holds organizations together. They're constantly seeking out new ideas and relationships that will help them experience life to its fullest. In the process, they express themselves candidly, getting everything possible out of life, and they inspire others to do the same. They offer their opinions freely, often spread a contagious spirit of friendship wherever they go, and are truly the optimists of the business world.

To summarize their inherent strengths, Type 4s:

◆ Are not afraid to make tough management decisions.

◆ Are highly optimistic, very self-confident, and accept others easily.

◆ See life as an experience to be enjoyed, and readily volunteer for challenging assignments.

◆ Are spontaneous thinkers with excellent communication skills.

◆ Are energized by large groups, such as work teams, and are willing to accept guidance from others.

◆ Demand action and productivity from others on key projects.

- ♦ Are high-energy individuals who inspire others to cooperate and excel.

- ♦ Are strong visual learners who are willing to compromise in order to get things done.

Type 4 Weaknesses

Of all of the personality types, Type 4s are the "light-weights" when it comes to work. They bolt through life focused on having fun in everything they do. They frequently fail to develop any meaningful depth in a job because their focus is on the easy street. One of their most serious limitations is their inability to make long-term commitments. They'll start more projects than any of the other personality types, but complete the least because of their dislike to make commitments that tax their endurance. It's difficult for them to concentrate long enough to earn trust in work-related relationships, and they have a similar problem committing to long-term personal relationships. Getting to know yourself is a difficult task for anyone because it involves painfully reviewing all of your personality strengths and weaknesses to develop a self-improvement plan. Although Type 4s may appear to start this self-analysis process, they'll end it before they ever really get started. Their commitment to establishing a true self-improvement plan is way down on their list of priorities. Having fun is always on top of Type 4s' list.

Their reluctance to take on responsibility for self-improvement leads Type 4s to believe this is someone else's job. They believe that it's management's responsibility to assure them of job security. Extreme Type 4s can become human sponges, feeding off anyone who will let them, such as relatives and friends. They are the people who will stay at your house and will live off of your kindheartedness—and your wallet—for as long as you will let them.

These charismatic individuals will openly give you all of the positive signs you are looking for to get them on the motivational track. Getting them to stay on that track is another matter. Motivating them is a challenge because they are uncomfortable with the pressures associated with responsibility. If things are not going their way, Type 4s will blame others. It's one of the many techniques they employ to avoid taking on responsibility. Their flighty disposition makes them restless individuals who find sticking with any one task to be boring. They're constantly looking for something new and exciting to do.

Type 4s often express anger if they believe that something in life is suddenly unfair to them and they become frustrated when problems aren't solved quickly. Although they will move into management positions, they often cannot be found in executive positions. Most Type 4s aren't interested in power positions. Those who are often do not have the discipline to use that power. None of the personality types are as naive or trusting as Type 4s. They are easily fooled by and are easy prey for the other, more sophisticated and calculating personality types. They trust everybody, like to develop intimate relationships, and can become devastated by broken personal commitments.

To summarize their weaknesses, Type 4s:

◆ Are self-centered, irresponsible, and unreliable.

◆ Talk a lot about what they are going to do yet provide little action to get it done.

◆ Can handle stress for only short periods of time.

◆ Do not like to commit to long-term goals.

◆ Often speak before thinking and freely interrupt others.

◆ Are unwilling to dedicate themselves to causes unless they are fun.

◆ Make insensitive jokes about serious and sensitive issues.

Motivating Type 4s

Type 4s are so spontaneous that they are always ready for whatever fun opportunities come their way. Their inherent desire to have fun makes them vulnerable to short-term motivational techniques. Any assignment you present that includes a fun-related reward for its successful completion will catapult Type 4s into instant action. Because of their love of celebrations, award dinner parties, letters of recognition, and group acknowledgments are some of the ways to motivate Type 4s. They are very talented individuals and love to receive applause for those talents.

Most Type 4s want to change. However, change demands a commitment from them that they will not readily make. If you can convince a Type 4 that the effort she needs to expend to implement a change would earn her applause from other departments, you can raise her motivation level several notches.

Motivational techniques for Type 4s are summarized as follows:

♦ Always be positive with them.
♦ Promote reward and recognition events for completing well-defined goals.
♦ Allow them to verbally express themselves, listening carefully to what they say.
♦ Don't be too serious or intense when criticizing.
♦ Totally control their schedules with regular follow-up sessions to make sure they're meeting their commitments.

Mixed Personalities

If you scored an equal number of points in two or more of the personality types on the test, you may have a mixed personality, as we all do to varying degrees. Very few people (one out of 10,000) who take the personality test score 100 percent in any one personality type. After taking the test, if you were unable to establish your dominant personality type, or if you consider yourself to be a 50/50 mixed personality contrary to your test score, don't be concerned. It simply means that the characteristics of your particular personality are harder to pin down. Use the table on page 43 to help determine your dominant personality type.

Improving Your Personality's Character

Although your personality is a feature that you're born with, it is shaped by character as you mature through life. Character is a powerful phenomenon with complex components, an individual's pattern of behavior that is dominated by his or her moral constitution. It displays one's moral strength, self-discipline, and fortitude. In general, character points to the positive, rather than the negative, attributes of your personality. It defines the type of positive or negative connections you make with yourself and others throughout your life. Your character is developed over the years by personal design and the level of

Personality Table

Personality Profile	Type 1 Power Players	Type 2 Team Players	Type 3 Diplomatic Players	Type 4 Party Players
Needs and Wants	Type 1s want to do everything right. The respect and approval of their peers is very important to them.	Type 2s want their feeling to be understood. Appreciation and peer-endorsements are very important to them.	Type 3s want to be independent and allowed to do their own thing. Peer support and recognition are very important to them.	Type 4s want to be popular with everyone they care about. Anyone who offers them an exciting opportunity will become their friend for life.
Summary of Strengths	Type 1s are committed to work, goals, and high levels of productivity. They like to be leaders and demand high work standards of others.	Type 2s are committed to people and to helping them achieve a quality focus. They have high integrity levels and they demand honesty from others.	Type 3s are patient with people and seek to solicit co-operation in everything they do. They are excellent communicators. They respect authority.	Type 4s are very forgiving. They enjoy life to its fullest and are the world's best optimists. They demand trust in their relationships.
Summary of Weaknesses	Type 1s can become highly insecure if anyone challenges their beliefs that are, to them, always right. They are very impetuous individuals.	Type 2s are self-righteous and highly judgmental of others. If others do not meet their expectations, they are unforgiving. They are easily depressed.	Type 3s can be insecure and hide their insecurities. They want to please themselves first before they strike out to please others. They limit their goals.	Type 4s appreciate the purpose of goals but don't like to set them. If they are involved in a situation that is not fun for them, they will become rebellious.

commitment you have toward life principles. Once character is established, it cannot be easily altered, and over time, becomes as solid as your personality.

Here's how character works in relation to your personality. Character can be deployed to override innate personality traits. For example, a Type 1 may rely on his character to tolerate differences of opinion, an act that runs counter to the Type 1 personality. A workaholic Type 2 stops working for a moment to join in on a fun celebration with his or her peers. An insecure Type 3 accepts a major long-term management role in the organization. An uncommitted Type 4 finally decides to get married. Individuals develop character strengths to supplement their more dominant personality traits as they progress through life. We become particularly attracted to character strengths that make sense to us.

We know that the development of character is a learned process. As a result, we should constantly be seeking ways to eliminate or neutralize personality weaknesses by applying positive character strengths. It then becomes practical to blend the five basic character traits to improve your own personality. They are: intimacy, power, communications, self-esteem, and commitment.

Intimacy

Types 2 and 3 have intimacy-oriented personalities. They are motivated by intimacy and tend to develop emotional connections to bond strong relationships with others in their personal and professional lives. They'll celebrate any occasion that will help them develop relationships with others. In business, they appreciate being noticed by others, which is one of the major reasons why they love celebrations.

Conversely, Type 1s consider personal relationships as "excess baggage" and believe intimacy disrupts their work and commitment to the job. Type 4s don't like to commit themselves to relationships that will disrupt the fun that they are having playing the game of life. However, the development of relationships is the glue that holds long-term motivational behavior in place. Without it, the best that Type 1s and 4s can hope for are short-term motivational bursts, which makes it difficult for them to meet their long-term goals. If you have a Type 1 or Type 4 personality, work on developing balanced intimacy characteristics into your personality. Types 2 and 3 would be well-advised to make sure that there is a healthy balance between their intimate and professional relationships, as well.

Power

Types 1 and 3 have power-based personalities and expend a lot of energy preserving the balance of power in their relationships. Subconsciously, they'll select the best strategic position in a situation that gives them the opportunity to control their power. However, Type 1s are much more aggressive in their pursuit of power than Type 3s. Type 1s should work on developing passive characteristics to help tone down their obsession with power. Type 3s will often employ a passive-aggressive approach to achieve power. Types 2 and 4 play the role of "bench warmers" who like to sit on the side-lines watching the power players vie for positions. Most Type 3s already know how to maintain a comfortable power balance. Types 2 and 4 should get off the bench and work on developing power characteristics that will serve them well if they want to aspire to more responsible positions.

Communications

How you communicate is a personality trait that is relatively easy to alter with learned characteristics. Type 1s and are more inclined to tell people what to do, whereas Types 2 and 4 are more likely to ask people to do things. Types 2 and 3 are comfortable seeking out advice from others while Types 1 and 4 prefer to be the ones giving the advice. Type 1s respond best to direct and logical communications while Type 2s prefer softer and more emotional communications. Type 3s prefer honest, low-conflict communications, and Type 4s prefer a casual communication style. To maximize your effectiveness, learn to develop communication styles that will allow you to adjust to the personality type you're addressing.

Self-Esteem

Self-esteem is the act of feeling good about yourself and is subsequently a critical component of motivation. All personality types seek self-satisfaction and self-esteem in everything they do. The act of feeling good is, at best, a difficult human characteristic to measure. Psychologists generally believe that Types 1 and 4 have higher self-esteem levels than Types 2 and 3, who are both more prone to self-criticism. At the other extreme, Types 1 and 4 are so busy criticizing others that they seldom have any time to do any self-analysis, let alone self-criticism.

On the surface, Type 1s are the most self-assured of all the personality types, but they also tend to be highly insecure. By lowering their high expectations of themselves and working at reducing their inherent insecurities, Type 1s would help ease this insecurity. At the other extreme, Types 2 and 3 need to control their self-criticism tendencies that often lead to depression. They should concentrate more on developing positive characteristics. Type 4s can get so wrapped up in their self-satisfaction syndrome that it becomes difficult for them to even know when they make mistakes. They need to be acutely aware of this situation and work at developing healthy self-criticism characteristics that will help them improve their personality.

Commitment

Commitment can take on several different shapes and forms. In the work environment, Types 1 and 3 like to focus on tasks that support their goals with specific deadlines. Types 2 and 4 are more concerned about their own creativity than they are about completing specific tasks. As a result, they are not interested in committing to anything that could disrupt their creative thinking. Although Type 2s will set some goals, they'll put restrictions on the complexity of the goals they set to help minimize their disappointment if they are not met. Type 4s will set goals if they are exciting to work on or if they are forced to by management. The moment one of their goals becomes boring, they'll immediately stop working on it.

The pursuit of personally meaningful goals is essential to the motivational process because goals provide the rewards that people need to maintain high motivation levels. Type 1s tend to rely too much on goals to meet their motivational objectives and would be well-advised to adopt some of the Type 2 creative characteristics. Conversely, Type 2s should try to acquire Type 1s' committed focus on goals to minimize their fear of not attaining them. Type 3s know how to set goals but don't like to work on them. They need to concentrate on setting goals that are important to them and to establish aggressive time frames in which to complete them. This will help build up their commitment to goals. Type 4 personalities need to get back to basics to learn what goal setting is all about and why goals are important to the motivational process.

The Final Analysis

Each personality type brings with it a unique set of strengths and weaknesses. By developing your character and understanding of all four personality types, you will be able to deal with the specific needs of each. Learning to facilitate relationships without jeopardizing your integrity is essential to successful management. After you understand your own personality, you should learn all you can about the other types. Learn to appreciate the unique strengths and limitations of each personality. Then study them so you can strengthen the inherent weaknesses of your own personality type. This will significantly improve your management capabilities. Whether you are selecting a candidate for a job or trying to make sense out of a parent-child relationship, the ability to recognize, appreciate, and understand all of the personality types is a unique asset that will serve you well throughout your career and life.

Chapter 3

Motivating Tactics for Yourself

Managers who feel good about themselves produce good results and inspire their employees to do great things. The greatest motivational challenge you have as a manager is keeping yourself motivated under adverse conditions. Have you ever seen a motivational speaker work a group of people into a state of cheering, yelling, and arm-waving hysteria? Effective motivators brim over with self-confidence as they assure their audience that if they believe in themselves, they can accomplish anything. Fortunately for motivational speakers, their spell-binding delivery gets much more attention than their words.

Inspirational speakers play on your emotions and get your adrenaline racing, which is why so many people go to see their performances. However, they are useless if your intent in seeing one goes beyond entertainment. When the presentation ends, you are caught up in the temporary mass hysteria. But minutes after the seminar is over, you head back into the real world and return to normal. This is precisely where the problem lies. Your excitement after your brief encounter with the motivational hype begins to dissipate in a matter of hours. Your challenge as a manager is to find a way to keep yourself motivated throughout the day, day after day.

George Custer was right when he said, "We really only have two choices in life. We can passively endure the arrows that come our way or we can try to do something about them!" This is also true of motivation. For example, you can passively endure the fact that your boss doesn't know how to motivate you, or you can figure out how to motivate yourself. Even if you are fortunate enough to have external motivation, such as good friends, don't skip this chapter; external motivators can change over time because you can't control them. You can, however, control self-imposed motivators.

Supplying your own motivation ensures that you are going to produce because you are working toward a goal that means something to you and not because of an empty reward someone else is offering. You've made a personal decision to achieve a goal and if there are any rewards, they are self-imposed.

Whatever your goals may be, it is important that you access who you are and want you want. Your goals then provide you with a sequential plan to get you where you want to go. The implementation of your plan begins once you have accepted the responsibility for your own motivation. Consider any motivation that you receive from external sources, such as your spouse, a bonus—something that you are not relying on to accomplish your objectives.

When you go through the self-assessment process, always remember you are working toward what you want, such as wealth, things you want to experience, such as a trip to the Australia, or to be highly regarded by others. There may also be things that you want to avoid, such as divorce or losing your independence. Whatever your collection of wants happens to be, it reinforces who you are and who you want to become, and subsequently, shapes the course of actions you'll take to get there. Motivation then becomes the fuel that you use to accomplish your goals. Following are scenarios representing different motivational problems. Review those that apply to your situations for help in finding motivation.

If You Can't Meet Your Goals

The ongoing successful completion of goals generates the fuel that drives personal motivation. Without the attainment of goals, there is no motivation. Unfortunately, the most common motivational problem managers have is setting and meeting their goals. For every goal that is actually completed, there are a million that were created and never attempted. To help you avoid the pitfalls of striking out on your goals, think about the following statement: The future drives the activities of the present! Bill Gates saw the future in a little computer program called DOS. IBM didn't. You know the rest of the story. Gates methodically established goals that would take him where he wanted to go in the future. You can rest assured that Microsoft is still following this same path today.

The Situation

You've grown tired of chasing your employer's goals because of some "dangling carrot" offered as a reward. Perhaps that is why you've developed a distaste for the entire goal-setting process and why you're only completing a small percentage of your personal goals. However, you've seen the light at the end of the tunnel and have decided to start meeting all of your goals for one reason—because you want to! How refreshing it would be to achieve a goal because it means something to you and not to someone else. If there are any rewards, they will be determined by you and not someone else.

Over the past several months, you have begun to realize how important it is for you to access who you are and what you want out of life. You know you can't get where you want to go without first setting the goals you'll use to get there. The implementation of your plan to reach your goals will occur now that you have accepted the responsibility for your own motivation. Along the way, you'll consider any motivation that you receive from external sources as a bonus or something that you are not relying on to accomplish your objectives.

Motivating Type 1s

If you have a Type 1 personality, you're ready to rise to the challenge of aggressively pursuing every goal you've set for yourself. As a Type 1, you are highly committed to goals and objectives. However, because of your tenacious nature, you will often over-commit to more goals than you can complete. As a Type 1, you demand action and results from yourself as much as you do from others and can become very frustrated when you realize you are not successfully completing those goals.

Reduce the number of goals that you have set for yourself to a more manageable number. For example, let's assume you have 10 goals that you want to accomplish over the next 12 months. In your own mind, you realistically believe that you only have time to complete five of the 10 goals. Select the five goals that you choose to work on and put the other five goals on the back burner. When you complete one of the goals on your list, replace it with one of your back-burner goals in order to keep your active goals to five.

Every now and then, remind yourself that your life won't end if you don't reach all of your goals. In fact, earlier you were encouraged to set aggressive goals, which may lead you to create unrealistic ones. That's okay! Scale them down until they are within reach and never confuse an adjustment with a defeat. If you're not making any adjustments, you're probably not getting anywhere.

Motivating Type 2s

If you have a Type 2 personality, you're highly disciplined and already have a strong goal-oriented personality. You're also a perfectionist, and as a result, are highly critical of yourself. As a Type 2, you are always "almost ready" to get started on your goals but worry that you can't complete all of them. You also have a tendency to set unrealistic goals. Over time, as insecurity sets in, you may start to challenge your own capabilities and hide your creative talent, which would be a strong asset in achieving your goals.

It's time for a reality check. Sit in a quiet location and patiently list all of the uncompleted goals you have set for yourself over the past six months. Next, record the original start and completion dates that you established, and in 10 words or less, identify why you have not completed each goal. Eliminate any goals that cannot be completed because of external events that are beyond your control. Concentrate on completing only the goals that you can control.

Show your refined list of goals to one or more of your trusted associates and ask her for a critical evaluation. Are your goals realistic? Can your planned completion dates be met based on your work plan? Have you clearly established the criteria for determining when each goal is successfully completed? Modify your list accordingly, establish new start and completion dates as appropriate, and go for it!

Motivating Type 3s

If you have a Type 3 personality, you have a tendency to select only low-risk goals you know you can accomplish. You tend to be uncommitted and are often unwilling to set goals because of your need to always feel secure. The potential failure to complete any goal you set may cause feelings of insecurity. As a Type 3, you do not want to introduce into your life anything with risk attached. However, you are very receptive to suggestions from people you trust.   ·

The most difficult thing for you to do is to establish a basic list of goals that are truly meaningful and important to you. This is the first step that you must take to get started. Openly solicit suggestions from trusted associates. Tell them what life issues are important to you and ask them to suggest goals that will help you accomplish what you want out of life. Explore all of the possibilities you can think of and read any material that you can find that emphasizes the importance of goals. When you have honestly convinced yourself the value of the goal-setting process, proceed.

Once you've decided what goals you want to work on, you must begin the process of actually beginning work on them. This is where the men and women are separated from the boys and girls, where you'll find out if you are capable of living up to your own self-assessment, your hopes and dreams. Pick one goal—not the easiest or the most difficult, but rather a goal that falls in the middle. Ignore all of your other goals and work on accomplishing that one. When you have successfully attained your goal, announce your success to your friends and celebrate. After the celebration, pick at least two new goals and start the process all over again.

Motivating Type 4s

If you have a Type 4 personality, you tend to be a bit disorganized, preferring to focus on more immediate issues and putter with minor concerns than to waste time developing long-term strategic goals. You find it difficult to commit to anything that takes priority over having a good time.

Despite your struggle with commitment, if you are uncomfortable about setting goals, go back to the basics. Read as much as possible about how to set goals. Learn all that you can about the process and then stop and ask yourself two fundamental questions:

1. Do I understand what I must do to commit to and complete the goal that I've set for myself?

2. Do I understand how important the overall goal-accomplishment process is to achieving the important things I want out of life?

If you answer no to either question, go back to the library and continue reading! If you answered yes to both, proceed to the next paragraph.

Before you establish the goals to achieve your dreams, focus inward on what it is you want to accomplish in your life. Break your wish list down into short-term (less than a year) and long-term (more than a year) objectives. Does each goal fit with where you want to go? Are your goals realistic? (For a goal to be considered realistic, it must have a 75 percent probability of completion.) Decide on a set of goals you want to accomplish, and proceed.

Armed with your list of important goals, determine which ones are short-term and which ones are long-term goals. Begin to develop, in writing, the steps and time frames that are needed to complete each goal. It is important to do this because you are then forced to take the goal-development process seriously. When your goals are written out and you are forced to look at them in black and white, you have a greater motivation to take action than if you simply think about the goals in the abstract. Write out each goal specifying what you need to do to complete it and when you'll do it.

(?) *Help:* Regardless of your personality type, here's a trick that will help you get started. Announce your decision to start working on a specific set of goals to someone you care about and who cares about you. Show her your written plan, complete with goal start and end dates. Set up review dates at which time you will disclose your progress on each goal.

Idea: Goals fill a number of needs and are the foundation for long-term motivation:

♦ They give order and structure to life.
♦ They measure progress.
♦ They give a sense of achievement.
♦ They provide closure and happiness.

(?) *Help*: There are four questions that you must be prepared to answer if you want to achieve your goals. They are:

1. Who am I and what do I want out of life in the short and long term?
2. What are my objectives in life and do I believe that completion of my goals will help me get there?
3. Once I establish what my goals are, do I have the determination to accomplish them?
4. Is my goal game plan realistic and do I have everything I need to win in place before I start?

Have You Lost Your Perspective?

Highly motivated people can become impatient with their perceived lack of progress in completing announced goals. They tend to judge themselves too harshly if they don't accomplish everything they set out to do. Like everything else in life, too much of anything, such as motivation, has its cost, such as burnout. You can wind up motivating yourself into disappointment if you don't keep a proper perspective about yourself and where you ultimately want to go. Every now and then, remind yourself that your life won't end if you don't reach all of your goals. When you do reach one of your goals, celebrate in your own way and raise the bar on the next goal that you set. To keep yourself motivated, plan on succeeding more times than you fail. Motivation causes success, and conversely, success causes motivation. For that reason it is vitally important to prevent your ambition from defeating your motivation. As long as you control your own motivation, you can accomplish whatever you set out to do.

The Situation

It was one of those days when anything that could go wrong did! For some reason, your alarm didn't go off and as you rushed to work to make the 8 a.m. executive staff meeting, you almost hit a pedestrian in the crosswalk. Nobody says anything to you when you slink into the meeting room 20 minutes late, but the glower on your boss's face tells you you're not going to be next on his promotion list. When the senior vice president asks you to comment on the sales forecast you prepared, cold reality sets in. In your haste to get to the meeting, you left your briefing file on the kitchen counter. Your apology is met with another icy stare that convinces you it's time to update the old resume. Until now, it had been a great month. You'd met all of your numbers and all of your projects were either on time or ahead of schedule. And yet the first 15 minutes of this meeting have destroyed your motivation. What can you do to get your motivation back on track?

Motivating Type 1s

If you are a Type 1, you want everything you do to go right. That is possible maybe 70 to 80 percent of the time. What you must recognize is that it's impossible for human beings to achieve 100-percent success in everything they do. The fiasco that you encountered at the executive staff meeting demonstrated this point. Put the event into perspective and don't dwell on it or it will continue to drag your motivation level down when you need it the most. You screwed up, but you have taken measures to make sure it doesn't happen again. Next time, you'll set two alarm clocks!

Motivating Type 2s

Your late arrival to the meeting and your inability to provide your comments about next month's sales forecast were met with a high degree of distaste by everyone at the meeting. As a result, your personal feelings, which are very important to you as a Type 2, have suffered some serious damage.

You need to take immediate action to restore your self-confidence. Start by employing your analytical capabilities and conduct a damage-assessment analysis. This is probably the first time you have screwed up in several months. You can explain to your boss why you were late. Keep in mind that everyone has suffered the consequences of an alarm clock not going off. The sales forecast numbers that were requested by the senior vice president can be produced after the meeting. An honest "I left them at home" should solve any credibility problem you might have.

Motivating Type 3s

Your Type 3 personality's need for recognition and support in this meeting was obviously destroyed when you showed up late and didn't have the sales numbers that the vice president needed. Your previous track record is good, and because you place a high value on honesty, you can explain to everyone what happened. Remember, it probably happened to them once, too, and unless they are really unrealistic and unsympathetic, they'll understand.

Motivating Type 4s

Your late arrival to the meeting clearly did not make you popular with the attendees. Since popularity is important to you, this event has adversely affected your motivation. A well-worded apology and explanation to your boss and the senior vice president as to why you were late should be sufficient to reinforce the fact that they still have confidence in you. They'll probably tell you that it has happened to them, too, at one time or another.

Do You Lack Commitment?

Many managers make life unnecessarily difficult for themselves. Rather than committing to resolve an issue that's bothering them, they'll waste time and energy fuming and fretting about it. The words "fume" and "fret" mean to boil up or to be agitated; "commit" is a take-charge word that neutralizes fuming and fretting.

The first step in this process is to stop fuming and commit to do something about the bothersome issue. Outline in detail the specific actions you need to take to get where you want to go. Next, establish a time frame for starting and finishing each step. Establish the indicators of each step's completion, and most important, determine the signs that will tell you that the original situation has been resolved.

The Situation

As you drive home from work, you are furious with yourself. That idiot Harry got the second-line management job that should have been yours. And the management review board didn't even have the courtesy to tell you that your application had been rejected. To make matters worse, yesterday was the last day to sign up for the stock option plan and you forgot to do it. That was stupid because you know the stock will split next month and you could have made a killing. As you slap yourself in the face, the word "commitment" comes to mind. You admit to yourself that for some time now, you have been having difficulty meeting your personal commitments. When you think about Harry, you realize that the man is committed. He's always at work when you get there in the morning and he's there when you leave. Perhaps it's time for you to take an honest look at your own level of commitment.

Motivating Type 1s

Commitment to work, personal goals, and objectives is extremely important to you as a Type 1. If you are a Type 1 but lack commitment, you will feel more helpless and lost than any of the other personality types. To restore your commitment to your personal and professional life, you need to resort to the goal-setting strength of your personality type. Review all of your goals. If appropriate, establish new estimated completion dates and revise objectives so that they mean something to you. Commit to completing the first goal on your list and do it! Then move on to the next set of goals.

Motivating Type 2s

If you're a Type 2, you may have lost your desire to be committed because of your innate fear of failure. After all, if you are not committed to anything, how can you ever be accused of failure? This irrational logic goes against your sense of better judgment. Use the analytical strength of your personality to determine precisely why you have become uncommitted, and then implement the steps necessary to restore your commitment to life.

Motivating Type 3s

You can quickly become uncommitted as a Type 3 if you become too relaxed with the way things are going. If you ask yourself why you have become uncommitted, you'll probably discover that it was because you didn't want to expend the extra effort to commit yourself to a given situation. If the situation didn't mean anything to you, then it's okay. But this was not the case presented. Make sure you have your priorities lined up and that you are fully committed to each priority that is important to you. Then commit to making it happen!

Motivating Type 4s

Unfortunately, it is a challenge for you as a Type 4 to commit to anything unless it is an easy thing to do. If you are a Type 4, recognize this fact as one of the inherent weaknesses of your personality type. Once you recognize your weakness, you are in a position to do something about it. Your first task should be to make a commitment to follow through with a goal until it is realized. Then double your commitments until they become an active part of your life.

? *Help*: If you need more ideas on how to become more committed, read Norman Peale's book *The Power of Positive Thinking*.

If You Feel Stressed Out

Job-related stress is a well-known aspect of the business world; it is especially prevalent in the management community. Psychologists blame the fact that managers, more than other professionals, have been forced to make behavioral adjustments to a faster pace of change in today's dynamic corporate atmosphere. Although some managers are aware of its harmful effects, few know how to control or prevent stress. Many managers, victimized by the stressful world in which they live, have accepted stress as a necessary component of their job.

However, there is a relatively simple way for managers to alleviate stress and thus control its undesirable effects. Relaxation will counteract the physiological effects of stress, and it can be elicited by a simple mental technique—motivation. For most of us, we link motivation to hard work, which can often lead directly to stress. This is incorrect. Motivation is a self-taught discipline that can be channeled in the direction thought best by you. In this next scenario, you will learn how to use motivation to conquer stress in your personal and professional life.

The Situation

As you head back to the sanctuary of your office at the conclusion of the day's meetings, the moment of reality comes to you. Your desk clock is moving toward 10 p.m. as you stare at the incredible mass of charts stacked on your desk. You're exhausted and you find yourself muttering, "This place is going to be a challenge." You reach for your binder and, in order to collect your thoughts, you scan over the nine hours of meeting notes you took.

Every presentation given during the meeting was negative and it is clear from the ensuing discussion that nobody knows how to solve any of the problems that were identified. Some employees didn't even know the problems existed. There is no strategic plan, the financial numbers are going in the wrong direction, employee morale is deteriorating, the competition is gaining market share, and the company has no viable new products or services to sell. The nagging question in your mind is, "How much longer can I stand it?"

As the smoke clears from your mind, you begin to understand the underlying problems and challenges that confront you. Without motivation, your employees are following the only game plan they know. They have no solutions and they certainly are not about to make any decisions for which they could be held accountable. They are clearly leaving that up to you. In the process, they've dumped several years of problems on you to fix. But that's why you're the manager making the big bucks. Knowing that you don't yet have the information to solve all the problems, you leave for home. You vow to show your staff how to get motivated to solve their problems as soon as you can figure out how to get yourself motivated first.

Motivating Type 1s

If you're a Type 1, it's not uncommon for you to be stressed out on a regular basis. You tend to work harder than you should and you're easily upset if the people around you aren't pulling their own weight. When any stressful situation occurs in your business world, if at all possible, walk away from the immediate situation and head for some quiet place where you can collect your thoughts. To help restore your motivation, always remember that if there were no problems for you to solve, you wouldn't be needed as a manager.

Motivating Type 2s

Type 2s can easily become overwhelmed with all of the problems of work, not to mention other worldly problems as well. If you're a Type 2, recognize this fact as one of the limitations of your personality. The key to your success as a manager is to learn how to quickly qualify the problems that confront you. Learn to separate your problems into three categories: 1) Problems that are urgent and require your immediate attention; 2) Problems that are not urgent and do not require your immediate attention; and 3) Problems that cannot be solved regardless of any action you take. Work on solving your number one problems first. Then, when you have the time, work on your number two problems. And forget about your number three problems. Delete them from your list.

Motivating Type 3s

One of the frustrations you have as a Type 3 is that you are often dependent upon others to help you solve problems. In the scenario, you are dependent upon your staff to solve a multitude of problems that they are not prepared to. They have subsequently sapped your motivation, which will make it difficult for you to help them. Once you recognize what has happened, step forward and take charge of the situation. Actively express to your employees your motivation and confidence that all of the problems identified will be solved. Motivation is contagious. Watch it catch on as your employees follow your example, become motivated and actively begin to eliminate the problems that were identified. Your stress level will be significantly reduced.

Motivating Type 4s

If you are a Type 4, you have suddenly found yourself in a situation that is not much fun. And as you already know, Type 4s like to have fun. No one wants to be inundated with problems that stress them out. Your best way out of this situation is to either resign from your management position or step up to the pump and determine what problem-resolution strategies to implement. Then, follow the same advice that we provided to your Type 3 counterpart.

Are You Burned Out?

Considering the responsibilities involved with managerial work, a manager's job is enormously complicated. They're often overburdened with obligations that cannot be easily delegated, and as a result, are overworked and forced to do many tasks superficially because of imposed unrealistic schedules. And the pressures of the manager's job are getting worse. In the past, managers needed only to answer to the owners and executives of the company. Now they must respond to empowered subordinates who continually reduce the manager's freedom to issue orders without explanation in order to get the job done. On top of the added subordinate burden, there are a growing number of outside influences managers must contend with, including consumer groups, and government agencies. In many instances, the manager has nowhere to turn for help. Perhaps this is why the number of managers who have left their positions has increased significantly over the past five years—because of burnout.

The Situation

All you have to do is answer the customer service phones for two hours to realize how stressful that job is and how important your representatives are to building customer loyalty. You begin to understand why your customer service employees are the first ones to burn out on the job. You also begin to understand your own burnout problems. Your customer service reps are being bombarded by people problems, just like you are, with two important exceptions. In most instances, customers' problems get resolved during the course of the telephone conversation and all of your reps leave at the end of their eight-hour shift. Most of the people problems that you confront take weeks to resolve, and a 60-plus-hour workweek is part of your typical schedule. You've got to figure out a way to reduce your workload before you burn yourself out.

Motivating Type 1s

Decide what you can do now to off-load work onto your subordinates. Do not fall into the Type 1 trap of convincing yourself that you're the only one who can do the work. If you do, then you will burn yourself out, probably destroy your health, and be of no use to anyone. Even if the initial effort of delegating the work requires more time on your part, in the long run, it will pay off in reduced pressure.

Is your organization doing some functions no longer required or that could logically be performed by another organization? Talk to your peers and boss about getting those functions transferred out of your organization. Be prepared to pare the responsibilities and head count of your organization down to the point where you are comfortable with your managerial role and your burned-out feeling subsides.

Motivating Type 2s

Analyze what your job consists of now, as opposed to what it was when you first accepted the position. What are you doing now that you didn't do then? Has anything really changed or are the changes just a perception that is causing you to feel burned out? If it is a perception, then you need to direct your attention at correcting your personal attitude. If the changes are real, then you need to determine if there is anything you can do to adjust your job accordingly. In either event, something has to change or you will burn yourself out and run the risk of damaging your health in the process.

Motivating Type 3s

Type 3s like to be free of pressure, which is certainly not the case in your current situation. To make matters worse, your job is no longer challenging and you feel insecure about where you are going. Your job may also be getting boring, which is causing you to lose your concentration on getting things done. You'll have to determine if you believe that things will get better in the near future and that your job will become challenging again. Can you delegate some of the work to other members of your staff so that you can reduce your work hours? If things don't get better and you're still burned out in a couple of weeks, it may be time for you to find another management position that more closely fits your needs.

Motivating Type 4s

Your job has grown to the point where it's overwhelming and you're not having any fun. What started out as a manageable assignment just keeps growing and growing to the point where you are almost burned out.

Perhaps your personal life is interfering with your work. Could it be that so much is happening at home you can't concentrate at work or vice versa? The real problem may not be the job so much as it is your personal life that is causing your burned-out feeling.

If You Feel Obsolete

Back in the days of the Wild West, there was an equalizer called the six-shooter. It enabled a small man to chop down a big man. In today's management world, the six-shooter has been replaced with an intangible component called desire. Desire is the equalizer that drives a person's motivation, allowing him or her to achieve whatever he or she wants regardless of who gets in the way. And like the obsolete six-shooter, obsolescence is the one process that can still neutralize one's desire to accomplish anything. Obsolescence is a mental frame of mind that allows people to convince themselves that whatever they desire, they cannot achieve because they have become obsolete. Although age is often associated with the word obsolete, in today's fast-moving business environment, it is becoming very prevalent for younger managers who are constantly challenged to keep ahead of the obsolescence power curve. If you are feeling obsolete for whatever reason, the next scenario will demonstrate how you can replace that feeling with desire.

The Situation

For 12 years you have built a lucrative career that has catapulted you into management. Until now, you have felt as though you were on top of the world and could answer any reasonable questions anyone threw at you. Not anymore! Last month, when you attended a three-day management retreat, you were overwhelmed by the breath of knowledge the younger managers displayed. Their knowledge of computers and the Internet left you standing in their dust on a subject you thought you understood. None of those computer nerds appreciated your probing question when you asked them if they knew what a keypunch machine was. That night at dinner with your boss, she asked you in her customary blunt fashion, "Based on today's meeting, do you think you're becoming obsolete?" Though her words shocked you at first, they also challenged you to privately assess her question and to determine if there is something you can do about becoming obsolete.

Motivating Type 1s

Obsolescence is a word that is unacceptable to all Type 1s who pride themselves on having the ability and intelligence to be on top of any subject that's within their sphere of influence. Just the possibility of becoming obsolete can prove to be devastating to a Type 1's motivation.

If you are a Type 1, make sure that you are not overreacting to the obsolescence issue. In the scenario, the Internet was used as the issue to make you feel obsolete. Ask yourself the question: "Do I really need to know the technical details about the Internet?" If your answer is no, then you can erase from your mind your concern about obsolescence. If your answer is yes, then solve the problem by attending one of the hundreds of courses that are offered on the subject and answer your innate desire to do something about it.

Motivating Type 2s

If you are a Type 2, your illogical mind is probably telling you that your obsolescence in certain areas is not important. In the scenario, the fact that you did not know anything about the Internet may not be important to your management function at this time. Therefore, your lack of knowledge should not cause you any feelings of obsolescence. However, carefully assess any threatening future obsolescence issues and, if they are real, mount a campaign to neutralize each issue. Take a class in the subject area to gain knowledge.

Motivating Type 3s

Your insecurity is further aggravated by your feelings of obsolescence. You probably also feel unenthusiastic about everything and lack direction as well. Perform a self-analysis test to determine if the problem is really your fear of becoming obsolete or if it's a result of your general frame of mind.

If you are facing a frame-of-mind issue, forget the concern you have about becoming obsolete and concentrate on solving whatever it is that is dragging you down mentally. If you are still left with the issue, determine what you can do to avoid becoming obsolete, such as training, and do it!

Motivating Type 4s

You have already gone through a good part of your life largely uncommitted to anything. It is no wonder that you may suddenly feel obsolete when forced to face certain realities. If you believe that the obsolescence you are facing must be resolved for reasons that are important to you, then you must be prepared to step forward and do something about the problem. That's a tough challenge for you, a Type 4, who would rather not work any harder than absolutely necessary.

Working for an SOB

How do you keep yourself motivated under adverse conditions when external forces are working against you and when you have nothing but your own motives to sustain you? What can you do when your SOB boss is constantly blocking you from achieving your goals, is paying you less than what you're worth, and is utilizing only a small percentage of your talents? Working for a boss who is constantly on your case and who offers you nothing in return for your hard work can prove to be devastating to your motivation.

The Situation

So you're working for John, a real SOB! You wonder if you have any options. Every time you try to communicate with this man, he jumps down your throat. Yesterday, he asked you how the Harding Project was going. When you started to tell him, he jumped on your case about why you didn't tell him about it earlier. Then he told you he didn't have time to listen to you now. What's a person to do?

Motivating Type 1s

If you have a powerful Type 1 personality, you may not be the easiest person to get along with either. Something has to change before the situation will get any better, and it will probably have to start with you first if you want to salvage your job. Remember that change is difficult for self-righteous Type 1s to accept. Think about how you might change to improve the situation. For example, adapt a less forceful role when you confront John and be careful not to say the wrong thing or intimidate him. If you're still running into a brick wall after you have given the situation your best effort, change bosses.

Motivating Type 2s

You may think that you are working for an SOB when all you really have is a boss with a personality and operating style that are different from yours. If you are a Type 2, you're probably analytical in everything you do and expect the same from anyone you work for. When John asked you to explain what was happening on the Harding Project, you provided him with an analytical analysis, which he may not understand or appreciate if he's not a Type 2 like you. Determine what his personality type is and communicate with him accordingly. For example, Type 1s like tables filled with facts and figures. Type 3s and 4s like to see the big picture in colored charts and graphs.

Motivating Type 3s

People with solid Type 3 personalities are usually very tolerant and patient with the people for whom they work, but you are having a real problem working for John. Perhaps you have done something in the past that irritated him to the point where he has turned against you. This places you in an unhealthy predicament. You have to find out what it was if you want to restore your relationship with John. When the setting is right, ask him if there was something you did to irritate him. You might start the conversation with a statement like, "John, I need your help. I have apparently done something to upset you and I want to correct the problem." Listen carefully to what he has to say in order to determine if you can reconcile the situation. If you feel you can't, find another boss.

Motivating Type 4s

Use the positive thinking side of your Type 4 personality to find out what has happened to your relationship with John. In all probability, he doesn't trust you for some reason. Find out what the reason is so that you can initiate corrective action. Have a one-on-one conversation with John and use probing questions to find out what's bothering him. If trust is the main issue, seek out his advice as to what you can do to correct the problem.

(?) *Help:* If you feel you are working for an SOB boss and need more information on how to deal with him or her, read *Problem Bosses* by Mardy Grothe and Peter Wylie.

Problems with Your Spouse

Most sane people attempt to go through life trying to avoid conflict, whether it be at work or at home. If you are married, conflict is inevitable, but it can also be beneficial as long as both understand the benefits. In today's fast-paced competitive world, knowing how to manage your spousal conflicts is critical to the success of both partners. Everyday arguments and disputes can be used as tools to not only improve the communications with your spouse but also the people who work for you and who work around you. The conflicting partners must be willing to share information and acknowledge each other's personality types. This cooperation will lead to innovative solutions, reduced stress levels, and improved personal relationships.

The Situation

"What a pain," you think to yourself. "I've got so many things to do at work, and a stubborn wife to contend with, too." After talking to your boss, you have finally gotten back to an unending list of tasks and meetings that you're sure will take you to the next promotion level. As you drive home, your thoughts return to your recent fight with your wife, Arlene. She is not buying the fact that with your new job responsibilities you're going to be working late most of the time. And quite frankly, her lack of support is disrupting your motivational drive at work. What can you do to correct the situation?

Motivating Type 1s

If you have a Type 1 personality, the respect and approval of your wife is very important to you. You also have a difficult time balancing your priorities between your personal life and work life. Clearly, Arlene does not approve of the late hours you are putting in at work. Somehow, you have to gain her respect for the personal sacrifices you are making to advance your career. A candid conversation between the two of you is the place to start. Ask her if the two of you will be better off if you do not take the steps (i.e., longer hours) that you feel are necessary to advance your career. If she feels that the loss of personal time during the week is the major issue, you might suggest going to work earlier in the morning so that you can be home at an earlier hour in the evening. If your longer work hours are short term (three to six months) with a real promise of a reward, such as a higher-paying position in the company, discuss the personal opportunities for both of you in the long term. Perhaps you will finally be able to afford that motor home or swimming pool you have always wanted. Type 1s are driven by goals and it is important that you realize that your goals must be shared by your wife before you can realistically expect her support, which is critical to sustaining your own motivation.

Motivating Type 2s

Type 2s are known for their moral conscience and you are no exception. The fact that Arlene does not appreciate the sacrifices you are making bothers you a great deal. That is the issue that you must address to restore your motivation. Arlene will need your assurance that she is more important to you than your job. A one-shot meeting won't get her motivated to accept your new job responsibilities. Make it a practice to constantly reinforce her importance to you over the job.

Motivating Type 3s

If you have a Type 3 personality, you can be a stubborn individual and will hide your insecurities from the people you care about most. The reality of the situation is that you feel compelled to work longer hours to ensure your own job security. The fact that you have not shared this concern with Arlene is probably the root cause of your problem. It's time to open up and tell her exactly what's causing your insecurities (for example, a boss who doesn't think you are committed to the organization) and what actions (i.e., longer hours) you have taken to reconcile the situation. She will understand and may have some viable suggestions that will help you regain your self-confidence.

Motivating Type 4s

If you are a self-centered Type 4, you may appear to Arlene as only thinking about yourself. Show Arlene how your new job responsibilities and longer hours will lead you to a promotion. Explain to her why your promotion is as important to her as it is to you. Perhaps it means that the two of you will be able to retire earlier than expected or it's a way to get that new house you both want.

(?) *Help:* Here is a plan to help resolve conflicts between your work schedule and personal commitments. At the beginning of each month, ask your spouse to provide you with a schedule of family and personal appointments over the next 30 days. Incorporate the schedule into your work schedule and treat it as a priority that you work around.

Problems With Your Kids

Work and your kids are often two distinct worlds that compete for your loyalty. Your relationship in your organization tends to be formal and task-oriented, while your relationship with your kids should be emotional and intimate. Some managers have difficulty separating these two worlds. They get caught up in the strong and often adverse relationships at work, which affects their relationship with their kids. Too often, organizations reinforce negative interpersonal habits that leave people unprepared to deal with their kids.

The Situation

The grades your son Gordon brought home from school last night hit you like a sledgehammer. How can he have a D average in high school and not think it's a big deal? The grades, combined with the drunk driving citation he delivered to you last month add to your frustration. You realize that your suppressed anger has been partially directed into an aggressive attitude toward your son. You've got him so scared that he won't talk to you. To top it off, you are finding it difficult to concentrate at work. You've got to take charge of this situation.

Motivating Type 1s

The intimidating nature of your Type 1 personality is what is causing Gordon to avoid having any kind of communication with you. If Gordon is also a Type 1, being the target of your anger will be extremely stressful and anxiety provoking to him. You have to settle yourself down before you can even begin to approach your son about his problems. For starters, invite him to go on an outing with you, such as to a ballgame or a movie, where the two of you can enjoy each other's company in a social setting. Avoid talking about Gordon's problems during the outing. Your mission is to regain your son's confidence in you. When the time is right at the end of the outing, you might say something like, "Gordon, we have had a great time today, but as we both know, we have some problems we need to address. Let's get together tomorrow and see if we can work things out." Remove intimidation from everything you do and say to solve Gordon's problems and to restore your own motivation.

Motivating Type 2s

If you have a Type 2 personality, you are usually sincere and honest when handling personal problems. In keeping with that trait, you may have described your feelings to Gordon in terms that were more vivid than he is presently prepared to deal with. To get at the root of Gordon's problems so you can arrive at a solution, share some of your personal feelings with Gordon, but emphasize your commitment to help him resolve his problems.

Once you have expressed your sincere and honest opinion, ask Gordon if he agrees with your assessment of the situation. If he answers no, continue with probing questions and conversation until the two of you reach an agreement on what is causing the problems. This will help your son focus on the situation, help him develop an action plan to resolve the problems, and will relieve some of your own frustration.

Motivating Type 3s

Type 3s are normally good listeners, but for some reason, you were not listening to Gordon when you confronted him about his problem. Anger has a way of eliminating a person's ability to listen, so eliminate your angry feelings as best you can before you confront Gordon about his problems again. Parents typically underestimate the impact their anger has on kids. To shield himself from your anger, Gordon will go on the defensive and will tell you whatever he thinks you want to hear just to get you off his back.

Your best approach is to ask Gordon to help you help him solve his problems. Be sure to celebrate the mutual achievement of meeting your son's goals to reinforce the fact that you are on his side.

Motivating Type 4s

Type 4s are reluctant to confront any kind of adverse situation, particularly ones that involve personal relationships. As a result, they tend to jump into conflict situations without first thinking through how they should handle the situation. Your failure to properly handle the situation with Gordon led you to say some things that may not have been appropriate at the time.

To help diffuse the situation, take personal responsibility for your actions and initiate a statement such as, "Gordon, I apologize for the anger I displayed when I received your grade report. However, let me point out a couple of reasons that caused me to be angry and maybe the two of us can work things out." You need to lead Gordon down a path that will correct the immediate problems that confront him if you want to alleviate your own anxiety. You do this by forming a partnership with your son.

If You Just Can't Get Motivated

The unmotivated quickly reveal themselves by making critical comments and displaying their jealous nature. They resent the success of others. One of the most noticeable attributes of unmotivated managers is the way they react to criticism and laughter. They can't stand it if they believe the criticism or laughter is being directed at them and will often react in a manner that is completely out of proportion to the act.

Unmotivated people are often uncomfortable when left alone. They've got to be going somewhere or doing something all the time to compensate for their drab behavior. Their lack of motivation reveals itself when they stop being competitive and adopt "I don't care" attitudes. They'll drag anyone they can down to their low motivation level and become absolutely dysfunctional when they're placed in positions of responsibility.

The Situation

That guy giving the seminar was right on and you can't stand that he was! When he told you that you were 100 percent responsible for controlling your own level of motivation, you knew intuitively that he was right. However, his comments about how you should get out of management if you can't get yourself motivated before you destroy your organization did not sit well with you. You like working with people and you believe you've got the talent to become a top-notch manager. Now if you could only get motivated.

Motivating Types 1 and 2

If you are a Type 1 or 2, you typically know how to set goals and have an appreciation for the importance those goals play in achieving the rewards of life. For whatever reason, your goals have become a demotivator for you. Perhaps you're not meeting the goals you've set for yourself, or after you set them, you lose interest in them.

Set goals that are realistic, and most important, mean something to you. When you set a goal and something inside you says "let's go," you're on the right track. In order for goals to be effective, they need to excite your motivational state of mind.

Motivating Types 3 and 4

Many Type 3s and 4s do not have a concrete set of goals that they strive to meet. If you are a Type 3, goals are sort of important and worth working on when you have the time. If you're a Type 4, goals mean very little to you and are considered a waste of time. And yet goals provide the fuel that drives motivation. It's no wonder you're not motivated.

A manager without goals is like a ship without a rudder—each will drift endlessly without direction. If you do not have any goals, you'll reap only a fraction of what life has to offer as you blindly follow the crowd in a circle to nowhere!

(?) *Help:* There are hundreds of excellent books that specialize in how to set and obtain personal goals. Pick one up or check out Zig Zigler's book *See You at the Top.*

Idea: The 2-Minute Morning Motivational Exercise. Spend two minutes every morning reviewing your routine goals and what you will do that day to help meet those goals. Routine goals are a continuation of what you are already doing or are expected to do; they are typically work-related, but they can also be personal.

Idea: The 2-Minute Midday Motivational Exercise. Spend two minutes every afternoon reviewing your problem-solving goals and what you will do that day to help meet those goals. What problems have you solved so far today? What new problems do you want to add to your list?

Idea: The 2-Minute Evening Motivational Exercise. Spend two minutes every evening reviewing personal goals and what you have done today to help meet tomorrow's goals. Also review all of the goals you have accomplished during the course of the day and congratulate yourself.

Chapter 4

Motivating Employees

The potential power of motivation is an amazing thing. Journals are filled with stories where people have triumphed against unbelievable odds, such as Helen Keller, who is dramatic testimony to the power of motivation. In addition to self-awareness, imagination, and conscience, motivation is the single most important human endowment required to achieve and sustain high levels of productivity. You can achieve increased productivity by applying short-term techniques, such as fear or cash awards, but you can only achieve sustained productivity by applying legitimate ongoing motivational techniques. If you remove the element of motivation, people will lose their drive to do anything but the bare necessities.

This chapter focuses on how to motivate employees in different situations. When reviewing the scenarios presented, concentrate on understanding the human issues that lie beneath the surface problems. For obvious reasons we cannot present problems that are identical to those you may be facing, nor can we represent every possible problem managers may face. But we can present the human issues that are behind most problems and the motivational techniques you can apply. For example, you are working with an employee who doesn't like his or her job. It does not make any difference what that job is—sales, production, or accounting. The motivational techniques offered should, in most instances, work regardless of what that job is, because they are based on the issues that lie beneath the specific job, or scenario, presented.

Low Producers

You are about to confront one of your employees who consistently produces at substandard levels. To make matters worse, all of the employees in your department are acutely aware of the situation and several of them have talked to you privately about the problem. You believe that their concerns are legitimate and promise to take immediate action to correct the problem.

The Situation

Kathy has been with the company longer than any of your other employees. She joined the company as a sales representative. Although she had no sales background, she possessed an innate ability to sell. Over the years, she consistently met or exceeded her sales quotas for her region. She likes her region and knows her customers well. Although she has had several opportunities to transfer to a larger region, she has always declined the offer, stating that her preference was to stay where she was.

For the first time in her career, for the past six months, she has consistently missed her sales quota. Until now, you have chosen to ignore the problem. Initially, you thought it was a temporary phase that would simply go away. Your rationale was based on the fact that Kathy has always been a good producer. You assumed that she was either encountering temporary personal problems that were disrupting her productivity or that sales were slow in her region. You now realize, with mounting pressure from your employees and concerns from upper management, that you must address the situation immediately.

Motivating Type 1s

Kathy is a take-charge individual and is trying very hard to do a good job. The fact that the other employees are on her case bothers her a great deal. Although she has not openly shared her concerns with you, the fact that she is no longer your number one sales representative is, in your opinion, a major cause of her insecurity. Her personality traits—hard working, likes to be challenged, and becomes bored with routine assignments—indicate to you that she is a Type 1 personality.

Type 1s want their managers to push them to be productive. In the past, Kathy was always productive, so there was no need for you to provide additional motivation. For some reason, she has lost her motivational drive and needs to be pushed. She may have become bored with the routines of her job (i.e., same customers or products). A challenging new job assignment may be in order for Kathy even though she wants to stay in her region.

Type 1s love to achieve competitive goals. Perhaps all Kathy needs is for you to develop a new set of goals that the two of you can agree on. The goals may be as simple as returning her region to quota by a specified date or as challenging as exceeding quota by 50 percent. The specific goals selected are not important as long as you and Kathy believe the goals are realistic.

Make sure that you and Kathy are in total agreement on how to identify when each goal is met. Add a goal-attainment incentive that adds excitement. For example, if Kathy meets her goals, an employee award in front of her peers may be very appropriate in light of the peer pressure that she has been subjected to.

Motivating Type 2s

From what you know about Kathy, you suspect that she has a classic Type 2 personality. She appears to be very sensitive and is openly upset over the fact that she is not being accepted by her peers. You hope that she is not too sensitive, in view of the pressure that is mounting on her to increase sales.

In your first one-on-one encounter with Kathy, she revealed more insecurities than you had time to listen to. This is typical of Type 2 personalities. Kathy's insecurities are affecting her productivity. The key to getting her back on track is to either eliminate or neutralize her insecurities.

In a follow-up session with Kathy, jointly prioritize all of her insecurities—most to least critical. Discuss any insecurities that neither one of you can do anything about. Develop a plan to eliminate the first or perhaps the first three issues on the list that are causing insecurity before you address the others. As you begin to resolve Kathy's key insecurity issues, monitor her productivity, which should increase.

Trust is important to Type 2s. Assure Kathy that you're on her side and, for her benefit, you'll be monitoring her productivity. Hold joint weekly or monthly meetings where you can review Kathy's productivity and progress in resolving her insecurities.

Motivating Type 3s

In view of the fact that Kathy's performance is not meeting your expectations, you have asked her to present her understanding of the problem. She begins by telling you, "As I stated earlier, our marketing and sales quotas are determined by the strategic plan numbers that the marketing department prepares." Based on Kathy's presentation, which was completely positive and did not address any of the problems she is encountering in her sales region, you are convinced that she has a Type 3 personality. Type 3s will do anything they can to bypass and ignore their problems.

Type 3s can be difficult to read and are often misinterpreted as not being aware of problems surrounding them because of their tendency to oversimplify them. In most cases, Type 3s are acutely aware of the situation and will hide their real feelings of fear and inadequacy. You need to get Kathy to openly communicate with you and address her problems. If she will not do this, you'll never be able to motivate her to solve her sales-quota problem.

If Kathy refuses to acknowledge the problem, try using a new approach: Appeal to the Type 3's need to feel good. State the problem and then emphasize the fact that you need Kathy's help in fixing it: "Kathy, you and I are both aware of the fact that sales are down significantly in your region. I need *you* to help me solve the problem." By taking this approach, you allow Kathy to feel good about solving the problem herself while reassuring her of your willingness to play an active role as her coach.

Motivating Type 4s

You ask Kathy to join you in your office for a chat. You ask her how things are going, adding, "Our sales performance this year has been pretty good. However, some of our sales regions missed their quotas by as much as 50 percent." You ask her what the reasons were for the wide fluctuations and variances in her region. After some deliberation, she appears hurt and gives you a rebellious reply: "I'm doing the best I can under poor management." You already have part of the answer that you were looking for—Kathy has a Type 4 personality whose feelings are easily hurt, which can cause them to rebel. You'll have to apply different motivational tactics to get her back on track.

Type 4s like to bound through life having fun and will frequently put their jobs in the "necessary evil" category. The job is required to supply the money they need to buy the fun things they enjoy. Kathy performed well on the job as long as it was relatively easy for her to meet her assigned sales quota. When the competitive environment changed, she wasn't willing to make the personal sacrifices to work harder. If this is the case, discuss the issues with her and get her to commit to a stronger work ethic.

Do not be afraid to remind Type 4s that everyone likes to play, but playing costs money, thus resulting in the need to work. Encourage, and even demand, that they reorganize their priorities—job first and personal fun second. That is not to say that they can't have fun on the job as long as it contributes to the overall productivity.

② *Help:* Low producers act similarly to unacceptable performers. Pay close attention to the next section and the similarities for motivational techniques that may further assist you in dealing with low producers.

Unacceptable Performance

Unacceptable performance is a subjective standard that must be carefully defined by individual managers. It is entirely possible to have an employee who thinks he or she is performing at an acceptable level even though their performance is less than acceptable to you. Although people in each personality type may view acceptable performance in a different light, it's up to you as their manager to set the standards for acceptable, and unacceptable, performance.

The Situation

Monday morning, you're sitting at your desk with a cup of coffee reading Bill's latest status report on the Harding Project. As you read through the report, you're dismayed that most of it doesn't make any sense. You can't follow Bill's logic, the sentences aren't clear, and you have no idea how he arrived at his conclusions. You're especially disgusted because this will be the third time this week you've had to tell him that his work is unacceptable. About one out of four jobs he does for you has to be redone. Whenever you talk to Bill about the problem, he always seems surprised that you think his work is below par. At one point, he even responds, "I thought I was doing okay."

Motivating Type 1s

Bill reacts to your criticism with the insensitive remark, "That's your opinion, which I don't think much of! I'm here to tell you I think it's a darn good status report." His flippant comment reinforces your belief that you're dealing with a strong Type 1 personality who becomes highly insensitive when anyone challenges his work.

Tell Bill exactly what he did wrong. If he becomes critical of others and attempts to pass the blame onto them, remind him of his responsibilities to the project and that you placed trust in him, rather than someone else, to get the job done.

Let Bill know that you are on his side and tell him what he did right. Do not back down on your original position that his overall work was not acceptable to you, but let him know you have confidence that he can perform to your work standards. Agree on what specifically will constitute the successful completion of the project and document, in writing, your agreement. Have Bill sign it, next to your signature.

Motivating Type 2s

When you confront Bill in a private meeting and inform him of your dissatisfaction with his recent status report on the Harding Project, you are disturbed by his silence. A full 10 minutes pass before he finally says something. When he tells you he did the best he could on the project and offers to turn the project over to whomever you designate, you know you're dealing with a self-righteous Type 2 personality. Your motivational challenge will be to somehow restore Bill's self-confidence.

Tell Bill the specific areas of the project that are bothering you and openly seek his advice on what action can be taken to correct the situation. Type 2s have good analytical minds. If they truly understand the problems that you are presenting, they will often come up with viable solutions.

If Bill shows any signs of depression as a result of your criticism, assure him that you need him on this project. Statements such as,

"Bill, you are the man for this job and I know you can do it," will go a long way toward dampening Bill's Type 2 tendency to become depressed over something he has done wrong.

Motivating Type 3s

The Harding Project is extremely important to you. You've got a promotion riding on its successful completion. When you explain to Bill your dissatisfaction with the way he has been handling everything, you're disturbed that he's too understanding about your concerns and readily agrees with everything you say. You're convinced you're dealing with a "too cooperative" Type 3 personality who will say anything he thinks you want to hear.

As the old expression goes, it's time to take the bull by the horns; show Bill where you want him to go. Prior to your meeting with Bill, develop a plan to get the project done, complete with a detailed schedule and specific definitions of completion milestones. You want to make absolutely certain that Bill understands what is expected of him and that he understands what needs to be done to complete the project.

Type 3s tend to be uncommitted to anything that does not have personal value. Make sure you solidify Bill's commitment to the project before you turn him loose for another try. Offer some kind of personally meaningful reward to Bill for successful completion of the project. Type 3s like to have time off, so an offer of a three-day weekend may be all that it takes. Also, inform him of the consequences (job demotion, termination, etc.) if the project is not completed on time.

Motivating Type 4s

When you confront Bill and inform him of your concerns on the Harding Project, he apologizes profusely for his performance. Halfway through his emotional outburst, you interrupt him and ask him when he can complete the project. When he gives you one of those puzzled looks and says, "I can't commit to a time frame right now," you know you're dealing with an uncommitted Type 4 personality.

Bill may honestly not know what is expected of him to complete the project, which is why he backed off from making a commitment to you. Review all aspects of the project with Bill and repeatedly ask him if he understands what needs to be done to complete the project in a time frame that you establish. Ask him questions to verify his understanding of the project.

Once you have Bill's commitment to complete the project within your time frame, ask Bill if he believes that your schedule is realistic. Type 4s are highly optimistic individuals. If Bill sounds too optimistic or doesn't challenge at least one part of the schedule, your guard should be up. He simply may be accepting your schedule as the easy way out of an awkward situation.

(?) *Help:* Unacceptable performers act in a very similar manner to low producers. Review the section on low producers for motivational techniques that may further assist you in dealing with unacceptable performers.

Idea: Tell Bill up front that you are going to regularly inform him how he is doing. Tell him what he did wrong and be specific, and then tell him what he did right, to reinforce that you are on his side. Make it clear that you support Bill and his success in your organization.

Mr. Tardiness

A person who is always late for work or meetings can set an adverse standard for your entire organization if the situation is allowed to continue. Tardiness is a highly visible event. If someone is habitually late, everyone is usually aware of it because of the vacant desk chair. If the tardy person walks into a staff meeting late, presentations have to be stopped and attendees turn their heads to look. In the process, they take mental notes like, "I wonder how much longer the boss is going to tolerate this situation." Tardiness can create an undercurrent in your organization that will undermine your best motivational efforts.

The Situation

It's happened again. As you walk through your work area a half hour after starting time, you notice that Sam's desk is empty for the second time this week. This has become an ongoing problem for him over the past several months. Because he didn't ask for any time off, there is only one conclusion you can come to—he's late again. The area gets quiet as you glance around and notice that everyone is watching you in anticipation. To dampen your employees' suspicions, you walk over to Sam's desk, pick up a piece of paper and look at it to show them that that is why you came into the work area in the first place. You then quickly make your exit. Twenty minutes later, you catch Sam sneaking in through the back door and scrambling to his desk. This has got to stop!

Motivating Type 1s

You have known Sam to display Type 1 personality traits in the past, so this behavior is troubling you. Type 1s are focused individuals who want to do everything by the book, including being on time. Chances are there is some external event in Sam's life that is causing him to be late for work.

Tardiness problems are potentially easy to correct in Type 1s. If Sam is consistently 20 minutes late for work, tell him to set his alarm clock 20 minutes earlier. Find out what specifically is preventing Sam from getting to work on time and then motivate him to correct the problem. For example, if he tells you he doesn't use an alarm clock, tell him to get one and start using it!

If the problem turns out to be a morning scheduling problem (for example, dropping the kids off at school), and Sam has no other alternatives, a possible change in his working hours may be in order.

Motivating Type 2s

Most Type 2s are conscious individuals who generally have no problems maintaining work schedules, or any other schedule, for that matter. They may simply not be aware of the fact that they are often late for work, and a reminder from you may be all that is required to solve the problem.

Because of the honest nature of Type 2s, you can often motivate them to solve tardiness problems by appealing to their integrity. Tell Sam that even though his tardiness may not seem like a big deal to him, it is sending a message to the other employees. That message may be that you don't care, are a weak manager, or any other that can cause damage to your credibility as a leader.

If Sam does not tell you when he will be late, counsel him to inform you each time so that you know what to expect.

Motivating Type 3s

The fact that you caught Sam sneaking into work through the back door tells you something about the man. He is legitimately concerned about what others think when he's late, representing a classic Type 3 personality trait. Have an honest talk with Sam and if you have been lax in handling the problem, admit it. However, make it clear to Sam that you cannot accept his tardiness in the future.

Do not disguise the consequences of continued tardiness. If job termination is the consequence, tell Sam, so that he can adjust his personal priorities to solve the problem. Clarifying consequences of unacceptable behavior can sharpen a person's motivation to change the behavior.

Motivating Type 4s

Type 4s don't like to commit to solving any problem, such as tardiness, unless they can clearly see that it is important to them. If the consequence of continued tardiness is job termination, let Sam know that in a nonthreatening manner. If he cares about his job, and most Type 4s do, he'll become highly motivated to meet the goal of arriving to work on time.

Don't put off talking to Sam about his tardiness problem. The rest of your organization will be watching you, not Sam, to see whether or not you'll deal with the problem and how effective you are at solving it.

Warning: If you get angry at Sam's habitual tardiness, delay your meeting with him until you feel you can listen objectively to what he has to say. He may have a valid reason.

Ms. Always Sick

In the late 1920s, the Oklahoma-based company Derrenger Enterprises created the first recognized sick-leave plan for its employees.

Harold Derringer was the CEO at the time, and he reasoned that a company had an obligation to help its employees should they become sick. Not only did he authorize company pay when employees were sick, but he also pioneered the nation's first company-paid employee health plan.

In those early days, the benevolent Mr. Derringer published very simple guidelines for his employees to follow if they wanted to take advantage of the plan. He stated, "If you're sick, I'll pay your expenses until you get well. If you fake it, I'll fire you." According to company records, nobody was ever fired for "faking it" because Derrenger employees understood that it was a privilege to work for a company that offered a sick-leave program. The company continued to prosper, even during the depression, and was later renamed Conoco, the oil conglomerate.

As American companies emerged from the post-World War II era and into the prosperous 50s, sick leave became a common practice offered by most major companies. It became known as a fringe benefit and took on a different connotation. Employees reasoned that if sick leave is a fringe benefit, it is something that they have earned. They further reasoned that if they did not get sick, then they did not get to enjoy the benefit. Therefore, they reasoned, they would take time off even if they were not sick.

By the end of the 1980s, it became common practice for employees to routinely use all of their remaining annual sick leave, whether or not they needed to. The cost of "faking it" to major corporations ran into the millions. When the corporate downsizing trend of the 90s took hold, many companies targeted sick leave as a way to reduce costs, and in some cases, reduced allowable sick leave by as much as 50 percent. And that trend remains with us today, even to the point where companies have renewed use for the phrase, "If you fake it, I'll fire you."

Of all the motivational problems that are addressed in this book, absenteeism probably draws the biggest yawn. In my opinion, managers expend less imagination in dealing with this problem than any of the others because many regard it as a nuisance rather than a problem. Absenteeism, though, is a lot worse than just a nuisance; it's a real drain on productivity.

The Situation

You are working for a company that has been through some good times and some bad times over the past 10 years. Fortunately for you, the company is prospering, thanks to some tough lessons learned during those bad times. All costs are closely monitored, down to every employee, piece of equipment, and paper clip. The excessive use of sick leave is a closely monitored statistic that every manager is acutely aware of.

Kristi is a habitually absent employee who is capable of convincing herself at any time that she's overwhelmed by whatever seems to suit her. Life's little difficulties are always just too much for her, and she learned long ago that the easiest way to deal with stress is to simply go back to bed. When she calls you on Friday morning, she sounds sincere when she says, "I feel terrible. Do you mind if I stay home today?" If it weren't for her consistent use of Fridays and Mondays for her sick days, you would have believed her. Over the past year, Kristi has enjoyed more three-day weekends than any other employee in the company, and the rest of your employees are resentful of that fact.

Monday, Kristi walks into your office and tells you, "I'm sorry I was out last Friday. I had one of those viruses that's going around. I'm still weak from the side effects." You tell her you hope she feels better, and as she exits your office, you pull her employee file to confirm what you already know. She always gets sick on either a Friday or a Monday. You wonder if she really was sick or just likes to have three-day weekends whenever it fits her needs. You have decided to confront her about the problem.

Motivating Type 1s

If you believe that Kristi is a Type 1, make sure you organize your thoughts before you confront her about the problem. Type 1s are notoriously organized thinkers, and if you confront them about a personal problem, you had better make sure that all of your facts are in order. Document the number of days Kristi has been sick over the past 12 months. If 80 percent of her sick time was taken on Fridays or Mondays, be prepared to show her how you arrived at the figure. Type 1s do not like to be compared to their counterparts if they are put in a negative light. If Kristi is using a significantly greater amount of sick leave than the average employee, show her the numbers to get her undivided attention.

When you have all of your thoughts organized, ask Kristi to join you in your office for a private meeting. You want to avoid a confrontation with a Type 1 on any sensitive issue, such as her abuse of sick leave, if at all possible. Your mission in this meeting is to determine if Kristi really has been sick. Your ask, "Kristi, I am puzzled about your use of sick leave over the past year." Briefly review the numbers and statistics that you have prepared and politely ask her to explain her pattern, listening carefully to what she has to say.

If Kristi tells you she can offer no explanation, you may conclude that she has been abusing her sick leave. Type 1s do not like to lie but they will seldom admit to any personal weaknesses. Your simple explanation of how sick leave should be reserved for times when people are really sick should be sufficient to motivate her to stop abusing her use of sick leave. If she tells you she really was sick, see the Warning notes on page 89.

Motivating Type 2s

Find out if Kristi has really been sick. Type 2s value integrity and honesty. Level with Kristi and tell her about your suspicions regarding her sick leave pattern. If she strongly protests her innocence, let her know that you believe her. Ask her if she can explain her pattern of sick leave use. Listen carefully to what she has to say—Type 2s are generally sincere if they trust you. She may have a valid reason as to why she is consistently sick on Mondays. Perhaps she is working with children every weekend and is therefore susceptible to catching common child-related illnesses. Determine with Kristi how much work she can do and set a reasonably reduced work schedule that you are both confident she can meet.

Motivating Type 3s

How are you going to find out if Kristi has really been sick? Type 3s are understanding and want to cooperate. Level with Kristi and tell her about your suspicions regarding her excessive use of sick leave.

If you know for a fact that Kristi has been abusing sick leave, when she misses a day, tell her how badly she was missed and about the hardships her co-workers had to endure to cover for her while she was gone. You might say something like, "We didn't realize how much work you did until we all had to cover for you. By the end of the day, we were all pretty tired." In other words, make her feel guilty every time she takes a sick day.

Type 3s will follow rules if they believe that the rules benefit them. The following explanation may motivate Kristi to stop abusing sick leave: "Kristi, let's assume that you decided to take a week's vacation and called in sick because you had no vacation time left. Two months later, you came down with the flu and missed a week's work without any sick leave benefits, which means no pay for that week. Would that cause you any financial problems? If you had not used up your sick leave for vacation time, you would have had it when you really needed it."

Motivating Type 4s

The important point to remember with habitual Type 4 absentees is that you have to give them lots of attention. The last thing you want to do is ignore them, which will only reinforce Kristi's conviction that her absence will never be noticed. You have given her no motivational reason to struggle in to work when she really doesn't feel up to it.

Our prescription for solving this problem is not much different than what you would apply to a child—gently encourage and mildly admonish. You should never ignore the situation because the habitual absentee has in many respects never grown up. Remind Kristi that she must do what the company is paying her to do, and when she doesn't, it hurts others.

Type 4s like to have fun; long weekends are an important part of their personal life. Tell Kristi to use her vacation time for long weekends. As a special motivator, let her know that if she will level with you and provide you with advanced notice (e.g., request for next Friday off), you will on occasion give her the day off without charge to vacation or sick leave as an incentive for not abusing sick leave, which is a practice you use to reward your steady employees, as well.

Warning: If several of your employees are sick at suspicious times (Fridays, Mondays, days before or after holidays, etc.), you may have a motivational problem that points toward poor morale and discipline in your organization. In a staff meeting, let everyone know what the rules regarding the proper use of sick leave are and warn them of the consequences associated with abuse. Actively seek out the advice of your management and supervisory team to help you identify specific morale or discipline problems.

Warning: It's irritating to managers to think that their employees can get away with abusing sick leave, but they can. It is very difficult to prove that a person is not sick. And the burden of proof is on the manager, should he or she terminate that employee for alleged abuse of sick leave. Request doctor's certificates from all of your employees who saw a doctor during their sick leave. If they refuse to give you one, make a note of it in their personnel file.

Idea: Compliment any employee who stops abusing sick leave as a result of your motivational efforts. You might tell her, "Since you have been feeling better, I have noticed a significant improvement in your personal productivity. If you keep this up, you should be in line for that promotion we have been talking about." Or, walk into the work area just before lunch on Friday and tell your rehabilitated employee so that everybody can hear—"Kristi, I appreciate your hard work and the fact that you are consistently here."

Antagonists

In Webster's New Collegiate Dictionary, an antagonist is described as a person who openly opposes the actions of others, often demonstrating hostility to the person they oppose. Antagonistic situations can occur anywhere at any time. For example, at a staff meeting, an employee makes a suggestion. The antagonist suddenly jumps up and tells him his idea is stupid. This could be the same person who walks into your office, shuts the door, and proceeds to tell you what's wrong with everyone in the company, from the president down to the night janitor. If you say something is black, an antagonist will tell you it is white just to start an argument.

Most antagonists are bright individuals with the potential to become highly productive, if only they can be motivated to spend more time worrying about themselves rather than others. If antagonists are allowed to continue down their path, they can cause serious motivational problems throughout your organization. Because antagonists like to do lots of talking and very little listening, effective communication is vital to motivating them. Communication is effective for a reasonable period of time when it is received, understood, and remembered by the employee for whom it was intended. If your message doesn't meet all of the criteria, you're not effectively communicating with antagonists and any of your attempts to motivate them will fail.

The Situation

You lean back in your chair, stare blindly at the ceiling, and sigh. Unfortunately, your talk with Dan went just as you had expected. He just completed a project for you and, although he did a pretty good job and met all of the tight deadlines, you know he could have done a lot better. When you broached the subject with him, he proceeded to blame several people who he contended got in his way and deliberately tried to prevent him from doing his job. You had to cut the conversation short when Dan got emotional and started referring to the people he was accusing as idiots and saboteurs.

In the interest of preserving your own sanity, you ask Dan to think overnight about what he has just said and join you for a follow-up discussion in the morning. You have overheard some of your employees privately refer to Dan as "the company antagonist" and now you understand why. Somehow you have got to find a way to motivate Dan to stop, or at least control, his antagonistic behavior.

Motivating Type 1s

When you meet with Dan again, ask, "Have you changed your mind about anything you said to me yesterday?" If he adamantly defends his position and starts to repeat his accusations, feel comfortable in the fact that at least you have properly identified Dan's personality. It is extremely difficult for Type 1s to admit that they are wrong.

When you talk to Dan about the problem, expect flak, listen to what he has to say, take notes, and keep the communications on track. Dan is probably performing as an antagonist to get attention. Appeal to the logical side of his Type 1 personality by demonstrating to him that the attention he is enjoying is the wrong kind of attention. Anyone who acts like an idiot can get attention, but it takes a real professional to get attention because he is admired.

Motivating Type 2s

When Dan walks into your office the next morning and spends the next 10 minutes apologizing for the way he acted and the accusations he made in yesterday's meeting, his Type 2 personality traits begin to show. Type 2s tend to be sensitive about the feelings of others.

Type 2s are team players. Dan's antagonistic behavior may be a result of the fact that he is not getting the payoff he expects from the other members of his team. Consequently, he may adopt a self-righteous attitude that allows him to feel he is always right, everyone else is subsequently always wrong, and hence, allows the emergence of his antagonistic behavior. If you honestly point this out to him in an open discussion, you should be able to motivate him to adopt a more appropriate behavior.

Motivating Type 3s

Type 3s will act in a manner they understand best if they feel there is a payoff. In any organization, there are a lot of opportunities for antagonists to act in the manner they understand best—tearing people down. In doing so, antagonists believe they will be seen as having greater importance, hence, the perceived payoff. As a manager, it's up to you to eliminate that perceived payoff by telling them that the reverse of their assumption will occur—their importance in the organization will ultimately decrease to a minimum. When that happens, they will be fired.

Before you tell Dan what it is you want him to do, invest some time and listen to what he thinks he's already doing, what he thinks he needs to do to solve the problem, and what motivational rewards he thinks he deserves if he eliminates his antagonism.

You can't motivate Dan to change his antagonistic behavior with a frontal assault. You have to first get his attention and get him to let his guard down. You do that by convincing Dan that you understand and appreciate his opinion.

Find an assignment that will require Dan to work with two or three people so that he can learn how to cooperate with others. Provide him with a book on the subject that will help him control his antagonistic behavior.

Motivating Type 4s

Dan is uptight when you discuss his antagonism problem the next morning, which is a classic Type 4 characteristic. You're asking Dan to dramatically change the way he likes to work. To do that, he will have to learn a whole new set of interpersonal skills. Encourage Dan to develop these skills. But remember that Type 4s do not like to extend themselves.

Find a seminar or training session that specifically addresses cooperative and interpersonal skill-building. Suggest to Dan that he attend the session. Make sure he understands that you care and that's why you are willing to spend company money for the seminar. At the same time, Dan must commit to you that he honestly realizes a need to change his antagonistic attitude.

(?) *Help:* Antagonists are like one-way radios—they have built-in transmitters with no receivers and are subsequently capable of doing lots of talking and very little listening. Effective communication is vital if you want to motivate antagonists.

Afraid of Change

As a manager, you must face the fact that change is disturbing to a lot of people. The natural tendency of your employees is to stick with what they know, play it safe, and gravitate toward familiar ground. Employees will often try to quash any idea that requires change or a suggestion for doing something differently. It's easy to understand why employees don't want to change. Uncertainty develops; employees try to resist and dig in their heels and stand steadfast against the proposition. All of these attempts at rejecting the idea carry a cost to your organization. They extinguish the sparks of innovation, enthusiasm, creativity, and ultimately, motivation, all so necessary for progress.

The Situation

Maggie left your staff meeting disappointed and dispirited. Unwittingly, your department head, Roger, had firehosed her idea to eliminate three of the 10 steps in the return-of-merchandise (RMA) procedure. Although you elected not to get caught up in the confrontation, you admit to yourself that Maggie's suggestion was right on the mark and could save your organization several thousands of dollars a year. By shortening the time it takes to process returned merchandise, customer satisfaction would definitely increase. Unfortunately, you sense that Roger's firehosing exercise was endorsed by many of your employees. You have two problems that confront you if you don't take immediate action: 1) It will be a long time before Maggie regains her motivation and makes another suggestion; and 2) Roger will be recognized as the firehose leader in your organization. This is the fifth time he's torpedoed attempts to introduce changes into your organization over the past two months and it's time for you to break the pattern!

Motivating Type 1s

Roger will become motivated to change if you can convince him to answer yes to the following four questions regarding Maggie's suggestion: 1) Will it pay off for me? 2) Can I successfully participate in and help implement the change? 3) Is the change worth the effort that it will take to implement it? 4) Do I trust the person who wants me to help implement the change? Your managerial challenge is to get Roger to trust you and convince him that yes answers to your questions are in his best interest.

Ask Roger to experiment with you. Type 1s love challenges, so invite him to help implement Maggie's change based on the fact that you believe it will be effective. Assuming that it is effective, Roger should be happy that he participated in enforcing the change, which will make the next change easier to accept. Ask Roger to recommend a constructive change at your next staff meeting.

Privately meet with Maggie and explain to her the action you have taken to prevent people from discouraging the ideas of others. Tell her you're going to implement her RMA idea.

Motivating Type 2s

Explain to Roger the specifics of the RMA change you're about to implement and why the change should be important to him and to your organization. Give him a chance to comment and patiently listen to what he has to say. No matter how good you think Maggie's idea is, recognize that the change is uncomfortable for Roger. Find out why.

Don't get angry at Roger if he demonstrates stubbornness at accepting change. If you allow the situation to disintegrate into a head-to-head confrontation between you and Roger, you'll both lose.

Motivating Type 3s

Here's a technique that works well for motivating Type 3s to change: Give them a compelling reason for the change. Tell Roger why you must implement the change and how you propose to do it. Tell him that if he has a better idea, you'll be glad to listen to his suggestion. Let Roger know that if he doesn't have a better idea, you're going to proceed with the change. If he comes up with a more viable idea, consider it, and if it warrants the replacement of Maggie's suggestion, implement it.

Pick changes that clearly benefit your organization and make sure they're effective. This will start to build Roger's and other employees' trust in you. Then you can start persuading employees like Maggie to continue making suggestions for change.

If you can't convince Roger that the change will help your organization, let him know in no uncertain terms that you are the boss and you're going to implement the change. If his opposition is really strong, ask him to come up with a better idea, which will put the ball back in his court.

Motivating Type 4s

People have very different reasons for not wanting to change. Listen carefully to what Roger has to say before you reach any conclusions. You can't motivate him until you know what's blocking him.

Although some people find change exciting, Type 4s are uncomfortable with it and even consider it threatening. However, don't conclude that this is the case with Roger until you have made sure his resistance isn't caused by something else. Once you have identified the cause, eliminate it as quickly as possible. A frank talk with Roger may be in order. Let him know when the change will go into effect and ask him if he will support it. If he gives you an affirmative answer, make sure it's sincere. Type 4s are not afraid to give phony answers just to get you off their backs.

If Roger answers negatively, be patient and ask him why he refuses to support the change. If he gives you a reason that you can do something about, such as extending the start date for the change, ask him if he would support it if you agreed to his request. If he continually comes up with other reasons, you won't have time to eliminate all of his road blocks. A transfer to another organization or his termination from the company may be in order if you cannot motivate him to support your changes.

Warning: Warn Roger of the concerns you have with his firehosing habit. Let him know up front that your organization will be going through numerous changes over time. If he can't accept that and agree to help implement the changes called for, tell him you'll help him find another job in another company.

Fighters

There are two basic categories of fighters. The physical fighters are the ones who are prone to get into physical conflicts with others for any reason. You address and resolve these situations with termination notices. The situation presented in this section deals with the verbal fighter (the employee who is one level away from becoming a physical fighter) because these are the people whom you have a chance to save through the motivational process. They verbally attack other people in an abusive manner that is often punctuated by four letter words and the potential threat of physical harm.

Some occasional group infighting is normal in any organization. Most groups are made up of talented individuals with strong and diverse personalities where there are bound to be disagreements that can lead to conflict. Your challenge as a manager is to recognize the difference between honest and harmful disagreement. For example, honest disagreement may occur when one employee confronts another with an appropriate set of diplomatic words: "Joe, although I respect your opinion, I must honestly tell you I disagree with your position for the following reasons...." Harmful disagreement that fuels infighting occurs when diplomacy is left out of the formula: "Joe, that is the stupidest idea I have heard in a long time. Here's my position and you had better listen." The infighting often begins with a shouting match between the two employees, and if the situation is ignored by management, it can escalate into hate and anger.

Serious infighting will devastate the motivation of not only your employees who are directly involved in the infighting, but the ones who are innocent bystanders. Fighters typically have short memories. Your communication with fighters has to be frequent and firm if you want to motivate them to stop fighting.

The Situation

Paul wasn't exaggerating when he told you how disruptive Dale has become. When left alone, Dale is one of your top producers, but as soon as you put him on a team assignment, everyone on the team comes running into your office to complain about him. He argues constantly with everyone he works with, and, to make matters worse, he openly uses abusive language. You're afraid if he doesn't learn how to control his flaring temper, he's going to hit somebody one of these days.

Motivating Type 1s

Most employees are sensitive to their co-workers' reactions to their thoughts and want their approval, but not fighters. They'll strike out at anyone who they feel is getting in their way with little regard for their feelings. This is particularly true if the fighter is a loner or perceives himself as someone the group doesn't like, which can be typical of people with Type 1 personalities.

Don't play amateur psychologist in this situation. Recognize up front that Dale may have a serious problem that demands psychological care. His fighting tendencies may be a result of complex personal problems that occurred when he was growing up that now need to be addressed by a trained professional. Seek out professional help for Dale.

Motivating Type 2s

Ask Dale to explain his behavior to you and listen carefully to what he has to say before you make any conclusions. Dale will probably tell you he's suspicious about the team's motives. When pressed for an explanation, he'll tell you that he honestly believes the members of the team are trying to sabotage the project and it's up to him to do something about it!

Confront Dale as soon as possible and inform him that you're removing him from the team. Self-righteous Type 2s will loudly object to this move but you have to think about the confidence the team has in your handling of this problem. Once this is done, you can address Dale's fighting problem head on. Tell him how disruptive he has become to your organization and let him know you're not going to tolerate it. If you cannot get him to acknowledge the problem and agree to work with you on a solution, you may have to terminate him.

Motivating Type 3s

Type 3s are crafty individuals who know how to leverage infighting to what they believe is their best advantage. Peer support and recognition are very important to them so they believe that arguing with anyone who will listen is a way to get their name known. Appeal to the cooperative side of Dale's personality and show him how good communication is a much more effective way to earn people's respect and advance through an organization. If none of the motivation approaches that you try on Dale work, you've arrived at the moment of truth. Advise Dale that if his infighting behavior continues, you will be forced to terminate him. That prospect may be enough to get him to change.

Motivating Type 4s

Before you take action, you must first determine the cause of the infighting. Is it the result of a personality conflict between just two of your employees? Does it bear the earmarks of organizational gang warfare where there are several employees ganging up on Dale, or worse yet, where there's infighting between two groups of employees? You will need to counsel each individual involved in the conflict, directly or indirectly, if you want to restore motivation in your organization. This will take some time.

? *Help:* To diffuse the immediate threat of infighting, you need to enforce a "cease-fire" within your ranks before you begin one-on-one consultations. Assemble all of the infighters in a meeting room, shut the door and tell them that, effective immediately, the infighting will stop! Strong management action is required to make sure each of your employees understands the personal consequences that will occur if the fighting does not stop. The following statement is not out of order: "If I catch anybody involved in infighting, it will be considered grounds for termination." You may choose to use a softer approach but the end result must be the same. Make sure that everyone is motivated to stop fighting. Let your employees know that you will be meeting with each of them to resolve the conflict.

Team Rejects

The popularity and growth of teams in today's organizations have been phenomenal. Almost everybody in business refers to the team concept; saying anything against teaming would be considered going completely against the grain. Managers boast of the number of teams they have organized, the problems they have resolved with these teams, and most important, how much money teams have saved the company. Teaming has become such a popular buzzword in corporate America that practically no one questions the effectiveness of teams in running an organization.

The Situation

Although you secretly believe that your company relies too much on the often overexaggerated benefits of teams, you're not about to buck the tide. Sure, working together is better than working against one another, but you believe your company may have confused the word "team" with "teamwork." Teamwork is always appropriate and desirable in any work environment. A formal team structure, in your opinion, is not always necessary to achieve what teamwork already accomplishes.

Teamwork is accomplished by simply making sure that cooperative and motivated behavior is positively reinforced within each member of your organization. As you stare at a spot on your office ceiling, you can't refrain from labeling Karen, one of your newest employees, a "team reject." For some reason, Karen is the laughing stock of every team you put her on. Even after the team assignment ends, Karen runs around asking, "What was the problem we were suppose to resolve on our team?" To make matters worse, she never completed a single team assignment she was given and seldom attended any of the team meetings. Your peer managers have picked up on the situation and when one of them confronts you in the cafeteria and sarcastically asks you if she can borrow Karen to head up her next team, you decide to solve the problem now!

Motivating Type 1s

To be successful, every team member must be a source of positive reinforcement for the others, a role that Karen is clearly not fulfilling. Team members have more contact with each other than their managers. Therefore, it is important that team members supply mutual reinforcement for each other. It can be more frequent, and more beneficial, because they are all working together. Unfortunately, if the team members believe one in their ranks is not a source of reinforcement, it can have a negative impact on the entire team's motivation.

Karen's Type 1 personality does not seem to fit in well with members of any team you put her on. Her arrogant attitude is turning her team members against her. This negative quality is an unfortunate twist of fate for the team; Type 1s have an inherent loyalty to task when in team situations. Counsel Karen on techniques she can use to control her arrogance. Suggest to her that she spend more time listening to the team discussions before she renders her ideas and opinions on the subject.

Motivating Type 2s

Type 2s can become too analytical when given a team assignment. When Karen continually asks what problem the team is trying to solve, recognize that she may be procrastinating. She would rather pursue a finite definition of the problem than work on its solution. The team members recognize this fact and allow her, as the "team reject," to pursue her search for a finite definition, while the rest of the team works on the solution. This issue needs to be brought to Karen's attention before you can motivate her to function effectively in a team environment.

Motivating Type 3s

Some team problems are better solved by people working alone on one or more of the tasks that the team needs to complete to meet its goal. Karen may be a greater asset to the team by working alone than she is in a group setting. This is a more comfortable role for many Type 3s.

Motivating Type 4s

Because of Karen's Type 4 personality, she is uncomfortable with the concept of empowerment and is not sure where it fits into the team process. It is up to you to point out to her that empowerment in a team setting is a process where decision-making is shared with all of the team members, including her. Point out to her that she is backing away from her responsibility, which is perceived by the other team members as a lack of interest. You must get Karen to endorse the idea of empowerment and accept her role before the team will accept her as a viable member.

Warning: The most important aspect in team effectiveness is the behavior of the team members. The team's assignment to implement change is much less dramatic than the need for the team members to change their behavior and performance. Human behavior is the single greatest cause of team failure. If the team members can't change their behavior to adapt to the other personalities on the team, such as Karen, then the team's mission may never be accomplished.

Rumor Mechanics

Rumor mechanics are those people who are experts at making up and starting rumors about anything under the sun. Every manager has them in their employ. These are people in your organization who you should not trust because they may try to undermine your organization. They're always planting false rumors about you or your organization.

One of the greatest managerial challenges you will face is to motivate someone you do not respect. This mission is particularly difficult when the person you dislike is one of your employees. The easiest solution would be to simply transfer that person out of your organization, make their life so miserable that they'll quit, or fire them. The tougher option is to take the initiative, overcome your discomfort with the situation, and embark on a mission to make an ally out of the rumor mechanic.

The Situation

You are dumbfounded when Brenda, one of you peer managers, tells you Harry, your best microprogrammer, is informing everybody that you have turned in your resignation. This is not the first time Harry has planted false rumors that somehow involve you. If it wasn't for the fact that he's one of the best microprogrammers in the industry, you'd fire him on the spot.

Motivating Type 1s

In your initial conversation with Harry, ask him why he planted the rumor about your resignation. Listen very carefully to his response and watch his facial expressions to help determine if he's telling the truth. If he looks away from you and tells you he heard it from someone else, you know you are dealing with a Type 1 personality, someone who is not afraid to lie.

Assuming that you still believe Harry is worth saving, make the terms of his continued employment clear. Tell him that if anything like this happens again, he will be dismissed. Invite him to inform you first about any rumor he hears so that you can deal directly with it.

Motivating Type 2s

If you want to motivate Harry to stop his rumor mechanic behavior, you've got to first find out why he's planting the rumors. He may simply not like you. Instead of putting him on the spot and asking him why he doesn't like you, ask a less intimidating question: "Harry, are there things that I might do or say that irritate you?" Use the same probing technique to find out what he likes or dislikes about your organization or the company. You need to find out what's bothering Harry before you can motivate him to stop planting rumors. For example, if he's doing it to get attention, show him how he can realize positive attention by completing key assignments on time.

Motivating Type 3s

Type 3s are normally very tolerant and patient individuals. The fact that Harry has been planting rumors about you is an indication of his dissatisfaction with something you probably did. Carefully review your relationship with Harry over the past six to 12 months. Did you give him a performance review that he did not agree with? Did you promote someone in your organization over Harry's objections? You must first find out what has turned Harry against you before you can motivate him to stop spreading rumors. He may not understand what your role is in the organization. It's time to explain it to him.

Motivating Type 4s

Type 4s love attention and they'll often do anything to get it. Harry may feel that this is the only way he can get that attention. Be careful—he may also have a secret agenda. He may hate his job, or you, for that matter. Document everything you tell him and make sure he understands that if he continues with this behavior, he will limit the opportunities he'll have in your organization. If he doesn't like his job, perhaps you can find a job that's more to his liking. If he doesn't like you and you determine that there is nothing you can do to change the situation, assist Harry in finding a position in another organization.

(?) *Help:* Be prepared for several rough sessions with Harry. If he is spreading rumors about you, he'll be willing to continue lying when you attempt to get at the bottom of what's causing his irrational behavior. Ultimately, he should be ashamed or embarrassed about his behavior and be willing to stop it. If he doesn't, you've done your best to salvage the situation and will have to terminate him.

Warning: This is an extremely serious situation that must be handled very carefully. Immediately notify your boss and human resources of the situation. When you meet with Harry to discuss the situation, always have another person present to witness the conversation. At the conclusion of each meeting with Harry, document your conversation in writing and file it in an official human resources file.

Hallway Talkers

On his death bed, J. Paul Getty was asked by an interviewer, "Mr. Getty, you're one of the richest men in the world, but I must ask you at this moment one last question. If you had your life to live over, what would you do differently?" Without hesitating, Mr. Getty said, "That's an easy question to answer—I'd spend less time talking and more time doing." Your commitment to doing rather than talking will be one of the single most important factors that will determine your success as a manager.

There is a direct correlation between the commitment you have as a manager to your company and the commitment your people have to you to achieve what needs to be done. You may have lots of people working for you who are busy but not getting the job done because they are spending more time talking in the hallways about the problems in your organization than they are solving the problems at their desks. For every employee you have wasting time, you need another who is busting his or her backside just to break even!

The Situation

Your desktop lunch is punctuated by incisive telephone rings in the outer office. As you peer out the door, you see two of your employees frantically trying to handle the inbound telephone calls. When you ask them where everybody is, they tell you they're out in the hallway talking. When you step into the hallway, there they are, clustered together listening to Linda, who is talking their ears off. When they see you, Linda stops talking, and before you can get the words out of your mouth to tell them to get back to work, the group disappears. As they scurry back to their desks, you wonder how many hours a day they spend conversing in the hallway about subjects that probably have nothing to do with work. And every time you catch them, Linda always seems to be orchestrating the meeting. It's bad enough that you're losing the commitment of one employee—Linda—but when she's dragging several other employees down with her, you've got a serious productivity problem in your organization.

Motivating Type 1s

When you confront Linda about the disproportionate time she is spending in the halls talking to the other employees, she does not deny the accusation. When you suggest that she seems to be leading the pack, she smiles and tells you you're right on! You suddenly realize that leadership qualities are inherent in Type 1 personalities.

Press Linda to find out why she is initiating hallway meetings. You may discover some interesting shortcomings within your organization. Remember that Type 1s like to be productive and Linda is probably not using hallway meetings to discuss nonbusiness-related matters. When Linda discloses an organization-related issue that she believes can only be resolved through group discussion, caution her that those issues must be brought to you before they are addressed with the other employees. Remind her that the hallway is not the place to do it.

If Linda doesn't show any signs of complying with your request to stop conducting hallway meetings, take firm action and tell her that this change in behavior is a condition of her continued employment. Type 1s respect authority and this may be all that you need to motivate her to stop the hallway talks.

Motivating Type 2s

Approach Linda about the hallway talks and ask her what is going on. She should give you an honest answer, which is typical of Type 2 personalities. She may tell you that the manager before you condoned hallway meetings. Over time, your hallway-talker employees learned to resort to these kinds of meetings as a way to relieve pressure.

If this is the case, identify the source of the stress. Are your employees being pushed to produce too much, or is the stress a result of management pressure you or someone else has initiated? Are there things you can do to remove the source of the stress to eliminate the need for hallway meetings?

Motivating Type 3s

If Linda tells you she and the others like the relaxed atmosphere of discussing the organization's problems in the hallway, you must look within your organization to determine if you are lacking a controlled mechanism that allows your employees to vent their frustrations in an open environment and participate in a constructive solution at the same time. Motivate them to discuss their problems freely at a meeting scheduled for just this sort of sharing exercise.

Motivating Type 4s

Redefine or establish break-time rules that would allow your employees to vent their feelings. Before you meet with Linda, decide in advance how you'll treat exceptions to those rules. Type 4s will trust you as long as they know that the rules apply to everyone in the company. Let Linda know why it is necessary for her to abide by the company's break-time rules and why you have to enforce the rules within your organization.

Offer Linda a constructive out. Tell her that if she would like to meet with a group of employees to privately discuss a problem within your organization, you'll allow that to happen. Make sure that she and anyone who participates in the meeting understands the ground rules. The subject of the meeting must first be approved by you.

Warning: If you hear your employees saying things like, "I hate this place," you have found the problem. Your employees have lost their motivation to work. However, more subtle negative talk will be difficult to detect and yet it indicates the same problem. Listen for other comments like: "We work under a lot of pressure here." "I've got too much on my plate and they are expecting more." "Why are we always the ones? Why aren't they asking someone else?"

Help: For additional ideas on how to motivate your employees, read *The Quick Motivational Method* by Thomas Quick.

Idea: Establish specific rules for employee breaks. This action probably demands nothing more than a restatement of the existing company policy.

Pessimists

Pessimism is the cancer that takes the life out of motivation and can destroy the work ethic in your organization. Pessimists are always thinking about defeat and are often referred to as obstacle people by their managers because whatever suggestion is made, their minds will instantly traverse to all possible obstacles that will prevent the suggestion from ever getting started. The pure pessimist will defend his position by telling you that one must always be realistic and aware of the possible failure that must be considered with every endeavor. The problem with pessimists is that they cannot see anything beyond the obstacles.

The Situation

You bite your tongue to keep from yelling at Willie as you stalk back into your office. This is the third time this week that this guy has told you an idea won't work because of a myriad of lame reasons. If you hear, "Besides, we've always done it this way" one more time, you are going to want to strangle this man. You've got to figure out a way to change Willie's pessimistic attitude before his pessimism permeates your entire organization.

Motivating Type 1s

Most pessimists will have a Type 1 personality and will draw from their opinionated nature. Getting them to even think about thinking positively is a significant motivational challenge.

Some of the obstacles that Willie has identified may be valid. Assign him the task of removing the obstacles that he has identified so that the project will succeed. If he insists that the obstacles cannot be removed, let him know that if he does not rise to the challenge, you will find someone else who can remove them. If Willie refuses to accept the assignment, you'll have to let him go.

Motivating Type 2s

Type 2s are subject to depression, and subsequently, make excellent pessimists. Although they will identify all kinds of reasons as to why a new idea won't work, they know exactly what needs to be done to remove the obstacles. Appeal to Willie's need to be wanted by telling him you desperately need his help. If you ask him to remove the obstacles, the obstacles will go away.

Motivating Type 3s

Before you start telling Willie what it is you want him to do, invest some time and listen hard to what he thinks he is already doing, what he thinks he ought to do, and what rewards he thinks he deserves for helping you. Your ultimate purpose is to change Willie's pessimistic behavior, but you can't do that with a frontal assault. You have to get his attention first by convincing him that you understand his concerns, and that you can help him—if he changes his frame of mind.

Motivating Type 4s

Lazy people make excellent pessimists and Type 4s fit this bill. Because they do not like to work any harder than they have to, they'll use their pessimistic attitude as a front to avoid getting involved with anything that they perceive will require more work. Do not negotiate with Willie on the viability of the project or the obstacles that he has presented. Tell him specifically what his responsibilities are and how you will hold him accountable for completing the assigned tasks.

? *Help:* Pessimists act similarly to employees who are afraid of change. Review the section beginning on page 92 for further assistance in dealing with pessimists.

Optimists

Optimistic employees provide their own form of motivation, as long as they feel that their goals have a decent chance of being fulfilled. If that feeling changes, they'll either find another job or suffer from a motivational collapse. To keep the motivation of optimists alive, you've got to help them manage their careers by helping them find tasks that interest them. If your optimistic employees feel they are right where they belong, you'll reap the reward of a high return on the time you spend keeping them motivated.

The Situation

As you sit back and wait for Steve to organize his charts, you reinforce your earlier impressions of him. He has a great deal of confidence in himself and works well with others as long as things are done his way. Steve interrupts your thoughts.

"Let me start my presentation by showing you Computech's organization chart. This will give you a point of reference throughout the balance of the presentations." As Steve starts off with an eloquent explanation of his responsibilities, Exhibit 1-1 appears on the screen in front of you.

"...and finally, administration is charged with setting company goals." You're glad he finally got to the part that he was supposed to address in the first place. "It is my department's responsibility to develop our strategic plan. We do it once a year as part of the annual budget preparation process. Here is how we develop our plan...."

You're fascinated with the simplicity of the final exhibit. You have never seen a strategic plan as simple as this one appears to be for a corporation of this size. Unfortunately, Steve's strategic plan does not include several critical components, such as the marketing plan for the company's new southeast market. Steve's optimism has once again overpowered his sense of what's really important to the company. How can you bring him back in line with the real world without destroying his optimism?

Motivating Type 1s

An optimistic Type 1 is potentially one of the best performers you can have on your team. In most cases, Type 1s are very logical in their thinking, meticulous in everything they do, and hard-working. However, if they become too optimistic, they tend to overlook important planning issues. Steve demonstrated this trait when he did not include a critical marketing program in his version of the company's strategic plan. You need to show Steve how to focus more of his attention on important details. Review with him the potential consequences that could develop if an important part of the strategic plan (i.e., the southeast marketing plan) is ignored. Optimists often move at such a fast pace that they overlook important issues.

Motivating Type 2s

Type 2s are detail-oriented individuals who pride themselves on exploiting their analytical capabilities to thoroughly cover all of the unknown issues of any project they're working on. However, if they become overly optimistic, they will bypass issues that they have limited knowledge of. In the above scenario, Steve probably felt uncomfortable covering the southeast marketing program in his strategic plan and allowed his optimism to override his sense of better judgment. In his mind, he felt that the marketing program would take care of itself and, hence, it did not need to be covered. When you point this out to Steve, he should have no problem understanding the importance of not letting his optimism disrupt his judgment.

Motivating Type 3s

Type 3 optimists will allow their optimism to cover up their indecisive nature, which was the case with Steve. Ask him why he did not include the southeast marketing plan in his strategic plan. If he tells you it was because he was unsure how he should address marketing, ask him qualifying questions to determine if Steve feels he has a limited knowledge of marketing. If that is the case, offer to send him to a seminar or course that teaches marketing principles. Coach him to solicit advice from his peers or the management team on subjects with which he may need help.

Motivating Type 4s

Type 4s will often play on their optimistic nature to bolster their charismatic and positive personality. Steve wants everything that he covers in his strategic plan to be positive. When you ask him why he excluded the southeast marketing plan, he will probably tell you it was because he's concerned that the sales department can achieve the plan's optimistic marketing projections. Point out to Steve that good optimists sometimes must play the role of pessimist. Potential problems cannot be corrected if they are not identified.

(?) *Help:* For more information on how to motivate optimists, read Saul Gellerman's book *Motivation in the Real World.*

Employees with Bad Habits

A significant part of most jobs is establishing and maintaining effective relations with people inside and outside of an organization. The personal habits of your employees can have adverse effects on their relationships in the work environment. When personal habits, whatever they may be, interfere with those relationships, the motivation of your organization is undermined.

The Situation

When Clarence walks into your office with a frown on his face, you ask him what the problem is. "I had a closed-door session with Martha last week to find out why the ledgers didn't balance. I honestly tried, but I can't stand to be around that woman more than a few minutes at a time. She smells and looks like she hasn't taken a bath in a long time. Is there anything you can do about it?" You tell Steve you'll look into the matter, and after he leaves your office, you admit to yourself that you have been procrastinating on this problem. Several of your employees have registered the same concern.

This scenario could have taken on many different forms, such as bad breath, humming, teasing, bad jokes, messy work area, fowl talk, or any other form of bad habits. Everyone probably has some bad habits that get on people's nerves. Martha probably doesn't even know she has this body odor problem, but you have a management obligation to help her resolve the problem.

Motivating Type 1s

When you talk to Martha about her odor problem, she'll quickly deny your accusation and probably show a fair degree of anger at you if she's a Type 1. Be prepared to suggest to her that she review the situation with another manager with whom you have previously consulted and who will corroborate what you have just told her. If she is aware of her problem, she will settle down and tell you, "That won't be necessary." Once she has acknowledged the problem, it should go away.

Motivating Type 2s

When you talk to Martha about her odor problem, she will reluctantly acknowledge it and will probably tell you she had no idea it was bothering anybody. Because of their strong moral conscience, most Type 2s will take the initiative to solve the problem without any more prodding on your part.

Motivating Type 3s

When you talk to Martha about her odor problem, the stubborn personality of a Type 3 will display itself. She'll first deny your accusation, and then say, "Even if it was true, its nobody's business but mine." At this point, simply tell Martha you understand her position but if the complaints continue, you will have to initiate corrective action, which could result in her termination.

Motivating Type 4s

When you talk to Martha, tell her up front that you have received complaints about her body odor. Initially, Martha will not take it seriously until you explain the impact of her offending habit on her work performance. Make sure you explain to her the significance of her work relationship with the rest of the people in your organization and with her performance review. This should motivate her to take action to correct the problem.

Warning: Be highly sensitive to the fact that when you are dealing with employees with bad habits, many of the problems that you must resolve are personal. Some personal problems can be better handled on a man-to-man or woman-to-woman basis. Actively seek third-party advice and suggestions before you approach highly sensitive problems.

Boss Squealers

Squealing on your boss as a matter of resolving conflict can carry high risks. It damages relationships and reduces organizational effectiveness, but continues to be practiced by some employees. What they don't realize is that they are placing themselves in a lose-lose situation.

As manager of this type of employee, you undoubtedly lose trust in them, as will your manager, for going behind your back to resolve a problem. There is one thing that you can count on, though. Your manager will dump the problem back in your lap for resolution. While there are a number of explanations for this type of behavior, one seems most probable: The boss squealer probably has had little or no personal experience with any other approach to conflict resolution. In his mind, squealing on his boss or the person with the highest level of authority above you is an acceptable way to resolve personal situations.

The Situation

Your boss catches you by surprise in the parking lot as you are heading home and asks, "What's going on between you and Ed, that new employee of yours? This is the third time he has approached me and told me he thinks the deadlines on his latest assignment are too tight!" You tell her that you'll look into it and you head for home. Whenever Ed doesn't get what he wants, he runs to your boss to plant the seed of dissent. If your other employees find out that Ed has gone around you, they'll be tempted to do the same thing. This situation is irritating you and you know that if you don't motivate him to stop running to your boss, your authority will continue to erode.

Motivating Type 1s

Always remember that Type 1s want things done their own way. If the assignments that you have given to Ed run counter to what he wants to do, he'll continue to go to your boss under the belief that you will eventually cave in to his wants. Check with your boss first to make sure he or she backs you on the stand you want to take with Ed. Then, tell Ed that if he continues to go behind your back, you'll assist him in transferring to another department or finding another job. If your boss won't back you, then your boss may be part of the problem as well.

Motivating Type 2s

When you meet with Ed to discuss the nature of the problem, ask, "Why did you tell my boss about the concerns you had with your current assignment rather that bringing it to my attention first?" Listen carefully to Ed's answer and be honest with yourself. Are you mistreating him to the point where he is so desperate, he feels forced to go over your head to resolve the situation?

If Ed did not voice his concerns to you before, ask him why. Unless he had a good reason for not talking to you, tell him that he should come to you first. Explain to him how the organization works and why you are in the best position to help him when the need arises. Logical explanations appeal to Type 2s.

Motivating Type 3s

If Ed is a paranoid Type 3, he may believe that you are out to get him and that he has nothing to lose by escalating his problems to your boss. Ask him what, if anything, you have done to lose his respect. The next logical question to ask is what you can do to reconcile the situation. If Ed tells you that his latest assignment is unacceptable, find out the specifics of why he felt it was unacceptable. Although the burden of proof is on Ed, if he gives you a reason with which you agree, consider accepting it as a valid reason as you search for a way to motivate Ed to discontinue his backstabbing behavior. Remember, Type 3s are insecure individuals. Ed honestly thought that by going directly to your boss with his problems, he was assuring himself that his problems were known. He's uncomfortable communicating with you, and that needs to be corrected.

Motivating Type 4s

In Ed's eyes, you are mistreating him so badly that he believes his only recourse is to bring the problem to your boss's attention. Type 4s will only do this if they are desperate, so do not underestimate the volatility of this situation. Ed believes that whatever you are telling him to do is so wrong that your boss ought to know what is going on.

Wait until you have your anger under control before you confront Ed. Objectively consider your own possible contributions to the situation. Have you given Ed any valid reasons to go to your boss? If necessary, tell Ed that if he goes over your head again without talking to you first, he undermines the confidence and trust you have in him as an employee. Type 4s are naive, so you have to introduce them to the realities of the situation. Make sure your boss will back you on this statement before you make it.

? *Help:* Your responsibility in this situation is to make sure you have not inadvertently contributed to the problem. What you may consider as a reasonable assignment may seem to another employee as unreasonable. When you delegate an assignment, ask your employees in a nonauthoritative manner if they understand the assignment and believe that the completion goals are realistic.

Idea: If you have talked with Ed previously about his going behind your back, and this situation is continuing to occur, your previous motivational techniques may require some reinforcement. Tell him that he will be terminated if he again goes to your boss without first trying to clear up the matter with you. Put this condition of employment in writing and ask Ed to sign next to your signature. If he refuses to sign the agreement, note that fact in writing, in Ed's presence, on the document. Then, get ready for his next offense, and make sure you are prepared to fire him.

Warning: Once you get the situation with Ed under control, you need to deal with your boss. If you have a good relationship with her, review the action you have taken with Ed and solicit her concurrence. If you are working for a boss who openly encourages interorganizational complaints, you may discover that she may not be supportive of the stern action you want to take. If you're working for a boss with this kind of mentality, be on your guard. Chances are, your boss may not have any confidence in your management style. Depending on your level of confidence, ask your boss with a leading question, "What would you do if I went behind your back to your boss and escalated an internal problem?" Listen very carefully to her answer!

? *Help:* For additional ideas on how to motivate boss squealers, carefully read the next section.

Backstabbers

Disagreement and dissension in an organization are not uncommon, particularly if the organization is undergoing changes normal in today's dynamic business world. However, deliberate attempts to undermine authority are not that common simply because most employees know that such actions carry a terminal risk to their jobs. Put in other words, it simply is not worth taking the chance.

You may, on occasion, run across a dissatisfied employee who thinks that backstabbing is the way to get ahead. If you run into this situation, you need to move quickly to eliminate the problem. Make sure you have just cause to salvage the employees before you embark on the difficult task of motivating them to change their behavior. If there is no justification to keep them (i.e., not a key employee), get rid of the problem by terminating them.

The Situation

"I think you should know what's going on behind your back," Betty says to you after everybody else has left your morning staff meeting. "Fran is running around trying to get people stirred up against you because of your decision to change our starting hours over the next two months. All of us, except Fran, know why you have to do it. She wants us to start using excessive sick leave to protest your decision." You've got a backstabber in your organization and you are going to have to move quickly to neutralize the problem.

Motivating Type 1s

There is a good chance that Fran may not like you as a person or as a manager. She may disagree so strongly with what you are doing that she'll resort to guerrilla tactics to stop you. Fran may be out to get your job and sees your current decision as an opportunity to discredit you among your employees.

If you believe that Fran's after your job and that this episode will be just one of many she will try in order to undermine your position, confront Fran and let her know that she has destroyed your confidence in her. A direct approach will quickly get the attention of a strong-willed Type 1.

To correct the situation, suggest to Fran ways she can earn your respect. A good start would be to come to you first with questions and concerns regarding your management decisions.

Motivating Type 2s

It's not pleasant to think that, for whatever reason, one of your employees is out to get you. Although you may recognize that the simple solution would be to fire Fran, you are more interested in discovering the root cause of the problem so you can prevent it from occurring in the future. Before you confront her, try to find out from your trusted employees what is bothering Fran.

When you confront Fran, let her know you're aware of the damage she's doing to your organization. Put her on the spot by asking, "Before I make a decision on what I should do to correct this situation, perhaps you can tell me why you did it?" Remember that sabotage only works when it is undiscovered. Once it is out in the open, it is a useless tactic. Explain to Fran how her efforts to sabotage you damage your organization and explain to her why mutual respect is critical in any organizational structure.

If she offers to make amends, you have a judgment call to make. Before you make the call, ask her a key question, "Why should I not terminate you for what you have done in my organization?" If she gives you an acceptable answer, watch her closely to make sure she is motivated to support you. If she gives you anything less than a satisfactory answer, eliminate the risk of backing Fran and terminate her.

Motivating Type 3s

Allow Fran a chance to tell you why she believes you are a threat to the organization. If she offers you a convincing argument, listen carefully to what she has to say. If the mishap is a matter of miscommunication on your part, correct the communication error with Fran and hand her a written warning that if she goes behind your back again, she'll be dismissed.

Make sure Fran understands why her actions are unacceptable to you and how they have damaged your trust and confidence in her. If Fran trusts you, she'll probably tell you what it is that is bothering her. If she plays it straight with you, tell her what you are willing to do to resolve the situation and what you expect from her in return. If Fran won't tell you what the underlying causes of her actions are, then you have no way of motivating her to change her behavior. It is now time to offer her a convenient way to exit the company.

Motivating Type 4s

This situation involves overtly hostile acts toward you by one of your subordinates that must be dealt with quickly to prevent your authority from being undermined. Your organization can't run without a leader who has the authority to set direction and change policy.

Fran simply may not like you personally and thinks you're doing a terrible job as a manager. She hates your organization and is not concerned about the risk she is taking of being fired by undermining your decision. It is like one of those "If you don't go, I'll have to go" kamikaze missions.

Helpless Souls

Walter Wriston, the former CEO of Citicorp, said, "Failure is not a crime, but failure to learn from failure is." The difference between the best of us and the rest of us is not determined by how many or how few mistakes we make, but by how much we learn from them. The sign of true champions on the athletic field is not just a great performance, but rather how quickly they respond to their failures and what they learn from them. In order to be innovative and to keep ahead of today's challenges, managers must be prepared to take risks and accept the mistakes that they will make in the process. The issue is not if you make a mistake, but what you'll do after you make the mistake that determines how well you will really do! Unfortunately, the helpless souls in your organization keep making the same mistakes and never seem to learn from them. How do you get them turned around?

The Situation

"What's wrong with Brandon?" asks James, your operations manager. "He used to be so calm under pressure. But lately, at just the hint of any pressure, he seems to go to pieces. It took us an hour to find him yesterday hiding in the men's room. When we asked him what was wrong, he gave us one of his blank stares like he didn't know what we were talking about. We have problems without his help on that front line and if it continues, we're going to have to replace him."

"Unfortunately, this isn't a new problem," you reply ruefully. "Brandon falls apart whenever the going gets tough, which I don't understand. He used to be such a good worker and I hate to get on his back when I don't know what's bothering him. But, I don't want to fire him either. That would really shake him up!"

Motivating Type 1s

There are very few jobs that don't require you to work under some pressure. Brandon is usually capable of performing quite well on the job. Type 1s are typically not afraid of pressure jobs. Something else outside of the job is bothering Brandon. If you allow him to escape to another job with less pressures, you'll reinforce his conviction that playing the role of a helpless soul will get him whatever he wants on the job. Sooner or later, it's almost inevitable that he'll be asked to perform under pressure and you'll get a repeat performance of the "helpless soul." Find out what it is that's bothering him and you have a chance of solving his problem.

Motivating Type 2s

When you meet with Brandon, explain why it is important that he not let the pressure of the job get him down. Make sure he understands the impact that his behavior has on other people who have to cover for him.

Explain to Brandon why you have to rely on him to perform well when the pressure is on and why his inability to cope is hurting your organization. Let him know that you will do whatever is necessary to help him resolve the problem as long as you have his full cooperation. Agree on an assignment for Brandon that will involve some job pressure; meet with him daily to monitor and coach him on his progress.

Motivating Type 3s

Brandon may be using the "falling apart" image to get himself out of unpleasant work. Type 3s don't like to work any harder than they have to. If his helpless state has resulted in people feeling sorry for him and bailing him out by doing the work for him, then he is likely to continue playing the helpless-soul role. Peer support and recognition are very important to Type 3s. When you explain to Brandon that his actions are not getting him positive peer recognition, he will become more receptive to accepting job pressures.

Motivating Type 4s

If you are working for a company that is like most dynamic companies, changes that used to occur a couple of times a year are now occurring daily. Brandon may not have the skills to deal with change that is going on at that speed. The mounting pressure to adapt to the changes is causing him to panic.

The next time Brandon is involved in a stressful situation, make sure you tell everyone on your staff not to rush in to help him. Give him a chance to gain his own self-confidence at performing well under pressure. Offer him advice along the way to help him improve his performance over a period of time. If he improves, even if it's slower than you had hoped, congratulate him.

(?) *Help:* A good course on stress-management techniques may be what Brandon needs to get back on top of his job. After he has taken the course, ask him what he plans to do to put the things he learned into practice. Test his grasp of coping with pressure by asking him how he would handle certain kinds of pressure situations that are likely to occur on his job.

Overconfident Employees

Peak performers know that you can't succeed without taking risks and they never confuse risk with chance. Pioneering sports psychologist Dr. Bruce Ogilvie completed a research project several years ago that shed light on the important distinction between risk and chance. Ogilvie studied several careers that involved risk, including sky diving instruction, aerobatics flying, and race car driving. He discovered that risk-takers are extremely cautious people who will spend an extraordinary amount of time preparing for their next risk venture. They'll analyze every factor that can operate against them. Such arduous planning increases their confidence, commitment, and self-control. Conversely, people who are overconfident check nothing, leaving everything to chance.

The Situation

"I can accomplish anything I put my mind to and nobody is going to tell me otherwise." You interrupt Sharon and remind her that she has been late on every assignment you have given her over the past three months. Sharon cuts back in, "Yes, I may have been late, but look at what you got. The quality of my work far out weighed the fact that it was a little late." To avoid a confrontation, you bite your lip and keep from telling Sharon her work rated a D- on the generous side. You would like to simply give her a termination notice and be done with the problem if it wasn't for the fact that her uncle is one of the company's senior vice presidents.

Motivating Type 1s

It's nice to think you are doing just great when the reality of the situation is that you are doing a lousy job. Sharon has allowed her overconfident behavior to dominate reality. Show her very specific examples of her unacceptable work and attempt to convince her that the reality of the situation calls for substantial improvement on her part.

Motivating Type 2s

Watch out for overconfident Type 2 employees. If you challenge Sharon's belief that she can do anything well, she will become very suspicious of your motives and could bring the problem to upper management, behind your back. Inform your boss of the problem before you consult with Sharon on a solution.

Motivating Type 3s

If Sharon is a Type 3, she will probably tell you she is aware of the fact that she is sometimes too confident and realizes that she needs to be more cautious when she approaches difficult tasks. If you approach her with a positive attitude, she'll ask for your help. This is the first step to solving her problem.

Motivating Type 4s

If you suggest to an overconfident Type 4 that her work is less than satisfactory, she'll go into a dormant mode. Sharon will avoid taking on any work that has even a hint of risk to it. Obviously, this is not what you want. Counsel her on what she is not doing right and show her specific things she can do to improve. Give her a trial assignment and coach her through the completion of all tasks. Always compliment her on her accomplishments and provide constructive criticism when she needs it.

Credit Stealers

People are territorial animals. We all want to stake out something to call our own and we will strike back with all the fury of a rattlesnake if our turf is threatened. In business, and even our personal lives, we get caught up in constant rounds of infighting to get more of what we think we deserve. As a manager, you don't want to smother these territorial and competitive instincts as long as everybody plays the game by the rules. On occasion, you will run across an employee who tries to cheat. Quite often, the act of cheating is subtle, where the cheater will steal someone's idea and try to use it to gain more turf. If he is allowed to do this unchecked, he'll stifle cooperation and competition in your organization.

The Situation

Joan walks over to your lunch table and without hesitation says, "Look at our company newsletter. It's all about James and the new inventory control system." You read the comments made by James, which include, "I thought we needed..." and "I did this...." Joan states her concern by saying, "When you read this, you'd never know this was a team effort and that it was my idea to begin with, not his. I'm here to tell you the entire team is fed up with James the 'credit stealer.'"

Motivating Type 1s

If James has a Type 1 personality, you have a tricky situation on your hands. Extreme Type 1s will do almost anything to make themselves look good. You must first recognize that this is also the goal of all employees in your organization. If they don't initiate action to make themselves look good, how can they expect to get promoted? James, however, has done it at the expense of his team members.

Type 1s can be tactless individuals, as James has demonstrated in this situation. When you meet with him, get him first to concur that the implementation of the inventory control system was a team effort. Once you have his agreement in hand, explain to him why the newsletter article was not appropriate and get his assurance that it will not happen again. Remember that most Type 1s want to do everything right. Explain to James how to properly earn credit on his own.

Motivating Type 2s

The self-righteous nature of Type 2s will propel them to take credit for something they may not have done. James may simply have concluded that he did most of the work and, therefore, deserves all of the credit. In spite of this weakness, Type 2s are loyal to people they trust. When you approach James, ask him how he thought the team functioned on the inventory control project. He will probably tell you that everyone was great and very cooperative. At this point, explain to him in very specific terms how the newsletter article undermined the team. If he understands what you are saying, he will be motivated to stop stealing credit on future projects.

Motivating Type 3s

The dishonesty trait that is instilled in the behavior patterns of Type 3s make them susceptible to becoming credit stealers. Motivating James to suddenly adopt an honest behavior when he has demonstrated a dishonest behavior is about as difficult as convincing the devil to go to church. Since word is out in your organization that James has taken credit for something that he did not do, it will be difficult for him to regain the trust of the employees in your organization. Type 3s are independent and want to do their own thing. However, they also like to receive credit. Show James how credit is earned by working with others.

Motivating Type 4s

Type 4s can be so self-centered that they don't honestly know when they are stealing ideas from others. Plan to have several lengthy discussions with James where you patiently explain to him how and why his peers perceived that he took credit for something that he did not do. Once you have convinced him that he did take credit for something that was not his, explain the consequences to him in terms of lost peer respect.

A public apology by James in your next staff meeting may be in order to mend the situation. After James makes his apology, appeal to his optimistic nature by showing him how to regain the trust and confidence of his peers.

Rebels Without a Cause

Have you ever known employees whose habitual reaction to management decisions was to dig in their heels to resist doing what they were told to do? This coping mechanism is a personality trait probably learned in early childhood in response to authoritative parents or teachers. Variations of this behavior pattern show up in the form of automatic resistance and disagreement to anyone's idea or suggestion. The rebellious and defiant reactions are motivated by a fear of being coerced or controlled. It is a protective posture, often fueled by suspicion or distrust of anyone with power. Rebels without a cause slow the group down because their arguments and disagreements must be dealt with. They can never be counted on to be constructive members of any team.

The Situation

"What's wrong with Simon?" Joe asks indignantly. "All I asked was for him to expedite a supply requisition. You would have thought I'd asked him to restructure the entire company! I thought you told me this order has top management priority?" Although you can sympathize with Simon somewhat because Joe is not your easiest manager to work for, you know intuitively that Simon has a problem. On repeated occasions he has refused to do tasks that are well within his job description. You've got a true rebel without a cause on your hands.

Motivating Type 1s

Type 1s are particularly insensitive and critical of others. Simon understands exactly what management has asked him to do and is deliberately ignoring the request. He may not agree with or respect you or Joe. In all probability, he really doesn't have a reason to rebel and is just doing it to be obstinate.

Formally write Simon up for disobeying a management directive and inform him of how serious the situation is if he disobeys a legitimate management request again. Type 1s do not like to take orders from someone they may not like or trust, which is probably the case with Joe. Explain to Simon why it's important that he obeys management directives if he wants to advance his career in the company.

Motivating Type 2s

Type 2s can be judgmental individuals who believe they have the right to question and refuse any assignment you give them. You need to adjust Simon's priorities. Explain to him that you are paying him a salary to perform certain job functions. Tell him that if he does not want to perform those functions, you'll be glad to help him find another position where the assignments are perhaps more to his liking.

Motivating Type 3s

Simon's stubborn and lazy behavior is a problem that you must contend with. Appeal to the obedient side of his behavior. Tell him he will be fired if he refuses to follow legitimate directions.

Motivating Type 4s

Some rebels will have Type 4 personalities and can be as obnoxious and rebellious as the other personality types. In all probability, Simon is demonstrating the obnoxious side of his personality. If you tell him he will be fired if he refuses to follow legitimate directions, he will immediately change his behavior to accommodate your request.

Company Saboteurs

Many companies are anxious to reinvent the notion that the company is their employees' home away from home. If you did your job right and stayed out of trouble, the company would take care of you. In the good old days when you found a company like that, you were lucky. Loyalty is a fine old concept whose time has passed. IBM provides us with the classic example of how it was and the way it is today. The real issue in today's corporate world is whether your employees' interests and the company's interests continue to coincide. If they do, then you and your employee can continue to be loyal to each other. If they don't, then it's your responsibility as a manager to look after the company's interests first.

The Situation

As you stare down at the 18th hole of the McCormick Golf Course, you can't believe what Doug has just told you about your company's pending acquisition of Sysmec, Inc. That information was extremely confidential. How did he know? You ask him a carefully worded question, "Oh, you must have read about it in *The Wall Street Journal?*" Doug replies, "No, actually one of your employees, Cindy Smith, told me all about it." Of course the article never appeared in *The Wall Street Journal* but your ploy got Doug to identify the saboteur in your organization. This is the second time Cindy has leaked confidential information out. If she wasn't so good at what she does, you'd have fired her long ago. If you can't motivate her to change her behavior, that's going to be your only option.

Motivating Type 1s

Type 1s are typically very loyal to whatever task they are working on. In this situation, Cindy has been working on part of the acquisition and has, for some reason, lost her loyalty to the company. Find out why Cindy leaked the information. A direct confrontation is in order here. Preface your conversation with a question: "Cindy, are you aware of the fact that this acquisition is extremely confidential?" Of course, you both know that you have already briefed everyone on the acquisition team about the project's confidentiality. So Cindy's answer will be very revealing.

If Cindy's answer to your question is not acceptable, you will have to fire her. If she provides you with acceptable answers, formally write her up and ask her to sign the warning. If she refuses, fire her!

Motivating Type 2s

Type 2s are very loyal to people they like and respect. The fact that Cindy has told an outsider about the acquisition places in question her loyalty to you. When you confront Cindy about this situation, put the conversation on a personal level. Ask her if she has lost her sense of loyalty to you and the company. If she has, you won't have the time it takes to restore her loyalty and the risks of further information leaking out are too great. You will have to fire her. If she tells you she didn't realize how sensitive the acquisition information was, you need to coach her on how she should manage her job responsibilities. Next time, before she says anything to anyone, she should ask you if she's unsure about the sensitivity of her job assignments.

Motivating Type 3s

Most company saboteurs have Type 3 personalities. The dishonesty trait inherent in their personality leads them in this direction. Dishonesty is an act that people employ if they believe they can gain something from the act. If Cindy leaked the information to Doug to gain something, like a better job with him, you'll have to fire her.

If Cindy honestly doesn't know why she committed her act of sabotage, find out if she is uncomfortable in a job that requires the handling of confidential information. Type 3s tend to become insecure when put under pressure, so transferring Cindy to a job that does not require the management of sensitive information may be appropriate. She must convince you that she understands the importance of confidentiality to your satisfaction or you'll have to terminate her.

Motivating Type 4s

Uncommitted Type 4s can engage in acts of company sabotage without even being aware of the seriousness of their act. If this is the situation with Cindy, you need to shock her back into reality. Tell her in no uncertain terms that she will be fired if she sabotages the company again. Trust is important to Type 4s and you will have shaken Cindy when she understands she's violated your trust. Show her how she can regain your trust by confiding in you any questions she might have on protecting confidential information.

Overempowered

Empowerment is one of today's most powerful business tools. When employees feel they are personally contributing to an organization's success, and feel they can influence the way things are done while being recognized for their efforts, they feel empowered. The empowerment process energizes people to tackle daily challenges, increase the quality of their work, and improve their productivity. Successful organizations are those best able to apply the creative energy of empowered individuals to achieve constant improvement. When people feel empowered, they are more likely to accept constant improvement, or change, as a way of life. However, overempowerment is a direct path to danger.

The Situation

George is good at what he does; but he needs to slow down. He has just one speed—fast. Whenever you give him an assignment, you can count on the fact that he'll show up at your office door, telling you he's done with the project a few days early, asking for another project. The problem confronting you is that several employees in your organization have complained about George's work tactics. If he asks them for something he needs to complete an assignment and they can't give it to him immediately, he goes behind their backs and takes whatever he needs. How can you motivate George to become more diplomatic without destroying his empowered drive?

Motivating Type 1s

Type 1s are committed to work, goals, and high levels of productivity. They like to be in the lead position and demand high work standards from others. The fact that George is overempowered simply means that he has an extreme Type 1 personality.

Since Type 1s can become highly insecure if anyone challenges their beliefs, you need to work with George on his people skills. Show him how to apply diplomacy when seeking support from others. He would be well advised to adopt some of the personality traits of a Type 3, the diplomatic player.

Motivating Type 2s

Type 2s want their feelings to be understood and appreciated by management. Your objective in this situation is to get George to back off a little when dealing with other people. George honestly thinks he is helping the people he pushes around to get whatever he needs.

Explain to him that people will only appreciate him if they understand why he needs their help.

Motivating Type 3s

Type 3s want to be independent and do their own thing, which is the primary reason why George believes he is totally empowered to do anything. He also needs management recognition and support of his empowered role. Tell George that although you support and appreciate the fact that he's empowered, you question the "steamroller" tactics he's using to get others to support him. Ask him if he will back off a little when dealing with others. Once you show him how, he will.

Motivating Type 4s

Type 4s want to be popular with everyone and believe that anyone who helps them achieve their empowered objectives is going to be their friend. George would be devastated if he knew that most of the people he's been pushing for support resent his efforts. Diplomatically explain to George how his actions can be misinterpreted by others as unwelcome encroachments. Show him how to ask for people's support in a nondemanding and noncondescending manner.

(?) *Help:* Overempowered employees act in a very similar manner to overconfident employees. Review the section on overconfidence, starting on page 119 for motivational techniques that may further assist you in dealing with an overempowered employee.

(?) *Help:* If you need more ideas on how to manage empowerment in your organization, read William Byham's book *Zapp the Lightning of Empowerment.*

Underempowered

A number of years ago, a philosopher by the name of Ed Rye said, "You are where you are because that's exactly where you want to be." Over the years, empowerment has received a great deal of attention, and a number of books have been written to show you how to become instantly empowered. The implication is that the motivated aren't satisfied with where they are in life and are striving to achieve a higher goal. Conversely, the underempowered and unmotivated are satisfied with where they are in life and want to go no further. If you believe this, then you can skip this section.

The Situation

Bill, your director of quality control, walks into your office and shuts the door. You can tell he is upset about something. He begins by saying, "After the employee-empowerment meeting, I spent some time roaming the halls and factory floors. I did a lot of listening and talking to the employees. They are excited about the concept and can't wait to see it implemented. However, there is another side of the coin. Every one of your managers is vitally concerned about what will happen to their jobs and responsibilities if empowerment is really implemented. The managers will do everything they can to block empowerment. And if they are successful, the employees will revolt. If the managers fail, you'll have a management revolt on your hands. As I see it, you're in a lose-lose situation."

Your morning staff meeting begins and you ask Bill to share his employee-empowerment concerns with the team. He agrees and repeats what he told you Friday evening. You thank Bill and start the meeting off with your opening remarks. "I know the decision to move more of the operational and day-to-day decision-making responsibilities down to the employees will not be an easy one to implement. But given today's productivity and competitive standards, we've got no choice if we want to stay in this industry." The confrontation that you expected from Jim, one of your department heads, begins as he stands up and says, "Quite frankly, I am concerned about our ability to pull this employee-empowerment thing off. The whole program runs counter to our basic management beliefs and principles." Jim is the most underempowered person you have ever known. What can you do to get him empowered?

Motivating Type 1s

It is unusual for a Type 1 to be underempowered. Most Type 1s have a strong conviction for work and are extremely goal-oriented. Knowing that, you figure there must be something in Jim's personal life that is causing his underempowered behavior.

A private conversation with Jim outside of the workplace is in order. Take him out to lunch and diplomatically express your concerns about his lack of motivation. Ask him if there is any work-related issue that is bothering him. If not, try to find out what personal issues are bothering him that you can help him resolve.

Motivating Type 2s

Type 2s are focused team players who have the innate ability to concentrate on whatever demands their attention in any given environment. Jim may have all kinds of personal problems that he's dealing with, but when he's at work, he should be able to focus on the task at hand in an empowered frame of mind. The fact is, he's not motivated.

Confront Jim about the situation and honestly express your concerns. Chances are, there is some work-related issue that is causing Jim to feel underempowered. Once you have identified the issue that is bothering Jim, work with him to find a solution to his problem.

Motivating Type 3s

Type 3s can quickly become uncommitted to whatever it is they are doing. When this occurs, they will go from an empowered to an unempowered state of mind overnight.

Approach Jim and ask him why he's no longer committed. Once you find out why he's lost his commitment, assuming there is something you can do about it, eliminate the cause to restore his commitment to empowerment.

Motivating Type 4s

Type 4s want to be popular with everyone. When they believe they are, they're empowered. Jim believes he's lost his popularity within your organization and has subsequently become underempowered. Find out why he feels this way and you'll restore his motivation.

Warning: Constant stroking will be required to maintain the motivational levels of your underempowered employees until they develop their own self-confidence. Personality Types 2 and 3 are the most insecure of the group and will, therefore, require the greatest amount of attention.

(?) *Help:* For additional ideas on how to motivate the underempowered, see page 145 for tips on motivating unmotivated people.

Summary

One of the greatest challenges you have as a manager is to find ways to motivate your people and keep them motivated during the course of the workday. In this chapter, we introduced you to a number of common and perhaps some not-so-common employee situations that required the use of a variety of motivational tactics. In some instances, our scenarios introduced specific employee problems that had to be identified first, and different techniques were used to motivate each of the four personality types. In Chapter 5, you'll learn how to handle the personal problems of your employees, which can and will affect their work performance.

Motivating Employees with Personal Problems

If you attended a traditional college or university, and most of us did, you were taught how to apply the quantitative aspects of management to solve business-related problems where you invoke plan A, B, or C to solve the dilemma. Your academic challenge was to resolve case-study problems that were relatively simple to decipher and typically did not include any serious human interaction problems. If human interaction was required, it was played on an organization stage where all of the players were expected to perform within the confines of their defined job roles.

Anybody who has been in management for more than a day knows intuitively that this is not the way it works in the real world. Personal problems can and will disrupt the performance ability of those most valued employees upon whom you are relying to implement your strategic plan. Your star accounting auditor will not be motivated to complete a critical audit if she is encountering disruptive personal problems. As an astute manager, you must be prepared to take charge of motivating your employees to resolve their personal problems.

Divorce

A divorce, or the pending possibility of a divorce, can devastate the morale of any one of your employees. Many noted psychologists believe that a divorce has the same, if not more devastating, psychological effects on a person's motivation than the death of his or her spouse. The bottom line is that if you have an employee who is going through a divorce or who has just been divorced, you are saddled with an employee who needs your help to regain his motivation.

The Situation

Ron is one of your best systems analysts. When he walks off the podium at the executive staff meeting in a huff after one of the executives asks him when the company's Internet project would be completed, you wonder where his mind is at. Ron's pending divorce has got to be causing him some problems. How can you help this guy get back on track? You're going to need his all-out effort on a major project that starts in two weeks.

Motivating Type 1s

Ron's Type 1 pride has prevented him from talking to anyone about his marital problems. If you approach him about the problem, you'll probably encounter an "I'm okay, just leave me alone" response. If you are not one of Ron's close and trusted friends, that is about all you will get. Let him know about the upcoming project that you need him to support and tell him that if he can't give you a commitment in one week, you'll find someone else. Although this sounds like a threat, it may be just what Ron needs to motivate him to get his act together.

Motivating Type 2s

Type 2s will move into deep depression during the early and late stages of a divorce. It is almost impossible to motivate them to accomplish anything important during this stage of their lives. Be patient with Ron during this cycle, but also inform him that you will be relying on others within your organization to perform the tough tasks. Ron will let you know when he is ready to offer you 100 percent of his support.

Motivating Type 3s

Type 3s will display premature "bounce back" symptoms to show that they are over their divorce. That will lead you to believe that Ron is ready for the tough assignments, which he may not be. Watch his performance closely to make sure he is truly on the emotional mend. Consult often with his close friends.

Motivating Type 4s

The bouncy, fun-loving nature of a Type 4 will have you scratching your head and wondering if his dissolved marriage had any effect on him whatsoever. It did, but because of his personality, it will be difficult for you to see the harm it has done unless you and Ron are very good friends. Be careful not to overload his work schedule until you are sure he is on a recovery path. Check Ron's progress with his close friends and solicit their advice.

Newlyweds

In busy times, it is standard practice for managers to ask their employees to work overtime. Most employees are acutely aware of their obligation to support their employer when things get busy. However, newlywed employees often have a different set of priorities that can drive the most patient manager up a wall. How do you motivate newlyweds to respond to the needs of their job?

The Situation

It's great to be a newlywed, but Helen seems out of control. Every time you walk by her desk, she's on the phone with her new hubby. Helen has been married for two months now and you were hoping that she'd get over her excitement about getting married and return to being motivated to get her work done. It hasn't happened, and in your opinion, the problem has gotten worse. It's time to have a little chat with Helen to set the record straight.

Motivating Type 1s

Close personal relationships are difficult for Type 1s to find, and when they do find them, they are ecstatic. Helen is demonstrating this personality trait by calling her new husband excessively during the day. When you approach her about the problem, do it in a casual manner. Say something like, "Helen, I congratulate you on your recent marriage, but I believe that your personal calls all day long are disrupting your work." You have to tell her exactly what you have witnessed over the past two months. Her personal calls to her husband should decrease.

Motivating Type 2s

Sensitive Type 2s will take offense when you approach them about a personal matter that, in your opinion, is disrupting their productivity. Be prepared for a semihostile reaction when you approach Helen about her excessive telephone calls to her husband. If you provide her proof of the number of times that she has talked to her husband on company time, she'll quickly back off on her objections.

Motivating Type 3s

If you confront a Type 3 about the disproportionate number of phone calls she is making to her spouse, she will display a high degree of embarrassment. Once you convince Helen that you know what is going on, her excessive phone calls to her husband will dramatically decrease.

Motivating Type 4s

Carefree Type 4s will view their excessive calls to their new spouse as a God-given right until they are caught in the act. Your firm statement to Helen that this is not an acceptable use of company time will quickly bring her back to reality.

Alcoholics

Most companies have well-defined policies covering alcohol abuse. The typical policy might state that no alcohol is allowed on the company's property unless it is a part of a company celebration, such as a Christmas party. However, most company policies stop short of alcoholic mandates during an employee's off-work hours for fear of invasion-of-privacy ramifications. To cover this ground, many companies include a caveat where a manager can terminate an employee who he believes perpetually comes to work intoxicated. However, the burden of proving this issue falls squarely on the manager's shoulders.

The Situation

Denise steps up to the podium to talk about the company's manufacturing operations, a subject that you've asked her to present at your staff meeting. Denise joined your company 10 years ago as a design engineer and progressively worked her way up through the ranks, landing the lead operations position four years ago. Over the years, Denise has acquired the reputation of being technically brilliant in the manufacturing engineering field and you don't want to lose her.

However, over the past several months, you have noticed the distinct smell of alcohol on Denise's breath when she arrives at work. Although she seldom goes out to lunch, you can count on the fact that if she does, her breath will have the smell of alcohol on it when she returns. In spite of your suspicion that Denise is either an excessive drinker or an alcoholic, you don't believe she's drinking on company property. Her job performance continues to be excellent even with her drinking problem.

Motivating Type 1s

When Denise tells you that the manufacturing division is the "tail that wags the dog" and it is therefore the most important part of the company, you are convinced that you are dealing with a Type 1 employee. When she tells you that every department in the company should ultimately report to manufacturing and that she intends to become the leader in that transition, you realize that you are dealing with a very strong Type 1 employee who will find it difficult to admit to any personal problems.

Type 1s do not want anyone to dictate their destiny or to tell them what to do. Given the scenario, you must break the rules in this situation. Confront Denise with the fact that, on several occasions, you have smelled alcohol on her breath and you want to know what's going on. Your short-term objective is to get Denise to agree that she's been drinking and to open up a dialogue with you to resolve the problem.

Type 1s have the highest degree of respect for quantitative and factual information. Alcohol abusers cannot be motivated to resolve their problems if you cannot get them to acknowledge those problems in the first place. If you confront Denise and she denies the problem or tells you she doesn't know what you're talking about, be prepared to show her a log in which you have documented the times and dates of each occurrence. If that doesn't work, invite her to talk to other people who will confirm her alcohol problem. If she admits to the problem, you have a chance to help her. Otherwise, see the warning at the end of the section.

Motivating Type 2s

Type 2s always want to be understood and will admit their weaknesses. The best way to motivate Denise to resolve her alcohol problem is to assure her that you will help her. If Denise believes that you understand her problem, you'll have a better chance of motivating her to solve it.

Type 2 personalities get along with each other more than any of the other personality types. If you have a Type 2 personality, you have an excellent chance of communicating well with Denise to help resolve her problem. Alcohol abusers cannot be motivated to resolving their problems if you cannot get them to acknowledge them. If you are not able to communicate effectively with Denise, refer her to one of your associates who has a Type 2 personality for help.

Motivating Type 3s

When you casually mention to Denise that you smelled alcohol on her breath, her response will probably be overwhelming. She'll profusely apologize, ask for your forgiveness, and will tell you it will never happen again. In fact, you may become so overwhelmed by her apologetic acknowledgment of the problem that you'll be lulled into thinking you solved her problem. Unfortunately, the smell of alcohol will again appear on Denise's breath.

Type 3s doubt themselves so much that they will do almost anything to be accepted by others, particularly their managers. If you confront Denise about the alcohol problem and probe a bit, she will acknowledge the problem. In the same breath, Denise may tell you she is on top of the problem and that it is about to go away. All you can do is give her encouragement and hope for the best.

Motivating Type 4s

Extreme Type 4s who are alcoholics lack innate motivation and will only respond to motivational tactics that have a clear and specific meaning to them. Their alcohol problem at work could be solved with the following scenario: "Denise, as we have both agreed, if I smell alcohol on your breath one more time at work, I'll be forced to ask for your resignation." Ask her to sign a note to acknowledge the warning you have given her.

The note that you ask Denise to sign simply states the time and date you told her about the consequences of her drinking problem. If Denise refuses to sign the note, indicate that on the note, as well as her reasons for not signing. Denise's refusal to sign reduces your chances of motivating her.

If you get a commitment from Denise to stop drinking, be prepared to constantly monitor her compliance. Watch out for Type 4s who may try to play every trick in the book, such as covering their alcohol breath with peppermint.

Warning: The resolution of an alcohol-related employee problem is a 90/10 proposition. That is, your employee must immediately acknowledge your concerns about the problem and agree to take immediate steps to resolve it in the short-term (less than 30 days). Advise her that she owns 90 percent of the problem and you own 10 percent. Let her know what the consequences are for noncompliance. If she doesn't resolve the problem, then exercise your 10 percent minority interest and terminate the employee.

Drug Addicts

Drug addicts often conjure up images of skid-row derelicts who have hit bottom. Since most of us don't have much interaction with such people, we comfort ourselves with the falsehood that we don't have to deal with drug addicts. However, drug addiction is actually the use and abuse of drugs that interfere with normal function, on or off the job. By this definition, then, drug addicts undoubtedly make up part of the working population. Based on this supposition, you either have or will have a drug-related problem within your organization.

Unfortunately, a common way that many managers choose to deal with drug addiction is to choose not to notice it. However, if you have an addict or potential addict in your organization whom you choose to ignore, the problem will eventually explode in your face. If you want to avoid the explosion, prepare yourself to deal with the problem face-to-face by first recognizing that you have a moral obligation to help drug-addicted employees. Here's why: The first signs of drug-caused deterioration are likely to show up at work even before they show up and begin to affect an addict's personal life. The quality of an employee's work is a sensitive indicator of how well his brain is functioning. You'll get an early warning of impending disaster well before most other people who are close to the employee, such as spouse or family members, will.

If no one intervenes during the early stages of addiction, a drug addict will continue to destroy himself. If, in your opinion, your employee's work has suffered as a result of his drug addiction, you have the right to demand that he admit himself for drug treatment, or if he refuses, to terminate him.

The Situation

You can't believe what you have just been told. Karl is apparently using drugs during breaks. "I've seen him go out to a remote corner of the parking lot on several occasions and sniff what I assume is cocaine," Tom tells you. You thank him for the confidential information and hang up the phone. You don't want to believe that one of your best employees is on drugs, but you admit to yourself that Karl has been acting strange over the past several months. His eyes seemed to have a glassy appearance, and in a presentation the other day, he seemed to slur every other word. The use of illegal drugs by one of your employees can cause all kinds of motivational problems in your organization.

Motivating Type 1s

If Karl has a Type 1 personality, he will deny that he is taking any kind of drugs when you approach him about the problem. Remember, the burden of proof is on you and there is not much you can do if he will not admit to the problem. If your company has a drug screening policy, ask Karl if he will take a drug test. If he won't, and the drug test is a condition of employment, be prepared to terminate him on the spot if he refuses to acknowledge the problem and accept your help.

Motivating Type 2s

If you are patient and control the way in which you ask your questions, you will probably get Karl to acknowledge his drug problem. He will also be very responsive to any professional help you can offer him. Remind Karl that this is a one shot deal: If he kicks the habit, he keeps his job; if he cannot, you'll have to let him go.

Motivating Type 3s

You won't get much of a reaction out of Type 3s when you approach them about drug-related problems. In fact, they probably won't say anything and will just glower at you in disgust. You may have to use the threat of a drug test to get them to start communicating with you. If this does not work, your ultimate weapon is their job. If they will not acknowledge the addiction problem, you have no way to help them. Tell them that!

Motivating Type 4s

Type 4s are some of the world's best optimists. When you confront Karl about his drug addiction, he'll quickly tell you that the problem has been resolved. If you push him to find out what specific steps he took to kick the habit, his story will get very weak. The suggestion that he take a drug test will probably be all you need to get him to tell you the truth. He'll readily agree to accept whatever professional help you can offer him. Your challenge will be to verify that he sticks to his convictions.

(?) *Help:* You as a manager have enormous motivational power over employees who have drug problems. That's because you control their paycheck, the financial vehicle that provides the addict with access to the drugs they need. Your mission is to get the addict to stop using drugs, because that is the only way they can keep their job. Insist that they seek treatment from a drug assistance program and inform them that their participation in the program is a condition of their continued employment with the company. If they refuse to enter the program, inform them that they will be fired. You motivate addicts with sincere, but direct, threats to their livelihoods. The best thing you can do for Karl, yourself, and the company is to motivate him to seek outside professional help. Many companies have programs where they will pay for the outside help for first-time offenders.

Smokers

Many corporations throughout the world are reviewing the escalating costs of health care for their employees and are becoming acutely aware of the high cost of health insurance to cover employees who smoke. In their neverending battle to reduce overhead, companies are implementing smoke-free atmospheres within the compounds of company property. As a result, it is becoming increasingly difficult for smokers to find a vent for their habit when smoking regulations are suddenly put in place. This can cause serious motivational problems for your smoker employees.

The Situation

Henry is openly violating company policy and he knows it! Last month, the company issued a new policy that forbids smoking anywhere on company property. And yet, there is Henry, standing against a tree in the parking lot smoking a cigarette for all to see. To make matters worse, he's openly defiant about the new regulation. On more than one occasion, you have heard him tell his co-workers that nobody is going to tell him where he can and can't smoke. You are about to burst his bubble!

Motivating Type 1s

There is a good chance that you are dealing with a strong Type 1 here. Henry is just waiting to vent his hostilities and frustrations because of his irritation over the no smoking regulation. To avoid a confrontation, neutralize the situation by telling Henry that smoking on company property is no longer an option. If he continues to smoke, he will be terminated.

Motivating Type 2s

When you confront Henry about his abuse of the company's policy, make sure he understands the seriousness of the matter. Type 2s respect authority and understand why companies need policies and procedures. Although he clearly does not like the no smoking rule, he will comply with your request.

Motivating Type 3s

The obedient nature of Henry's Type 3 personality should come out when you politely inform him that if he is caught smoking on company property again, he will be fired. If Henry is a heavy smoker, he may not be able to comply with your request and will probably start smoking in his car while he reads the help wanted ads.

Motivating Type 4s

Henry will continue to think that the company's no smoking policy is a joke until you inform him in writing what the consequences are for continued violations. If the company offers assistance programs for stopping smoking, make sure you offer the program to Henry.

Financially Challenged

Financial independence. That's a goal many people would like to achieve, and they will go to great lengths to get there. Some will work for corporations or government agencies, while others will choose to become entrepreneurs and move into the private business sector in a relentless drive to reach their goal of independence. For those who make it, happiness and the ability to get the most out of life is theirs forever. Unfortunately, most will not even come close to meeting their goal of achieving complete financial independence to the point that they will never have to work again. Their biggest financial challenge will be to simply keep a positive balance in their checkbook from payday to payday. Financially challenged employees are difficult to motivate unless you can help them get on top of their financial problems.

The Situation

"Elaine, I can't help it if you are not making enough money here to make ends meet at home. I just gave you a raise, which you told me at the time was more than generous, and now you're telling me it is not enough." Elaine gives you that hurt look and bolts out of your office. As her manager, you find yourself scratching your head to find a way to help this lady solve her financial problems. She's an excellent worker and you don't want to lose her to a higher-paying employer.

Motivating Type 1s

It is very difficult for a Type 1 to admit to the fact that she has lost control over her personal finances and it can have a devastating effect on her motivation. It will help Elaine put the problem in the right perspective if you can show her how widespread the problem is and suggest that she take a class on personal financial management.

Motivating Type 2s

The analytical and focused minds of Type 2s should keep most of them out of financial problems. If Elaine is a Type 2, she is going to be extremely frustrated and will need outside assistance to help her solve her problem. Refer to the Help section on page 145.

Motivating Type 3s

Many of your financially challenged employees will have Type 3 personalities because of their tendency to avoid establishing firm financial goals. If Elaine demonstrates a lazy or uncommitted personality trait, then there is probably nothing you are going to do to help solve her problem. Even if you direct her to a class on the subject, she probably won't go unless you offer her a reward for going. Give her the day off. Once she starts going to class, she'll realize the importance of financial planning.

Motivating Type 4s

Many of your financially challenged employees will have Type 4 personalities because they do not like to plan anything unless it's a party. Show them how financial planning can also be fun. Demonstrate how they can watch their money grow in different interest-bearing accounts and how easy it will be to chart their financial progress. Once they realize the process can be fun and may only require a few minutes of their time a day to maintain, they'll implement a financial plan.

(?) *Help:* If your company does not offer a course on personal financial management for its employees, try to establish one or compose a list of programs that are available in the local communities. Check with the community colleges, universities, and chambers of commerce for program sources. Your local library will have dozens of books that cover all aspects of personal financial management.

Unmotivated Mules

Getting the attention of someone who possesses no motivation can be a challenging and frustrating task for any manager. An old story illustrates our point. A lady was driving through the country when she came upon a farmer who was beating a mule over the head with a two-by-four. She quickly got out of her car and demanded to know why the farmer was abusing the poor mule. With a sigh, the farmer explained that he was just trying to get the mule's attention. To get the attention of someone with no apparent motivation, your methods have to be a lot more subtle than a two-by-four. Unlike the farmer, your problem is not the thickness of a mule's skull, but rather reaching the high activity level of the human brain.

The mind you are trying to reach has been stuffed with lots of other ideas. One of the most difficult motivational tasks is to change someone's attitude, especially when that person has strongly held convictions. You can't come at her with a frontal attack. She will view that as an attack on her judgment or self-esteem. Because you can't motivate her by challenging or exposing her faulty reasoning, you might begin the motivational process by agreeing with her. Listen first and talk later. The ideas that are inside someone's head have a momentum of their own. The key to your motivational plan should be to contrive a way to make your ideas a welcome intrusion. Most communication failures occur the instant they are initiated because the message is not wanted by the recipient.

The Situation

As you stroll unobtrusively through your accounting department, you notice the lack of industry from one of your employees, Judy. Once again, you find her staring at her computer monitor. Her hands

145

are resting on the keyboard and nothing is happening. In fact, if her eyes weren't open, you would have thought she had fallen asleep. Back in your office, you review the last two months of Judy's production. She's processing less than half the invoices of anyone else in the department and has been consistently late closing out her portion of the accounts receivable ledger. When you review Judy's personnel folder, you also take note of the fact that she has a consistent record of complaining about the company's compensation plan.

Motivating Type 1s

The quickest way to snap Judy out of her unmotivated frame of mind is the tell her exactly how unsatisfactory her performance is.

Motivating Type 2s

Type 2s are typically blessed with a commitment to work. It's doubtful that Judy has lost her commitment, even though it may appear she has when you find her staring at her computer monitor. Chances are, some external event is dominating her mind. Diplomatically ask her what's distracting her from her work; chances are, she's probably confronting a personal issue. If she is confronting significant personal problems, she might need your assistance in obtaining outside professional help.

Motivating Type 3s

Type 3s have a lazy streak in their personalities. There is a good chance that Judy's poor production numbers are a reflection of the fact that she's feeling lazy. Although you may not choose to accuse her of being lazy when you confront her about the problem, show her how her performance compares with that of the other people in the department.

Ask Judy for an explanation as to why her productivity is down. She probably won't have one because Type 3s will not acknowledge that they can be lazy. To motivate her to increase her productivity, explain to her how her job performance and productivity are used to determine her compensation. Let her know when her next performance review will take place.

Motivating Type 4s

The irresponsible nature of Type 4 personalities is most likely causing Judy's behavior and low productivity numbers. Type 4s have to be constantly reminded that you are not paying them to be irresponsible. Make sure she knows exactly what she must do to meet minimum performance standards and specify everything in writing.

⑦ *Help:* For additional ideas on how to motivate unmotivated mules, see page 128 for tips to motivate underempowered employees.

Nearly Retired

Yogi Berra once said, "The game isn't over until it's over, but eventually, it's over." For nearly retired employees, that day may come long before their pension checks gets processed. It comes when they reconcile themselves to the fact that they have risen as high as they are going to rise, regardless of whatever they do. Creeping retirement can become a cancer that eats away at an individual's motivational well-being. The challenge to motivating near-retirees is to convince them that setting performance records should be very important to them. The best way to end a career is not in terms of where one has ended it, but in terms of how far one has come.

The Situation

Good old Ed is driving you crazy. When you ask him to do something, he just looks up at you, smiles, and tells you he'll look into it. When you tell him you don't want him to just look into it, you want him to do it, he keeps smiling and gives you his standard speech that you've learned to hate: "I've been here a long time. This company will continue whether I complete this project or not. Trust me when I say I'll look into it before I retire in six months." Unfortunately, Ed's the only one qualified to handle this assignment or you would have given it to someone else.

Motivating Type 1s

If Ed has a Type 1 personality, he was probably a real power player in his day. You can rest assured that he knows how to play the manipulation game with the best of them and he's manipulating you in this situation.

If Ed has a lot of contacts from his years of employment with the company, be careful. If you have a confrontation with him, he may discredit you with as many of his contacts as possible. Remember, he has nothing to lose because his career is almost over. You have everything to lose, so play along with Ed as best you can until he retires.

Motivating Type 2s

If Ed has a Type 2 personality, he's extremely loyal to the company. His seeming lack of urgency for the assignment you have given him is just a cover. He really wants to be appreciated and to know that he can still provide a valuable function to the company.

To excite his loyalty traits, explain to Ed how important this assignment is to the company. When you tell him he's the best one qualified for the job, stand back and watch Ed perform.

Motivating Type 3s

Even though Ed appears to be dancing around the assignment you've given him, the obedient nature of his Type 3 personality provides you with a way to get him back on track. In a firm tone, tell Ed that you don't want him to look into the assignment—you want him to do it! Don't be afraid to tell him that if he can't give you the commitment you need, you'll find someone who can. Ed will rise to the challenge.

Motivating Type 4s

People with Type 4 personalities are friendly individuals who also like to be cute, as immature as that sounds. Ed thinks he's being cute when he tells you he'll look into your assignment. He also believes he can get away with it in view of the fact that he's about to retire.

If you don't take control of this situation, Ed will continue to play his friendly, cute role. Ask Ed if he wants to be treated just like every other employee in your organization even though he plans to retire in six months. When he says yes, tell him that if he cannot commit to your assignment, you'll write him up, just as you would any other employee in your organization.

Grieving Individuals

In an office high above the city streets, two managers were having a serious conversation. One, heavily troubled by a personal crisis, paced the floor relentlessly and then sat down, a picture of despair. He had come to his trusted friend for advice. Together they had explored the problem from every angle without coming up with any solutions. This only deepened the man's discouragement. "I guess there is no power that can help me."

His friend reflected for a moment, then spoke rather defiantly. "I wouldn't look at it that way. I believe you are wrong in saying there is no power that can save you. Personally I have found there is an answer to every problem. Why not try prayer power?"

As managers, many of us have been taught that there is a separation between church and state and between church and work, which is most unfortunate. How can you ignore the spiritual needs of a human being just because he is at work? The situation that follows will give you some ideas on how to handle a difficult situation with one of your grieving employees.

The Situation

When Jake tells you his wife of 23 years has just been diagnosed with terminal cancer, you automatically approve his request for the rest of the week off. He's the proposal manager on a project that is critical to the company, but you can certainty figure out a way to cover for him for a week.

When Jake calls you Monday morning and requests more time off, you ask him how much time he needs? He tells you he doesn't know, and you start to panic. You've got no one to immediately replace Jake on the proposal team and you estimate your chances of winning the proposal will drop 50 percent if Jake is not there to provide his technical support and leadership.

Grief at the thought of losing a loved one is one of the most powerful and disabling events to those who experience it. It would be wonderful if you could just tell Jake to take off all the time he needs to recover, but you can't.

Motivating Type 1s

Jake is acutely aware of the problem that his absence from the proposal team is causing, but that doesn't alleviate his grief. Gently insist that Jake set a regular schedule where he can come into the office daily to meet with the proposal team. It may also help him deal with his grief by giving him an outside interest.

Motivating Type 2s

The high emotional state of Type 2s may make it difficult for Jake to come into work, even on a part-time basis. The solution might be to let him work on his part of the proposal at home. The risk you take is that he may be less able to concentrate at home than he would at work.

Motivating Type 3s

The extreme insecurities that Type 3s feel when emotionally threatened by the death of a love one may preclude you from wanting to bring Jake into work on a part-time basis to work on the proposal. The best approach might be to offer him a leave of absence and find yourself another proposal manager.

Motivating Type 4s

If Jake's a Type 4, he's devastated by the terminal illness of his wife. You won't see it on his face because he'll hide it inside. There is nothing you can say to him that will get him back on the job under the current situation. He will probably agree to meet with his replacement on the proposal team to turn over key information.

Liars, Cheaters, and Thieves

Every once in a while, we are reminded by perhaps a headline in the morning's paper that business life doesn't always bring out the best in everyone. In the daily scramble to get ahead and make a buck, some people don't play by the rules and become liars, cheaters, or thieves. Inevitably, the loss of old-fashioned values gets blamed for causing the problem as we desperately search for a universal solution. The reality of the situation is that there is no universal solution.

Ethics problems that occur within an organization must be identified and dealt with on a one-on-one basis.

The Situation

Allison, the vice president of personnel, walks into your office and asks if she can speak with you. She shuts your door, takes a seat, and proceeds to tell you some things about your organization that you find appalling.

"As you know, our CEO asked my department to conduct an integrity audit on the company. Let me tell you what I found in your organization: Twenty percent of your people are cheating on their time cards and 36 percent lied when they were asked on the company's life insurance form if they were smokers. Sixty percent of the calculators that were issued to your staff over the last three months cannot be located. The assumption is your people have taken them. I'm sorry that I have to be the one to dump the bad news on you, but better that you hear it from me first, rather than from the CEO."

You agree and thank Allison for informing you of the dismal news. You ask her to conduct another audit after you have had a chance to address the problem with your staff. She agrees, and as she leaves your office, you can't help but wonder if your organization is made up mostly of liars, cheaters, and thieves.

How do you go about motivating an entire organization to change a dangerous set of habits? You plan to hold a series of meetings with everyone in your organization to stamp out the problem before it stamps you out. Because all four personality types will be present in each meeting, you decide to present each issue in a format that will get the attention of each personality.

Motivating Type 1s

To grab the attention of your Type 1 employees, show the dismal percentages that Allison gave you. If your people are under heavy work pressure and are exposed to situations that are fraught with ethical risks, be on your guard. Constantly brief your Type 1 employees of the ethical responsibilities that they have. Remind them that you are trying to prevent dishonesty.

Motivating Type 2s

Because of their analytical mind-set, your Type 2 employees may question the accuracy of Allison's statistics. Plan to spend your initial presentation time showing them why you believe the numbers are statistically accurate. When you have their attention, tell them what actions you are taking to prevent this from happening again. Audits will continue until the problem has been resolved.

Motivating Type 3s

You'll lose the attention of your Type 3 employees unless you address the commitment that you expect from them. In your initial presentation, get tough and mandate a cease and desist order. Back your order up with a warning, stating that any employee caught lying, cheating, or stealing from the company will be immediately terminated.

In the normal course of working with your subordinates, periodically ask them if there is an ethical conflict with what they are doing in their job, such as processing cash transactions. Sensitize them on how important ethical issues are and how easy it is to overlook them.

Motivating Type 4s

As a manager, you are responsible for making sure that all of your subordinates are aware of the company's ethics. Periodically remind your Type 4s about these ethics because they will quickly forget them. Your Type 4 employees may not take you seriously until you tell them that periodic audits will be conducted to determine who is violating company policy.

Warning: Hard-core motivational tactics designed to halt lying, cheating, and stealing need to be constantly addressed to maintain the integrity in your organization. To assure your credibility, be prepared to fire the first person who lies, cheats, or steals from the company.

Help: Although you can't wipe out skullduggery altogether, you can take steps to cut it down to a manageable size. To keep most people on their best behavior most of the time, eliminate the conditions that encourage unethical acts in the first place. Add safety guards to deter those who are exposed to conditions such as cash transactions that could lead to unethical conduct. It's a lot easier to eliminate or minimize tempting conditions than it is to figure out who will pass or fail an ethics test.

Prima Donnas

Almost every business has at least one of them. Startups and growing companies actually need them—the supremely self-assured stars, the people with all of the answers, the prima donnas of the world. If properly motivated, they are very productive, imaginative, and effective individuals. But their huge thirst for acclaim and autonomy, while driving them to excel, can also spark tension, lower morale, and kill productivity in your organization. Prima donnas are the kind of people you don't like to fire because of their productive value. How do you drag your superstars back down to earth?

The Situation

Bob, one of your salesmen, is driven and phenomenally productive. The trouble is, he knows it and he's been driving his co-workers nuts with temper tantrums, rudeness, and other displays of bad behavior. Things have gotten so bad that several of your employees have complained to you about the problem. Apparently, he is so demanding and disruptive that nobody is able to get any work done. You can no longer afford to have a prima donna on your staff. You must motivate him to change his behavior.

Motivating Type 1s

Type 1 prima donnas can take lots of different forms, from the raging egomaniac to the more subtle passive-aggressive. The one thing all Type 1 prima donnas possess is a tendency to put themselves ahead of the team. Like a wild mustang, you've got to break them of that habit. Call Bob into your office and tell him, point blank, what the sales team thinks of him. If he challenges your accusations, invite him to attend a meeting with his peers to hear what they have to say about him.

Motivating Type 2s

If you believe you are dealing with a Type 2 prima donna who thinks he is the greatest thing on earth, hang on for the ride. Extreme Type 2s want to know that their feelings are understood by everyone. If you burst their bubble and tell them that, in spite of their exploits, nobody is behind them, they may instantly hand you their resignation. If you want to keep Bob in your organization, handle this situation with kid gloves.

Motivating Type 3s

Type 3s can be very insecure. It is not uncommon for them to use a prima donna front to hide their insecurities. You need to find out what is causing Bob to feel insecure before you can break his prima donna behavior. Exploit the cooperative side of Bob's personality and ask him to divulge one of his insecurities to you. Then together identify possible solutions to alleviate the insecurity and agree on a plan to make it happen.

Motivating Type 4s

Type 4s make excellent prima donnas with their obnoxious, self-centered personalities. One of the best ways to handle them is to confront them early and candidly in an unthreatening manner. Type 4s want to be popular with everyone and Bob thinks that his prima donna front will gain him popularity with his peers. Explain to him why his perception is wrong—tell him how others really perceive the obnoxious behavior of prima donnas.

Summary

Motivating employees with personal problems is one of the toughest challenges you will face as a manager because each situation will be unique and will involve different personalities. In this chapter, we presented several typical situations that you may have to contend with and offered a variety of solutions. When dealing with these situations, the most important piece of advice we can offer is this: Listen carefully to what your employees have to say and ask as many questions as necessary before you offer your advice. In Chapter 6, we will address the related topic of how to motivate employees through adverse change.

Motivating Employees Through Adverse Changes

Adverse changes are internal and external events that negatively affect the motivation of your organization. When people are bothered by something they cannot control, they lose motivation, which affects their work. Some may be distracted from concentrating, while others will spend excessive time venting their feelings, both of which are counterproductive. Adverse changes have widely varying effects on the different personality types. Aggressive Type 1s may treat change as an opportunity, whereas insecure Type 3s may become apprehensive about the unknown aspects of change.

For example, executive management is in the process of negotiating an acquisition. It may be viewed as a negative event by some employees who are concerned about perceived layoffs or changes in their benefits. The threat of an acquisition is disrupting their motivation. In some cases, the events are internal in nature, such as our acquisition example, or they may be external. External events are usually completely outside of the control of company management, such as inflation or world conflict, but they can still have a devastating effect on employee morale.

In this chapter, you'll learn how to motivate employees, regardless of their personality type, to overcome stress and fear brought by internal and external changes that are outside of their control.

Corporate Downsizing

As we head into the last years of the 20th century, we see more and more companies downsizing by offering early retirement plans to get rid of the older employees who are paid more than the younger ones. Some companies will try to wriggle out of their pension commitments because of their staggering costs, much to the shock of older workers. For the younger workers, downsizing has some dismaying implications, such as who you can trust.

People differ in their ability to cope with cold, hard facts and you can't treat them all alike. For those who are tough enough to confront corporate downsizing, your best approach to motivate them might be to tell them, "If the lifeboat sinks, everyone's on their own. So let's all do what we can to keep it afloat." For those who are terrified by the situation, you might have to dampen your approach and tell them, "This is going to be a tough storm, but if we all pull on the oars, the captain of the ship will navigate us out of this mess." How you motivate employees with different personality types to cope with downsizing is what this section is all about.

The Situation

You're halfway through your staff meeting and as you conclude your comments regarding next week's work schedule, you ask if there are any questions. George jumps up and anxiously asks if there is any truth to the talk he's been hearing about downsizing. "We want to know if we're all going to lose our jobs." You admit that there may be some truth to the rumors, although nothing has come through the official channels yet. Financially, the company is not doing as well as Wall Street would like, and you have sensed mounting pressure to reduce costs in order to boost the financial standings. Your boss has told you to anticipate several downsizing mandates by the end of the week.

Motivating Type 1s

Let your information-hungry Type 1 employees have all of the facts they need to make plans for their future. Be sure to distinguish between what you know as confirmed information about the company's downsizing plans and unconfirmed rumors or tentative plans. For example, if the company is planning to announce layoffs on July 1, you have a firm date to present to your employees. If the magnitude of the layoffs is undecided, you can't provide them with any information regarding the size of the planned layoffs. Reject any request to speculate.

Motivating Type 2s

The best way to combat downsizing rumors with your Type 2 employees is with the truth, which is difficult to do if you are not sure what the truth is. Just because you are in the management chain does not give you access to all of the privileged information, so you may have to do some digging to find the truth. In the interim, explain to your Type 2 employees as best as you can what's going on. Keep them motivated and focused on their current assignments. You might tell them, "I am aware of a potential plan to downsize the company. In recent months, the company has suffered some financial setbacks that have been publicized in the news media. That may be the source of the speculation about downsizing. Ignore the rumors. I will keep you informed. In the meantime, if you focus on your work, that's the best job security you can have."

Motivating Type 3s

To diffuse the immediate concerns of your Type 3 employees, assure them that you will look into the situation and address the subject in your staff meeting next week. Encourage them to discount any rumors they may encounter while you gather the facts, and make sure they understand that the best job protection they can have is by demonstrating their own good performance.

Motivating Type 4s

Inform your Type 4 employees about the company's layoff policy to help minimize their insecurity over the situation. Special provisions, such as early retirement or extended leaves of absence, may have been put into place to cover the downsizing activities. Ask senior management to clearly explain the rules before you address the concerns of your Type 4 employees.

Idea: Reassure your employees whose jobs you believe are secure and counsel them on what they need to do to maintain their current level of employment. Discourage them from participating in complaint sessions and tell them to concentrate on maintaining superior job performance. Take whatever steps you need to assure that they are motivated to perform well during the adversity caused by the downsizing activities.

Warning: If you tell any employee that they will not be laid off, make sure you can make that commitment. Your credibility as a manager relies on their confidence in your integrity, so be careful about making "forever statements." For example, your boss may have signed off on your list of employees whom you believe should be excluded from the pending layoff. If you then tell them that they will never have to be concerned about being laid off, you're making a commitment that goes beyond the current layoff period and one that you clearly cannot make.

Help: For additional ideas on how to motivate employees through downsizing activities, see the section on layoffs that begins on page 163.

"Rightsizing"

We have often been taught to leave well enough alone—"If it ain't broke, don't fix it!" But how well does this advice hold up as we confront the challenges of the future and the computer age? It's easy to succumb to the idea that we'll enjoy the sweet smell of success indefinitely if we don't mess with it, but this is bad advice. In our highly competitive world, following these old axioms will leave you and your company in the dust. To build a bridge into the future, many of the more aggressive companies have created the concept of "rightsizing" where they are constantly testing the size and fit of everything. Do they have the right number of people? Are they in the right markets? Are they targeting the right customers? And so on. The point is, because rightsizing is a daily, weekly, and monthly exercise, what may be right today could be wrong tomorrow and, therefore, must be instantly changed. Instant change puts pressure on an organization's employees, who must be prepared to adapt quickly to the changes as they occur.

The Situation

The bigger your company becomes, the harder it is to tell how your employees feel about their jobs. It's frustrating you because you are losing contact with your people, and it is becoming increasingly difficult to gauge their feelings about all of the company's rightsizing activities. To help you get back into the communication cycle with your troops, you decide to implement monthly "town hall" meetings and invite everyone in your organization to attend on a voluntary basis. The format of the meetings will be simple. Anybody in your organization can anonymously write a question on a piece of paper for you to address during the meeting and/or present questions from the floor. One of your primary concerns is to address each question in a format that is responsive to the needs of the mixed personality types in your organization.

Motivating Type 1s

In a rightsizing environment, things are moving fast and there are lots of activities that are constantly going on within an organization. It's the perfect environment for action-oriented Type 1s. Openly share with them where your organization is going, and they'll support 100 percent of the changes.

Motivating Type 2s

The fury of rightsizing activities bothers Type 2s, who tend to get emotional if things are moving faster than they would like. They are detail-oriented individuals who like to analyze everything before it happens, which is impossible in a rightsizing environment. To help them get accustomed to the changes that are occurring, provide them with as much detailed information as you can.

Motivating Type 3s

Because they are unsure of themselves in the first place, Type 3s are thoroughly confused by the avalanche of changes that are occurring as a result of the rightsizing activities. They won't know which way to go and what to do unless you lead the way and tell them exactly what they must do. Tell them to ignore the adverse publicity as best they can and concentrate on improving the productivity of their respective jobs.

Motivating Type 4s

Like their Type 3 counterparts, Type 4s lack direction and tend to be disorganized under the best of circumstances. All of the rightsizing activities will be confusing to them unless you constantly explain to them what's going on. Remember, they're followers, not leaders.

Bottom-Line Fallout

The sharing of information from the company's income statement with the rank and file can prove to be a powerful tool for motivating them as long as they understand the numbers. However, if they don't, the reverse can be true and bottom-line fallout will occur. That's when employees who have no access to the financial records of the company must rely on financial hearsay to make operational decisions. These decisions are often based on emotion rather than facts. If the accountants in the organization are allowed to, they'll lump everything on the statements together, into a bottom line, and issue a call to reduce expenses by some huge percentage across the board. In their dogged pursuit of the bottom line, they will firehose innumerable good ideas.

The Situation

"We don't have passion in this company anymore. Instead of passion, we have bean counters. They've killed the financing for our research and development effort and everyone's motivation to work in the process." You ask Art to sit down so that you can explain to him what's happening. This will not be an easy sell because the bottom line zealots, or bean counters as Art calls them, are in charge of the company.

Motivating Type 1s

If Art's a Type 1, you don't need to spend a lot of time with him. Confirm to him what he already knows—the bean counters are in charge and hence, their bottom line wishes will be carried out.

Motivating Type 2s

Art's speech demonstrated the unforgiving attitude of his Type 2 personality. Convince him to back off in the interest of protecting his job. If the bean counters get wind of his attitude, he's history. Tell him these situations tend to get resolved in the short term and to be patient.

Motivating Type 3s

Normally, Type 3s are very patient individuals. Calm Art down by explaining to him the reality of the situation. He'll quickly come back to his senses and will be willing to wait until the bottom-line fallout has been neutralized.

Motivating Type 4s

Type 4s are afraid of adverse facts that could disrupt their belief that everything should be fun. Convince them that sometimes it is best to know the facts today so you can work on improving things for tomorrow. The belt tightening that is required today will assure them that they will have jobs tomorrow.

Acquisitions

When two companies merge, there's often a temptation to gloss over tough questions about which company's culture will dominate after the merger. The failure to resolve differences in corporate cultural issues can lead to hostile problems down the road. The acquired employees are often uneasy about their new boss and their job security, which frequently translates into low morale. To avoid these pitfalls, when Bruce Mancinelli, CEO of VM Systems, acquired another software company, he conducted welcome interviews to make the new people felt at home. He listened to their concerns and offered them official letters of employment, promising them their current salaries, similar job responsibilities, and a comparable benefit plan. Within a week of the acquisition, both companies were in the full swing.

The Situation

Your attention is suddenly drawn to what has been happening in the local stock market. The bulls jumped into the market yesterday, which presents some hostile takeover challenges to your company's management team. They moved quickly to grab the bull by the horns in a valiant effort to shake off the hostile takeover attempt. But just when you thought they had everything under control, things take a turn for the worse. In a strategic move that happened almost overnight, your company is acquired by your arch rival. The announcement was immediately followed by the resignation of your company's CEO and the senior vice president, two good friends of yours. To survive the aftermath of the acquisition, you find yourself trying to salvage your own motivation and the motivation of your employees.

Motivating Type 1s

It's easy, particularly for a negative person, to find the downside of an acquisition. The best way to motivate your Type 1 employees is to convince them to accept the acquisition as a positive event. Tell them of the upsides, such as new growth opportunities or larger market share. Type 1s will get excited about an acquisition if they think there is something in it for them. Maybe you can get yourself excited in the process.

Motivating Type 2s

Acquisitions make Type 2s very nervous. After the acquisition has been announced, they'll immediately go into their analytical mode in an attempt to find out why the acquisition occurred in the first place. Get them to change their focus and concentrate on the future rather than the past.

Motivating Type 3s

Your Type 3 employees will want to know if the acquisition will place additional demands on them. Tell them that that should be the least of their concerns at a time when there could be layoffs. Convince them that they should be directing their attention at proving their worth to the new owners of the company, if they value their jobs.

Motivating Type 4s

To vent their irritation over the acquisition, your Type 4 employees will, in all likelihood, make fun of the acquiring company and its management team. In the process, their derogatory remarks can reflect on you and your organization if your boss finds out that your people do not endorse the acquisition. Remind them that if they value job security, they should keep their opinions to themselves.

Layoffs

Some problems have no painless solutions, and managing a layoff is not one of the exceptions. It has long been a trend of American business that when sales or profits decline, the first element of cost that gets reduced is labor. Labor usually translates into the lowest paid employees. In instances where drastic cutbacks were needed, it included white-collar workers, who were traditionally not included in the cutback formula. In recent years, all of that has changed. You are expected to minimize the harm layoffs cause to an organization. In this section, we'll show you some of the techniques that you can use to at least dampen the trauma that is associated with layoffs.

The Situation

Your company has ordered a 10 percent across-the-board reduction in its work force. The announcement appeared in this morning's newspaper, where you heard about it for the first time. When you arrive at work, you find your office flooded with employees all demanding to know what's going on!

To gain control of the situation, you tell everyone you plan to meet with them in small groups later in the day to discuss the news release. Your plan is to split your employees up into their respective personality types and then meet with them in those groups, where you can customize you presentation to address their unique personalities. Once you complete these sessions, you'll hold a department-wide meeting to make sure you communicate key layoff issues to everybody in a central setting.

You return from a hastily called meeting in which your boss explained the nuts and bolts of the layoff announcement. As you suspected, it boils down to Wall Street's dissatisfaction with the company's bottom line and its stock performance. You've been told that 10 percent of your people must be laid off within the next two weeks and that you must maintain your existing production quota with the re-duced head count or you will be included in the layoff numbers. How do you motivate your people when you find your own motivation slipping?

Motivating Type 1s

The potential threat of being laid off is a direct assault to Type 1s, who believe they are always right. For them, the prospect of a layoff implies that they may have been wrong, which can have a devastating effect on their motivation. To neutralize this situation, you need to explain to them in very logical terms that this layoff is directed by Wall Street and has nothing to do with them personally.

Be honest with your Type 1 employees. Tell them that your department will be reduced by 10 percent and that you will still be required to maintain current production levels. Type 1s love to push each other to be more productive, and if you provide them with the proper motivation and challenges, they'll produce beyond your wildest expectations once the layoffs have been announced.

Motivating Type 2s

The layoff announcement has emotionally shaken your Type 2 employees. In the early stages of a layoff, they will be in a depressed state of mind.

They'll probably tell you they feel responsible for the layoff mandate. To motivate this group, you have to address their guilt and dispel any responsibility they feel they have for the layoff.

If you can successfully dispel the group's self-imposed guilt and responsibility for the layoffs, you have a chance of restoring their motivation. If you are not successful at accomplishing this objective in the first meeting, schedule a second meeting, or as many meetings as it may take, to restore their faith in themselves and in the company.

Once you have restored the faith and confidence of your Type 2 employees, you can motivate them by appealing to their greatest strength, their commitment to relationships. Type 2s will do anything they can to salvage a valued relationship. If they believe the company does care about them in spite of the announced layoffs, they'll do anything they can to assure its success.

Motivating Type 3s

Type 3s want to feel good all the time, and clearly a layoff announcement is not sitting well with them. They like to operate in a self-serving environment in which it is difficult to tell if they are the manipulator or the manipulated. They are shrewd actors and can play either role with finesse.

The quickest way to get Type 3s back on the motivational track is to tell them when the problem will go away. For example, if you tell them that the layoff announcements will be made exactly one week from today, they'll accept that and go about their business.

If you cannot provide your Type 3 employees with a layoff target date, their insecurity will continue to grow.

Motivating Type 4s

Type 4s always want to look good socially. The fact that the company's layoff announcement was published in this morning's paper did not sit well with them. As one told you when you walked into the meeting room, "I've got a lot of explaining to do to my friends and family. What am I going to tell them?"

Type 4s are, by nature, uncommitted individuals. Chances are that every one of your Type 4 employees updated his or her resume within minutes of reading the announcement in this morning's paper. They will leave you the moment they find a comparable job. If you are looking for voluntary attrition to help meet your 10 percent layoff quota, your Type 4s will help you out with voluntary terminations.

Type 4s look like they are always having fun regardless of adverse situations. They will be the first to come up with jokes about the pending layoffs. However, they tend to be highly insecure people on the inside. If you have key Type 4 employees whom you don't want to lose, consider meeting with them privately and telling them that they are not on your layoff list.

(?) *Help:* For additional ideas on how to motivate employees caught up in layoffs, review the downsizing section on page 155.

Inflation Spiral

When things get tough, conventional wisdom offers us a lot of free and useless advice, including such favorites as "don't make waves" and "play it safe." Inflation is like a cancer that feeds on your paycheck. All of the conventional wisdom in the world can't erase the fact that with run-away inflation, similar to what we experienced in the late 1970s, people are forced to take a pay cut everyday. The first things that they are forced to cut back on are the things they enjoy, such as vacations and entertainment. Inflation can devastate the morale of your best people, who may take their anger and frustration out on your organization.

The Situation

Your finance manager, Susan, comes into your office to talk. She asks, "With all of the inflation going on right now, I'm having a devil of a time keeping up with my bills. To be honest with you, I'm actively looking for a higher-paying job." Susan has had a solid track record as a chief financial officer. Her academic background is impressive. She is a CPA and has recently earned a master's degree in computer science. You don't want to lose her to the competition.

Motivating Type 1s

Type 1s like money, but they will accept a viable long-term opportunity over a short-term money option. If you can convince Susan that you have big plans for her within your organization, she may drop her job search.

Motivating Type 2s

If Susan is a Type 2, she'll lock in on exactly how much money she needs to beat inflation today. Her number will change tomorrow. Find out how much she needs. If you can match it, you'll keep her until she hits you up for more money. If you can't match it, or convince her that inflation is temporary, wish her good luck on her next job.

Motivating Type 3s

Susan demonstrates an uncommitted attitude typical of a Type 3 when she tells you to give her a raise or she'll leave the company.

Before you tell her to shut the door on her way out, find out why the raise has become a paramount issue in her mind. Chances are she already has an offer from another company and is indirectly challenging you to match it. If she is a valuable employee to your organization, you may want to offer her the additional money she feels she is worth to prevent her from leaving. Money is typically not a lasting motivator. Look for other ways to motivate Susan (for example, recognition for good performance or key job assignments) if you want to keep her for the long term.

Motivating Type 4s

The last thing a Type 4 wants to do is spend time and energy finding another job. They are most likely bluffing, so if you call their bluff, they'll probably back down. That, however, is not the way to motivate a good Type 4 employee whom you want to keep. If you can't meet Susan's salary increase request at this time, tell her when she can realistically expect a performance and salary review. Advise her of specific issues she can work on in the interim to improve her overall performance rating.

Lost Market Share

Every company's financial position is affected by the actions of its competitors. In our global marketplace, more and more companies are learning to break away from costly old habits. A particularly bad habit is to let your competitor define your market, causing you to lose market share. For example, Levi Strauss's menswear division was competing unsuccessfully in a market created by Haggar, the long-established leader in men's slacks. Levi's mounted an all-out assault to no avail. Their division president explained, "It seemed that there was no passage up the face of Mount Haggar until we discovered Dockers and created our own Mount Docker."

The Situation

Sharon tells you that your arch-rival competitor has just taken the $2.5 million Intel account away from your organization. She goes on to say that everyone in your organization just heard the news and they are paranoid about what's going to happen to them. You wonder

167

how you are going to be able rebuild the motivation of your troops and rally them around a recovery plan.

Motivating Type 1s

Your recovery plan calls for you to develop an aggressive marketing campaign that you can direct at your competition to regain your lost market share. Employ the power of your aggressive Type 1 employees to help you put the plan together. They'll rise quickly to the challenge.

Motivating Type 2s

Your market share recovery plan must be implemented with people you can count on. Your Type 2s are the best ones for the job. They are dependable and extremely reliable. Assign the key tasks in your plan to Type 2s to ensure that they will get done.

Motivating Type 3s

Strategic plans must be creative to be truly great. Call on the creative talents of your Type 3 employees to come up with ideas to regain your lost market share. If they are properly motivated, they'll find inventive ways that you hadn't even thought of.

Motivating Type 4s

The charismatic nature of your Type 4s can be called on to help keep everybody in your organization motivated while creating and implementing your recovery plan. Use your Type 4s to help organize motivational meetings, public relations events, and special programs to maintain the motivation in your organization.

Key Management Resignations

For any organization to run successfully, two elements are essential. One is good leadership at the top and the other is good leadership throughout the organization. The same requirements apply to manufacturing companies, service businesses, professional firms, nonprofit organizations, social service agencies, educational institutes, or volunteer groups. The need for good leadership throughout an organization is universal. Conversely, the loss of a good leader can prove to have a devastating effect on the employees within that organization. In this section, you'll learn how to restore your employees' motivation after they have lost a cherished leader.

The Situation

At the end of the day and after a number of long and stormy confrontations with Steve, you accept his resignation. You decide to eliminate the position of vice president. Many company insiders contended that Steve's career got stalled in the quality quagmire. He tried to cancel TQM (top quality management) because of the lack of impact he felt the program had on customer satisfaction. He had the backing and support of everyone in your organization. When he resigned, you sensed an abrupt halt in all of the motivational progress you had made in your organization. Because of Steve's immense popularity with your people, you need to handle his resignation with diplomatic gloves to restore motivation in your organization.

Motivating Type 1s

Your power-oriented Type 1 employees will tell you how much they're going to miss Steve and then they will ask you for his job. To keep them from slipping off the motivational track, be prepared to provide a good explanation as to why you are eliminating Steve's position in your organization and discuss other opportunities that will become available either within your organization or the company.

Motivating Type 2s

Many of your Type 2s will be legitimately emotional over Steve's resignation. Without breaching any personal confidences, explain to them why Steve chose to leave. That will help to diffuse the situation and allow your Type 2s to get back to work.

Motivating Type 3s

Most of your Type 3s will be uninvolved in Steve's resignation, and they probably won't care about it. If they were working for Steve, they will show some concern about who their new boss will be, so tell them how you plan to merge Steve's department with one of your other departments.

Motivating Type 4s

Your charismatic Type 4 employees who liked Steve will be very upset when they learn about his resignation. When you tell them that you do not plan to replace him, they will want to know whom they will be working for so that they can determine whether their new boss will measure up to the standards they have set for Steve. Provide them with that information as soon as possible to help minimize rumors and speculation.

Key Employee Resignations

We've all had key employees we have admired. They are the ones who have seen it all and have been with the company since the beginning of time. Anytime anyone has a question that he or she can't answer, they run to the key employee who always seems to have the right answer. Over time, they build up a tremendous amount of respect with the rank and file. When they resign, your people will wonder why the key employee left the organization and will begin to question if they should stay themselves. When people start thinking about leaving an organization, their productivity takes a serious nose dive and their motivation disappears. How do you restore the motivation in your organization after a key employee resigns?

The Situation

Betty is one of the best employees you have ever had working for you. When she tells you she has accepted a job at another company, you use every trick you know to try and convince her to change her mind. In the end, you wish her the best of luck. Her resignation leaves a hole in your organization that's going to be hard to fill. She was admired and respected by everyone in your organization. During the course of the week after she left, several of your employees expressed concern over Betty's resignation and have even expressed an interest in finding another job. You don't want this thing to get out of hand and drain the motivation from your organization.

Motivating Type 1s

Type 1s are always driven by events and circumstances to try and improve their position in life. They respect Betty's decision-making ability and believe that if she made a decision to leave the company, then it must have been the right decision. The reality of the situation was that Betty left for personal reasons. When you explain to your Type 1 employees that Betty left for personal reasons, they'll stop looking for a job just because Betty did.

Motivating Type 2s

Type 2s may feel that they were partly responsible for Betty's resignation. This may be difficult for you to understand, but it is consistent with the loyalty side of Type 2s' personality. Betty was their good friend. Your extreme Type 2s may even try to find a job at the company were she is now working. To stabilize the situation, make sure your Type 2s know that Betty left for personal reasons.

Motivating Type 3s

Type 3s tend to be unsure of themselves and so relied on input from Betty more than any of the other personality types. Now that she is gone, they're lost. Set up weekly meetings so that you can listen to their concerns and offer advice just as Betty did. Over time, they will find a replacement for her.

Motivating Type 4s

The spontaneous nature of your Type 4s will come into play shortly after Betty leaves. If they can find another job within a short period of time after Betty's resignation, they'll take it. After that, those who are still there will forget about Betty and latch onto her replacement, once one is found. Immediately after Betty's resignation, meet with any of your Type 4 employees and tell them why Betty left.

Threatening News

The news was devastating. August 30, Florida City: A young couple walked through rubble where their house used to stand, the same house where the young man had been a boy and where his father had grown up. Now it was just a pile of wood and bricks. Looking around, they saw ripped up hunks of aluminum siding from trailer homes.

Hurricane Andrew was a disaster greater than most of us will ever experience. The scars it left will be slow to heal. Unfortunately, it is a fact of life that there will be other hurricanes in the future, as well as earthquakes, forest fires, and world conflicts, all of which gets lumped under the heading of threatening news. It's threatening because some people develop a natural fear that it could happen to them. Fear is one of the worst demotivators and you must be prepared to deal with it in your organization.

The Situation

As you pull into the parking lot at work, there are clumps of people standing around talking about Hurricane Andrew and all of the damage it did. You can tell this is going to be one heck of a productive day. With everyone wrapped up in the news about the hurricane that pounded Florida last night, nothing is going to get done today unless you can quickly create a diversion.

Motivating Type 1s

Tell your task-oriented Type 1s that you want them to organize a hurricane relief effort where the people in your organization can donate food and clothing to the victims. Make sure they understand that this project should not get out of hand and disrupt productivity. They'll rise to the challenge.

Motivating Type 2s

When you inform your Type 2 employees of your efforts to organize a relief program, you'll instantly lift them out of their state of despair. They love the opportunity to help someone else. Give them the task of assisting your Type 1s in organizing the program and watch their motivation level climb to record heights.

Motivating Type 3s

When your Type 3s hear about the relief effort, they'll accept it as a great way to help the victims of the hurricane. They'll start thinking about what they can donate to the cause, but they will stop short of volunteering to help put the program together.

Motivating Type 4s

Happiness will return to the faces of your Type 4 employees when they learn about the relief program. That is all they will need to restore their motivation and get back to work. They'll also stop talking about the hurricane during working hours because they really don't like to talk about anything that depresses them.

Intense Competition

The global market boom is almost free of the limits on growth that we have known in the past. International boundaries are becoming less of an obstacle with Western Europe's drive for unity and the removal of the borders in Eastern Europe. Many U.S. companies are now developing businesses throughout the world. Technology not only allows corporations to make startling advances, it also offers them many new international opportunities.

Recently, Levi Strauss found a new customer in Hungary where its new plant is making a profit and providing Hungarians with jobs. To take advantage of the pending global opportunities, companies of all sizes are positioning themselves to be competitive and technically alert. Many will have gone through painful downsizing exercises to make that happen and they have developed into lean, mean, competitive fighting machines. They are capable of destroying any competitive company that gets in their way.

The Situation

You are finally even with your competition in terms of market share, but you're not satisfied. You are tired of always having to chase your competitors, so how can you get ahead of the pack so that you dominate the market? What can you do to increase your market share when the domestic market is becoming saturated? How can you motivate your people to develop ideas that, when implemented, will help you get where you want to go?

Motivating Type 1s

If you tell your Type 1 employees that you are organizing a team that will be empowered to devise a way to increase your market share, they will all want to be the team's leader. If you have an urgent need to come up with a viable program, a Type 1 will make a good leader. Pick a Type 1 who is not too aggressive or you'll run the risk that he or she will burn the team out before they complete their mission.

Motivating Type 2s

Detail-oriented Type 2s like to participate on teams. When it comes to making sure that all of the options have been considered, nobody does a better job than Type 2s. Their loyalty to your organization will give you the added assurance that the job will be done right.

Motivating Type 3s

Type 3s typically do not make good team members. They are independent and always want to do their own thing. If you have a special assignment that you can give them, they'll do well by you. Perhaps you can employ their creative talents to work on an ad campaign for the marketing program your team is developing.

Motivating Type 4s

To spark some enthusiasm into your newly formed marketing team, make sure you assign at least one Type 4 to the team. Their optimism and enthusiasm will be important if the team starts to falter because of the long hours they will be spending on this assignment.

Summary

Adverse changes that are often outside the control of management can occur at any time and often without warning. When they happen, part or all of your organization can be adversely affected by the change and the motivation of your group usually suffers. In the beginning of this chapter, we described an adverse change as an internal or external occurrence that your employees cannot control. As a result, they often become frustrated as they search for the cause of the change. Ultimately, it is up to you as their manager to work with your people to help them restore their motivation, even though you have no more control over the adverse change that has occurred than they do. The whole process presents interesting and creative management challenges that we demonstrated in several unique scenarios. In Chapter 7, we will show you how to take charge of and motivate your peers to do what you want them to do.

Chapter 7

Motivating Your Peers

Because of our competitive nature, we often expect management power to be wielded with as much forcefulness as possible, as if toughness were synonymous with success. This may explain the popularity of professional football with managers (men and women alike), who feel that the manipulative nature of their work calls for the same kind of physical courage and toughness that football players need. This is unfortunate in many ways. The skills of a chess player might be more useful as guides to success than those of a football tackle where the courage to make a decision is very different than the desire to stop the receiver in his tracks. Knute Rockne's famous quote, "When the going gets tough, the tough get going," aptly applies to the football field. On the management playing field, it may be more sensible to say, "When the going gets tough, the *smart* get going."

A peer is an equal, and in many cases, a rival manager whom you may have minimal influence over within the confines of your company. Like a football player, you can play the management game with a vengeance to destroy or humble your peers, or you can play it smart. The tougher, but far more effective strategy to implement, is to motivate your peers to help you win the Super Bowl—that promotion where your peers now report to you! The management issues that we address in this chapter are directed at techniques you can employ to motivate your peers to do what you want them to do. The situations presented in this chapter cast you into a range of scenarios from resolving hostile peer relationships to soliciting your peers' needed support. The ability to effectively control and motivate peers to do what you want them to do is essential for anyone who wants to move up the corporate ladder.

Personal Conflicts

Conflict within an organization is like the temperature within a body. As long as the temperature is warm, the body is alive and presumably functioning. Conflict is a sign that the organization is alive and that people are doing what they are supposed to be doing, to arrive at the best possible solutions to problems. However, conflict between peers can be problematic, especially when the infighting involves a personal challenge to your level of competency or your management ability. Whatever its cause, these kinds of internal conflicts consume valuable time, drain energy, and are universally disliked in any organization. We deliberately chose not to create a character scenario in this situation, but rather decided to give you some broad guidelines on how to deal with the different personality types to resolve personal conflicts.

Motivating Type 1s

The dominant operating style of Type 1 managers will inevitably cause personal conflicts. Because they think they are always right, you will have a difficult time injecting your own opinions unless you take advantage of their weakness—their need to always be right. Even if you disagree with their reason for what is causing the personal conflict, tell them that you agree with their opinion. They will start to purr like a kitten, which will place you in an advantageous position to begin motivating them to do what you want them to do.

Motivating Type 2s

Type 2s must have a solid reason in their minds before they will get into a personal conflict with anyone. Perhaps there is something that you have said in the past that offended them, or maybe you did not provide the support they needed on a project. You need to find out what they think you did that caused them to write you off so that you can neutralize the situation and eliminate the personal conflict.

Motivating Type 3s

The stubborn nature of Type 3s will often cause them to display an aggressive nature that results in personal conflicts. Type 3s are not easy to upset, so don't take lightly the issues that may underlie their conflict with you. Play on their pleasant nature to open up a dialogue so you can find out what you did to offend them.

Motivating Type 4s

You have to push a Type 4 to the extreme before they will engage in any kind of personal conflict with you. Chances are you were the one who was responsible in the first place because Type 4s will do anything they can to avoid conflict. Think back to determine what you did wrong and correct the situation.

When You Need Their Support

Forbes magazine's annual corporate survey last year showed that 90 percent of companies admitted that their management training programs left a lot to be desired. One of the exceptions was Tassani Communications, which encourages managers to spend time with other managers on a recurring basis. Managers are given the option of selecting a peer manager to shadow, or having the group's executive pick one for them. In either event, the objective is the same—following a peer for a day to learn what he or she does so that you can broaden your perspective as a manager. It's a great way to get everybody in the company involved in training, it doesn't cost a lot of money for the program, and it encourages support among managers.

The Situation

You have just been given a new assignment to spearhead the marketing introduction of a new product that your company has developed. You are acutely aware of the fact that many of your peers consider marketing an unnecessary overhead function and you are tired of hearing them accuse you of always trying to sell something nobody wants. If you can figure out a way to motivate your peers to help you introduce this new product successfully, you'll be in line for a senior vice president slot.

Gordon, who is fondly called "Flash Gordon" within the product-development ranks of the company, always seems to bristle with enthusiasm. Over the past five years, the company has gone through four product development managers. Roy was hired away from a major competitor nine months ago and is the newest member of the management team. Gordon's department developed the product that you have been assigned to introduce into the market and he has no interest in marketing. You don't know anything about the technical features of the product and Roy has the technical knowledge you desperately need to ensure its successful market introduction. How are you going to be able to motivate Roy to help you?

Motivating Type 1s

You have scheduled an informal meeting with Roy because you are interested in learning how new products are introduced into the company. You enter Roy's office, and before you can sit down, he starts his presentation. "As you can see, Exhibit 1 on the board is a flow chart that shows how our company analyzes and develops new products. Ideas for new products can come from any department but all ideas are carefully screened by my engineers to determine if they are viable and offer marketing opportunities for the company. We're the only ones qualified to make that call." You quickly determine that Roy believes he's always right and therefore fits the classic mold of a Type 1 personality.

Healthy relationships with Type 1s often exist and flourish within a friendship. During the course of your conversation with Roy, look for things that are of common interest to the two of you. For example, if both of you like to fish, perhaps a fishing trip would be in order to help earn Roy's friendship. Over time, develop a legitimate friendship with Roy, and you will be rewarded with his undying support and assistance in introducing new products into the market.

If you decide that you are not interested in establishing a personal friendship with Roy, you need to find another way to motivate him to help you. Type 1s like power and influence. If you present your product support case to Roy and refer to it as his product, the support that you need from Roy will fall into place. Type 1s want to be the leaders in everything they do, so let Roy think he's the leader of the project.

Motivating Type 2s

You manage to catch Roy having lunch by himself in the cafeteria and ask if you can join him. After several minutes of meaningless conversation, you ask him a question that has been nagging you. "Roy, do you involve any of the other departments in the product development process? For example, do our finance and accounting people review your production cost numbers? Is any research done by our marketing department to test the market potential of new products that are under consideration? Does the sales organization participate in the pricing analysis?" Roy tells you, "I actively solicit support from any department that can contribute to the successful introduction of a new product. I'm a team player, always have been, and always will be." Roy told you what you wanted to know. He is a team-playing Type 2 personality.

Type 2s value intimacy. If you present Roy with a list of concerns you have relative to new product introduction, he will go out of his way to offer advice and any resources he has to help you resolve problems, as long as he trusts you.

Type 2s consider themselves to be morally good people. If you lie to or deceive Roy, he will cut you out of his communication channel and if given the chance, do anything he can to discredit you.

Motivating Type 3s

By chance, you happen to attend a meeting where there is a confrontation between a sales manager and Roy. The sales manager registers his dissatisfaction with Roy's newest product line that apparently is not meeting expectations. In a demanding voice, he asks, "Roy, why don't you show the sales figures for the last 10 products that your group has introduced? That will give us an indication of how unsuccessful you've been at developing marketable products." Without showing any emotion, Roy tells the sales manager, "You're entitled to your opinion," and abruptly leaves the room. Based upon what you have observed, Roy wants to be understood and appreciated. A confrontation with the sales manager would not have accomplished his Type 3 personality desire to always please others.

The gentle nature of Type 3s shines through regardless of confrontations. They like to be respected. Tell Roy you are on his side and that the sales manager was wrong. That simple statement may be all that is needed to earn Roy's trust and support, and to help introduce your new product into the market.

Type 3s like security. Tell Roy he'll get partial credit for the successful market introduction of the new product, which will go a long way toward solidifying a positive relationship with him.

Motivating Type 4s

Based on the research you conducted, the historical cost of introducing new products has exceeded projections by a whooping 35 percent. When you consult Roy on this issue, he provides you with an answer that establishes his personality type. "If our working model passes the feasibility test, we use the model to determine production cost. At this point, we work closely with operational people to make sure all costs are covered. It's up to them and the bean counters in finance to come up with the right numbers. If they are wrong, it's not our fault. They clearly own the problem." Since Roy is obviously not interested in taking responsibility for any problems, you believe he has a Type 4 personality.

Type 4s do not feel comfortable with the pressures that often come with a responsible position. Blaming others is one of their classic patterns. The best way to motivate Roy to help you in this situation is to assure him that you will take full responsibility for any problems that develop during the market introduction phase of the project. You can appeal to a Type 4's need for praise by assuring Roy that he will share in the celebration that will occur once the product successfully hits the market.

When You Need Their Advice

Many times you may think you know what you are doing and you don't need anyone's help, when actually you are unwittingly choreographing your own defeat. In these situations, without realizing it, you refuse to admit to yourself that you don't have all of the answers, refuse the notion of getting someone else's opinion, and strike out on your own. When you finally make that critical decision, and then later face the aftermath of a bad decision, you ask yourself why you didn't seek out the advice of someone who knew more about the situation.

Part of the blame stems from the fact that it is often difficult to get a competing peer manager to take the time that's necessary to offer consulting advice. Although seeking the advice of others does not always ensure that the right decision will be made, it can dramatically improve your odds.

The Situation

"You expect me to believe that the reason you want my advice is because we're supposed to act as a team?" Dan, manager of the marketing department, says in disbelief. He stops short of losing his temper. You respond, "Look, it's what we're trying to accomplish here that's important. It's how the company will succeed; it's about the direction the CEO wants us to take." You know your frustration is showing, but how many times have you tried to get Dan's advice without any success? Your personality clashes with Dan have not helped the situation but you desperately need his advice now on how to define a target market for one of the new services your organization is about to introduce.

Motivating Type 1s

Dan is an insensitive and calculating Type 1. As far as he is concerned, you are a competitor who is working against him for an upper management slot. In his mind, he has absolutely nothing to gain by helping you. You need to come up with something that you can trade for his support. It could be a business favor, such as agreeing to loan him one of your employees whom he needs to complete a project, or it could be a pair of hard-to-get football tickets.

Motivating Type 2s

Dan is obviously very emotional over something that probably goes beyond your request for his advice. You must have done something in the past that really irritated him. Find out what it was so you can correct the situation and get him to help you solve your problem.

Motivating Type 3s

Most Type 3s will jump at the opportunity to render their advice on anything when asked. Chances are that you approached Dan at the wrong time, when he was probably depressed or angry. Let him cool off for a day and approach him with your same request for help.

Motivating Type 4s

Type 4s don't want to give out any advice for fear that they may be committing themselves to something that will require more work. Hence, they'll avoid getting caught up in conversations that, in their opinion, could result in more work. If you can assure Dan that all you want is his opinion and not his commitment, you stand a chance of getting him to talk to you.

When You Need to Get the Truth

One of the biggest inhibitors preventing us from taking risks and confronting the many challenges facing us is the lack of truth. If you do not believe you are getting a straight story, you'll stop turning your innovative ideas into actions, following your dreams, and performing well under pressure. You will be afraid that you won't accomplish your goals or make it to the top if you're given bogus information. The need to get your peers to tell you the truth when you need it can be a difficult challenge.

The Situation

"I like being direct," you say as you enter Glen's office and shut the door. "If it isn't Mr. Conflict at work defending the innocent and protecting the helpless," you tease. "Yes, people like me and people like you," Glen snaps back and you both enjoy laughter together, which is a rare moment for the two of you. It hides the conflicting differences you have had with Glen for some time now. You are acutely aware of the fact that Glen has been openly sabotaging your effort to consolidate two of your departments into one group, and you cannot understand why. Your objective in this morning's meeting is to find out why he's doing it, and this time you want the truth.

Motivating Type 1s

Lying Type 1s are usually insensitive and calculating individuals who must be handled with all the care you would give to handling a rattlesnake. The only way to get Glen to be honest with you when he gives his advice is to promise something in return.

Motivating Type 2s

Glen's emotional outburst in our scenario is fairly typical of Type 2s. The fact that he got emotional places you in an advantageous position. While Glen is in a relaxed mood, ask him for his honest advice.

Motivating Type 3s

Glen clearly doesn't like you and whatever he says will be a lie unless you can direct his attention toward something he likes. Your approach might be, "Glen, although our relationship has not been good, I need to get your opinion on something, not for myself but for our company. We have both been given the mandate to reduce department overhead costs, which is what I am trying to do by consolidating two of my departments. Why do you oppose the idea?" Listen carefully to Glen's answer.

Motivating Type 4s

Type 4s can be extremely obnoxious people who think it is clever to not tell the truth when someone desperately needs it. The only way to get them to be honest with you is to convince them of the seriousness of whatever it is you need their advice on.

When You Need Their Employee

Cooperation is one of the most powerful words in the English language if it is properly understood by both parties involved. For cooperation to work, people must believe that their goals are positively related, so that as one moves toward the attainment of his goal, the other person also moves toward her goal. Both parties understand that if one succeeds, the other succeeds. People who are involved in cooperative activities want each other to succeed, because they understand that if one loses, the other loses as well.

The Situation

You've done your best to prepare for your meeting with Elaine by gathering every piece of information she could possibly need. There is only one person in the company who can give you an outside chance of pulling this research project off—Billy. Unfortunately, Billy doesn't work for you, he works for Elaine and you need to borrow him for six months. You're dreading this session with Elaine because she's hard enough to get along with even in the best of times. The fact that you need one of her employees to assist you in a project that she feels should have been assigned to her anyway is not sitting well with her.

Motivating Type 1s

One of the strong attributes of people with Type 1 personalities is that they have a loyalty to task and a strong commitment to whomever they are working for at the time. In your effort to motivate Elaine to loan you Billy, open your request like this: "As you know, Elaine, we're here this morning to discuss the company's performance in research and our crying need to do something about it. I need one of your employees to help me successfully complete our latest research project, which will set a precedent in this area. Can I count on you for your support?" By appealing to the loyalty trait that all Type 1s have, you should be able to get her support.

Motivating Type 2s

If you believe that Elaine has a Type 2 personality, keep in mind that Type 2s are intensely loyal to people they trust. If they believe you are loyal and sincere, they'll go out of their way to support you.

Your approach to motivate Elaine to loan you Billy might start out with a statement that is designed to show your sincerity and to gain Elaine's support: "Elaine, I am truly sorry that you did not get this assignment, but as we both know, that decision was made outside of our control. The fact is, I have the assignment and my chances of successfully completing the assignment are greatly reduced if I don't have the technical expertise that I need from one of your employees. Will you help me?" This should appeal to her team-player nature and motivate her to loan you Billy.

Motivating Type 3s

Concentrate on minimizing the insecure feelings Type 3s have for anything that is new. Because of her inherent insecurities, Elaine is reluctant to loan you Billy. She doesn't believe the project will succeed regardless of what you do. She's concerned that she, too, will be dragged down in its eminent failure if she is even remotely associated with the project.

The best way around this dilemma is to have Billy officially assigned to your organization as one of your employees for the duration of the project. This action protects Elaine from any project failures that could occur. On the other hand, if the project is a success, she stands to gain from some of the fanfare when you transfer Billy back to her organization. You both win!

Motivating Type 4s

Type 4s are traditionally uncommitted individuals. If Elaine is a Type 4, you are dealing with a peer manager who may have no commitment to the company. Therefore, if you attempt to motivate her with, "By helping me, you're helping the company," your words may fall on deaf ears.

A more viable approach might be to appeal to Elaine's need to always be popular. Suggest to her that by loaning you Billy, senior management will know that she has taken an active stand to support the successful completion of the project. Remind her of the celebration that will occur if the project is completed on time. Tell her she's invited!

When They Are Physically Threatening

Anger can be a healthy experience if it is managed, because anger promotes problem confrontation, dilutes the emotions in a problem, and fuels solutions. When someone gets angry with you to the point where they may physically threaten you, they are at a distinct disadvantage. They know intuitively that their behavior is irrational and not acceptable in a business environment. In short, the person who is angry is off balance, and if approached properly, can be motivated to adopt whatever behavior you choose because angry people are desperately looking for anything that will make them feel good again.

The Situation

The shouting match that ensues in your office gets worse when the two of you stand up and proceed to shout your objections in each other's faces. When Mack blurts out, "If you were just a little younger, I'd knock your..." He stops short of completing his sentence and knocks you with his shoulder in his haste to get out the door.

As you fall back into your chair, you wonder how you could have gotten yourself into this situation in the first place. You almost got into a fight with this man and you haven't been in a fight since you were 7 years old.

Motivating Type 1s

Physical conflicts are rare, but if they do occur, they will probably be with a Type 1 personality. Nobody wins in physically threatening situations, so do your best to avoid them. The easiest way to diffuse the situation with a Type 1 is simply to agree with him at that moment to diffuse the situation, which will buy you valuable time to determine how to best handle Mack.

Motivating Type 2s

Type 2s have to be pushed very hard before they will react in a physically threatening manner, so you may be the one at fault here. In any event, if you apologize to Mack, things will quickly return to normal and you should be able to continue with your discussion. Mutually agree with Mack to avoid repeating whatever behavior set the two of you off.

Motivating Type 3s

Like Type 2s, the diplomatic behavior of Type 3s will preclude them from demonstrating physically threatening behavior. If it does occur, follow the advice given for dealing with a Type 2.

Motivating Type 4s

It is completely against the nature of a Type 4 to demonstrate physically threatening behavior. In fact, it is so unusual that you need to be extremely careful as to how you handle the situation. An irate Type 4 could not only hurt you, but he could physically harm himself. Do whatever you need to do or say to neutralize the situation.

(?) *Help:* Physically threatening peers act in a very similar manner to emotionally threatening peers. Carefully read the next section for motivational techniques that may further assist you.

When They Are Emotionally Threatening

There are times you may think you are acting in your own best interest, when instead you are unwittingly choreographing your own defeat. If you allow yourself to get involved in an emotionally threatening situation, without realizing it, you are mentally setting yourself up for defeat.

Sharp managers know that emotional thinking that's often based on quick decisions is subject to error and must be replaced with more rational thought.

The Situation

When Jim, the vice president of personnel, calls you a fool in front of your entire staff, you decide to abruptly close out the meeting and ask Jim to join you in your office. For the next two hours, you share your concerns with Jim about the company's employee turnover rates that you were addressing in your staff meeting. During the discussion, you show him several charts that illustrate the cost to the company of poor employee morale. Several times during the conversation, Jim threatens to leave your office. "If you're accusing me of being responsible for our high turnover rate just because I'm in charge of personnel, you're barking up the wrong tree. Maybe the problem is you!" By the end of the meeting, Jim is still upset and as he leaves your office he threatens to escalate the problem by going to the CEO. Reluctantly, the two of you agree to meet tomorrow to see if you can work things out. You're emotionally drained as you drive home and can't help but wonder what you can do to save what appears to be a hopeless situation.

Motivating Type 1s

In all probability, you are dealing with an aggressive Type 1 personality. You invited Jim to your staff meeting to comment about employee turnover. Although your intent was to show Jim that you value his input, he misinterpreted the invitation as an affront to him (i.e., he's responsible for the turnover problem). Tell Jim why you invited him to the meeting, which may be a repeat of what you told him before. For some reason, he may not have understood you. You need his help to solve the turnover problem in your department. When you admit to Jim that you own the problem, he will provide you with all of the support that you need.

Motivating Type 2s

Jim is probably reacting to you emotionally because he doesn't trust you or is suspicious of your motives. If the issues that the two of you are arguing about are not important in the overall scheme of things, tell Jim whatever you need to in order to end the confrontation. If important issues have to be resolved, find out why Jim doesn't trust you before you continue with the discussion.

Motivating Type 3s

Jim's lack of direction is probably what is causing him to react emotionally to your comments and what he perceives to be accusations about his performance as a manager. If you don't believe that he is at fault for the high turnover rate, let him know that to neutralize the emotional element in your conversation.

Motivating Type 4s

Since Type 4s typically have no direction in their career path, they can become extremely upset if anyone tries to steer them toward a long-term commitment. Employee turnover is a long-term issue that you want Jim to acknowledge and help you resolve. He won't do it unless you agree to take on ownership of the problem and his role is prescribed as consultant or advisor. Assuming that Jim has some of the expertise that will help you solve your employee turnover problem, this is your best option.

? *Help:* Emotionally threatening peers act in a very similar manner to physically threatening peers. Review that section beginning on page 187 for motivational techniques that may further assist you.

(?) *Help:* If you need more ideas on how to manage conflicts in your organization, read Dean Tjosvold's book *Learning to Manage Conflict.*

Employee Affairs

Complacency is the last hurdle any winner must overcome before obtaining potential greatness. It is also the disease of success. It takes root when you are feeling good about what you are doing and selectively choose to ignore difficult situations that you should do something about. As a manager, problems come to you in all shapes and sizes. Most of us have been trained to handle the traditional problems of business, all of the stuff that can get in the way of the bottom line. We have not been well-coached on how to deal with the personal side of business where our employees often step into uncharted territories, such as openly having an affair with another employee.

The Situation

As Jenny leaves your office telling you how relieved she is to get the current situation off her mind, you wish she had dropped the bomb somewhere else. Jarold, one of your best friends and peer managers, is having an affair with your employee Carol. To make matters even worse, they are both married! What in the world could be on Jarold's mind? Word travels at twice the speed of light and you know that everyone in your organization already knows about the affair. The monkey, or rather gorilla, is clearly on your back to resolve the situation. Why Carol is having an affair with a peer manager isn't particularly important here even though you may be emotionally involved. You are not responsible for Jarold's side of the problem, but because she works for you, you must deal with Carol's side of the problem. Focus on her situation and the motivational problem that she is causing in your organization.

Motivating Type 1s

Let Carol know that you are aware of the situation. If she denies your accusation, be prepared to identify the specific employees who have brought the situation to your attention. Listen carefully to what

Carol has to say before you offer her any advice. If she tells you her personal life is none of your business, tell her you agree, as long as it does not disrupt your organization's motivation. Inform her that when it does, you will be forced to become actively involved in the situation.

Motivating Type 2s

When you confront Carol about her affair, she won't deny it and will be somewhat apologetic for having caused concerns and rumors within your organization. Explain to her what the potential ramifications are and listen carefully to her response. She may have already anticipated the potential magnitude of the problem and be in the process of breaking off the relationship or moving on to a new job.

Motivating Type 3s

When you approach Carol about the affair, her stubborn Type 3 nature will probably come out. She'll tell you, "It's nobody's business but ours." She is absolutely right; tell her that. Carefully explain to her that the affair is disrupting the motivation of the people in your organization. If she believes that she is involved in a long-term relationship, perhaps the best solution would be to work out a transfer for her to another department.

Motivating Type 4s

If Carol has a Type 4 personality, she will tell you that this whole affair is no big deal and that everyone has blown it out of proportion. To set the record straight, tell her that you, as her manger, consider it a big deal because it's affecting the productivity of your organization. When she asks you what you want her to do, be frank and offer her some options: 1) resign; 2) end the relationship; or 3) keep the relationship out of the office.

Warning: Affairs between managers and subordinates require kid-glove treatment because of the possibility of coercion and because of the relationship's effect on the other employees. Do the employees in your organization feel they have been harmed by the affair? Is Carol getting preferential treatment from Jarold?

When They Cheat Your Subcontractors

Mistakes, forgivable sins by management, are not to be confused with malicious acts made by your peers. A malicious act is strategically plotted with the sole intent of adversely affecting someone within the boundaries of the organization. For example, many organizations rely heavily on their subcontractors to provide them with needed products and services. Cheating a subcontractor ranks as one of the worst management deceptions. What do you do if a peer manager cheats one of your valued subcontractors?

The Situation

"Charlie, I can't believe that we have anyone in our company who would pull a dumb stunt like that. I can certainly promise you I'll look into the situation, find out what happened, and get back to you within a few days." You slam the receiver down and start for the door. You can't believe that Art, one of your peer managers, would try to cheat one of your key subcontractors by giving them procurement numbers from your organization that were completely fabricated. Art got your subcontractor to commit to prices based on the new volumes that were completely unrealistic. You call Art and tell him you're on your way over to see him.

Motivating Type 1s

When you inform Art that you know he has been cheating your subcontractor, he may deny the accusation, but he will also not do it again. Type 1s are not stupid, and Art intuitively knows what the consequences would be if he got caught a second time.

Motivating Type 2s

If Art has a Type 2 personality, he will have a very specific reason as to why he cheated your subcontractor. He may not trust the subcontractor or he feels that they have been cheating the company in some other area. You have to find out what the problem is before you can get Art to back off.

Motivating Type 3s

Your Type 3 cheater simply sees his cheating of your subcontractor as an inventive way to save the company money. If you tell Art that you may take the situation to a higher level of authority, he'll plead with you not to make a big deal out of it and will promise to stop.

Motivating Type 4s

If cheating happens to provide Type 4s with an opportunity to save the company money, they'll see nothing wrong in doing it. Patiently explain the facts and consequences to Art, and he'll probably stop.

Jokers

Corporate managers have to be particularly sensitive to what they say. Newspapers are quick to report stories of managers who are being accused of racism or sexual harassment because of something they said, something that was meant to be a joke. The corporate legal guns will become involved in the situation and whoever is being called a racist will not enjoy a lasting career with the company, regardless of whether they are innocent or guilty.

The Situation

"If I hear Ellen tell that joke about the Oriental and the Polock one more time, I'm going to strangle her." You can tell from the look in Nuygen's eyes that he's furious. When you ask him if this is the first time he has heard Ellen tell racial jokes, he tells you that any time she is over in his work area, she's telling jokes to anyone who will listen. Ellen is one of your peer managers whom you personally don't like. It would be a lot easier to just turn this situation over to her boss. But instead, you plan to meet with her tomorrow after the manager's meeting to discuss the problem with her.

Motivating Type 1s

If Ellen is a Type 1, she probably has a power-oriented personality. She's using jokes as a way to exercise her power. Demand that she stop telling the offensive jokes. If she refuses, tell her that you will escalate the problem. She'll stop!

Motivating Type 2s

Self-righteous Type 2s think that it is their right to say just about anything that comes to them, including racial jokes. When you talk to Ellen about the problem, suggest to her that she review what the law has to say about her conduct. If she understands that her actions could result in her termination, she will stop. If she doesn't understand what you are telling her, bring the problem to her boss.

Motivating Type 3s

The easy-going attitude of Type 3s will cause them to say just about anything that comes to mind, even if it is not in good taste. Warn Ellen about the consequences of her racial jokes. If she says she doesn't know what you're talking about, suggest to her that she go to the local library and read some of the historical material on what has happened to managers who've been identified as racists. Advise her that they have traditionally not enjoyed long and successful careers.

Motivating Type 4s

To Type 4s, telling any kind of joke, including racially oriented jokes, is their way of showing off. When you tell Ellen that if the racial jokes continue, she'll get herself fired, she'll stop!

Power Mongers

Power is the faculty, strength, and potency to accomplish anything you want. It is the vital energy one employs to make choices and management decisions. If power is properly channeled, it can prove to be the source of energy one needs to overcome deeply embedded habits and to cultivate higher, more effective ones. Over the years, the term "power monger" was coined to describe managers who employed illicit means to gain access to power. To a power monger, employees are nothing more than expendable soldiers and anybody who gets in the way is considered to be the enemy. They'll kill your career on contact if given the chance.

Management is a power game where the object is to know what you want and how to get it. The moves of the game are complex and can involve the manipulation of people and situations to your advantage. The unwritten management rule is that good managers do not abuse their power positions. In this section, you'll see how to deploy the ultimate weapon of motivation to control, and if necessary, destroy power mongers.

The Situation

Before joining the company three years ago, Jim managed a chain of credit and collection offices. His collection offices consistently outperformed competitive agencies. You walk into Jim's office for your planned meeting and he begins the conversation on an aggressive note when you ask him what he thinks about management in general. "It's the job of my organization to make sure the company gets its worth out of everyone who works here. Let's face it, with the exception of some managers, most people fall into a pattern. In my opinion, the average employee nowadays has an inherent dislike for work. You just can't motivate them. They have to be coerced and threatened to put forth adequate effort toward achieving the company's objectives. Most employees want to avoid responsibility and prefer to be directed in everything we want them to do. They have relatively little ambition, but they want job security. We can use the job security issue to our advantage and bolster productivity. What do you think?"

You look at the year on your notebook calendar to verify that you are, in fact, operating in the late 20th and not the early 19th century. "Jim, your outlook on human relations has been, to say the least, enlightening," you say sarcastically. Jim beams with his perception of what he thinks is a compliment. "What kind of employee turnover rates, such as voluntary termination, are we experiencing annually?" After rummaging through his notes, Jim gives you a number that sends you to the roof: 25 to 30 percent. "Isn't that high number an indication of low employee morale?" Jim gives you the answer that you were afraid of hearing: "Yes, but it allows us to hire replacements at cheaper rates than what we were paying the ones who quit. Most of the quitters were dissenters anyway, so it's no great loss."

Your boss has asked you to work with Jim to come up with ideas that will improve the overall productivity of his division. How do you convince a power monger like Jim to adopt a softer approach where legitimate motivational tactics are applied to improve employee productivity and reduce turnover?

Motivating Type 1s

Almost without exception, power mongers will have extreme Type 1 personalities. They are demanding and very critical of others. As the scenario with Jim points out, Type 1s are impatient with human inadequacy and feel that nothing short of efficiency should be tolerated. Jim believes that employees' fear of losing their jobs should be exploited to improve productivity. Somehow, you have to figure out a way to break into the logical side of Jim's Type 1 personality if you want him to help you improve the productivity of your department. Ask him if he knows of any highly productive employees within the organization. He'll enthusiastically come back with several names of individuals who he believes are highly productive. Now that you have the bait dangling in front of him, suggest that he help you make an example of their success in a training seminar on productivity. He will grab the bait and help you!

Motivating Type 2s

Type 2s are judgmental power mongers, one of the worst kinds. If, in their opinion, they judge your actions or statements to be wrong, they will do everything in their power to either stop you or get you terminated. Appeal to the creative side of Jim's Type 2 personality. Challenge him to help you devise a plan that will increase the productivity and reduce turnover in your organization.

Motivating Type 3s and 4s

It is highly unlikely that you will have to deal with a Type 3 or 4 power monger because the trait is not inherent in their personality. However, watch out for the exceptions. They will become power mongers if they have a sponsor, such as a father, relative, or close personal friend who is higher up in the organization. They will report to their sponsor whatever you say that they don't like or actions they don't believe in. Be diplomatic when you attempt to persuade a Type 3 or 4 to help you. If they believe in your cause and also believe that there is something in it for them (for example, executive recognition, publicity, etc.), they will help you in any way they can.

Summary

Motivating your peers to do what you want them to do is vitally important to the success of your management career. It may simply entail motivating a peer manager to loan you one of their key employees for a day to a more complex situation of backing you on a major project. The techniques that you employ to effectively motivate peers rely heavily on your ability to predetermine what type of personality they have. Once you know that, you will be in a better position to determine what turns them on and off before you approach them with your request for support. We'll show you how to use similar tactics in Chapter 8, which addresses how to motivate your boss.

Chapter 8

Motivating Your Boss

The early Greeks had a magnificent philosophy that embodied three words: ethos, pathos, and logos. These three words contain the essence of what you need to do to effectively motivate your boss. Ethos (character) represents your personal credibility, the faith your manager has in your integrity and competency. The trust that you inspire into your manager motivates him to do good things for you, such as giving you a glowing performance review. Pathos is the empathic, or the feeling, side of the relationship between you and your manager. It ensures that you are in alignment with the emotional trust of your manager. Because he trusts you, he's willing to confide in you. Logos (rational principle) represents the logical part of the relationship. It governs that your strategies, plans, and presentations are logical and well thought-out.

Most people will refer right to logos in an attempt to impress and subsequently motivate their boss. They'll try to convince him of the validity of their logical solution without first taking ethos and pathos into consideration. How many times have you heard the statement, "I had the only logical solution but the boss didn't buy it. Instead, he chose that other guy's solution over mine"? The other guy may not have had logos working for him, but you can rest assured he had mastered the ethos and pathos part of the relationship. In this chapter, we focus on techniques you can employ to motivate and direct your boss to move in a direction that's favorable for you.

Micro-Managers

Each boss's personality type must be dealt with differently, so successfully motivating any boss is a matter of figuring out how he is likely to react in different situations. Be careful not to jump to any conclusions about what type of personality your boss has. Micro-managers, those managers interested in every minute detail of things happening around them, are quite capable of changing their personalities to throw their subordinates off guard. They can show all of the aggression of a Type 1 and quickly change into a loyal Type 2 or the relaxed behavior of a Type 3 or 4. If a micro-manager finds himself in an adversarial relationship with an aggressive subordinate, he'll lull the subordinate into complacency with all the expertise of a Type 4. However, most micro-managers will have predominately Type 1 or 2 personalities. Their love for minute details is a common characteristic in these two personality types.

The Situation

When the company formed its new southeastern region, the president's choice for general manager was Cheri, a dynamic salesperson in her late 30s. Cheri joined the company last year and rapidly rose to a middle-management position. Her general manager appointment was controversial because it rocketed her past several more senior managers. In your first staff meeting with Cheri and her cadre of 15 other subordinate managers, she explains what she expects from her organization. "You are all highly qualified for your jobs or you wouldn't be here. The subject of this meeting is to tell you how I expect you to do your job and what I will require to control this division. Effective immediately, my signature must be on all expenses over $100. I also want to review and preapprove every project before it is started. And finally, monthly status reports will be replaced with weekly status reports. Are there any questions?" There are none, and as you walk out of the room, you realize you are working for a micro-manager.

Motivating Type 1s

With rare exception, Type 1 micro-managers have no idea as to how they are viewed by their employees. This is in part because Type

1s are poor listeners, only hearing what they want to hear and insulating themselves from feedback.

The key to motivating Cheri to get off your back is to provide her with indirect feedback. For example, when the opportunity presents itself, instead of saying, "Cheri, you are a micro-manager who is stifling creative thinking in your organization," you might try a more diplomatic and indirect approach: "Cheri, I am concerned that you don't have any confidence in my capabilities." When she asks you what you mean, seize the opportunity. Show her how her micro-management approach has led you to that conclusion. Type 1s are proactive individuals, and if you address your concerns to Cheri in the proper manner, she'll trust you and back off.

Motivating Type 2s

Most micro-managers will have Type 2 personalities. Remember that Type 2s love to be very analytical in whatever task they take on. Their requirement for micro-data from you on a recurring basis is the input they need to support their analytical habit. There is not much that you can do to change this personality trait.

The best way to stop Cheri from micro-managing you is to convince her that what she really needs from you is a micro-status report submitted on a timely basis. Convince Cheri that your status report will contain everything she needs to know about your projects. She may want you to submit the report weekly, as opposed to monthly, which is still better than fielding her daily phone calls. If Cheri agrees with your status report alternative, make sure you include lots of details in every one.

Motivating Type 3s

Type 3 micro-managers tend to feel insecure about their jobs, which is the reason why they became micro-managers. It's their way of making sure that nothing slips by them that could get them into trouble later on. By the same token, Type 3s are inherently lazy and subsequently don't like to wade through reams of detailed reports.

The solution to motivate Cheri to get off your back is to show her how you can make her job easier. This gives her the level of security she wants. Arrange to formally meet with her on a regular basis, perhaps once a week, to review the status of each one of your projects.

Motivating Type 4s

Type 4 micro-managers honestly believe that they are helping you perform your job better by micro-managing everything you do. It is Cheri's way of showing you that she is your friend and that she trusts you. How do you convince her that you don't need all of her help while preserving her trust in you?

When appropriate, discuss with Cheri your need to have more space. Point out to her how important it is for you to feel you are running your own organization, with her help of course. However, somewhere in the course of the conversation, make her aware of the fact that she is micro-managing everything you do and that bothers you a great deal. Type 4s are appreciative of people who will honestly share their feeling with them. Cheri should be willing to back off from her micro-management stand with you.

Macro-Managers

In the previous section, we talked about micro-managers, those individuals who want to know something about everything going on around them. In contrast, there is the macro-manager who is only interested in the big picture, what's going on in the entire organization, and its aggregate output, often measured in bottom-line terms. They have blatantly little interest in details, a quality that often gets them into trouble.

The Situation

"I'm so furious," you say to your friend. "I asked my manager, Greg, to review a couple of key journal entries before I posted them to the ledger and he tells me they're not important! When I snapped back, he told me the only thing that counts is the bottom line. It's as if my job isn't important. No wonder he spends most of his time with the finance manager, George, who plays up to him by always talking about the big picture."

Motivating Type 1s

Most macro-managers will have Type 1 personalities. Type 1s like to perceive themselves as power players, and they perceive that macro-managing is the way to get to the top. As was demonstrated in the situation, Greg has very little interest in details and only wants to address the big picture.

If you are working for a macro-manager, your chances of winning his esteem are going to be slim to none. The only possible way you can motivate Greg to appreciate you is to wait for the right opportunity to convince him that the small picture can be more important than the big picture.

For example, suppose you discovered several accounting errors that significantly overstated the company's income and you brought this to Greg's attention just before he was about to go into an executive meeting to present the numbers. That should get his attention and earn you his respect.

Motivating Type 2s

Type 2 macro-managers always seem to be talking about the big picture, but they have an appreciation for all of the processes, including the accounting functions that must be in place to make it all happen. If Greg is a Type 2, chances are that when he rebuffed your request to review your journal entries, he was preoccupied with some other more pressing matter.

Approach Greg in a nonconfrontational manner and simply ask him why he wasn't interested in reviewing the journal with you. Listen carefully to what he has to say. He will probably apologize for his abrupt action and will be more motivated to assist you in the future.

Motivating Type 3s

Type 3s think that the act of independence is the key to getting to the top of the management ladder. A few Type 3s will revert to macro-management tactics as their perceived way of establishing their independence. This behavior provides Greg with the perfect excuse. By telling you he was focusing on the big picture, he's demonstrating his independence by not having to deal with you at the time.

If you politely inform Greg that his reaction to your request for help upset you, it will probably not happen again. Cooperation within their organization is very important to Type 3 macro-managers.

Motivating Type 4s

It is unlikely that a Type 4 would be a macro-manager because most of them do not want to be independent or enjoy working with everyone on anything. However, if Greg is a Type 4, you can rest assured that his rebuff to your request for assistance had nothing to do with you personally. There was something else on his mind that distracted him from helping you. When you confront him for an explanation, that is exactly what he will tell you. You'll also get an unsolicited apology from him and his commitment that it will not happen again.

(?) *Help:* Macro-managers act in a very similar manner to wimp and chameleon managers. Review those sections, beginning on page 206 and page 223, respectively, for motivational techniques that may further assist you in dealing with a macro-manager.

No-Action Managers

A particularly irritating type of manager is the one who takes no action, that manager who is always promising to do something but never does. No-action managers are totally incapable of making any kind of decision. The discussion about how to motivate a no-action manager points us back to *The Peter Principle*, written by Laurence Peters and Raymond Hull. The authors point out that we all live in a hierarchy where employees tend to rise to their level of competence. If you apply this principle to your boss, you will quickly discover that nothing fails like success. This is what happens when a competent employee becomes the boss. They will eventually reveal their incompetence as a leader when it becomes apparent that they are incapable of making any management decisions.

The Situation

Your boss, Nick leans back in his chair, clasps his hands behind his head, and nods at you. "Okay, I canceled my golf date to come in here to hear what you have to say. It better be good. So let's hear it!" You have been working on what you consider is a great idea and a solid opportunity for the company. However, for some reason, you have never been able to motivate Nick to back you on any of your previous ideas. What is going to make your latest idea any different? As you begin to carefully arrange your presentation charts, Nick impatiently cuts in. "Come on! What's your great idea?" You take a deep breath and lean forward. "What we're going to do is start publishing a monthly newsletter for every one of our customers beginning next month." Bolting into an upright position and slamming his fist on the desk with eyebrows raised halfway up to his forehead, Nick cuts you off.

"A newsletter? Are you out of your mind? You dragged me in here and made me miss my golf game for a stupid idea like that? We're not a publishing company or a newspaper, in case you haven't noticed. We're a manufacturing company. You've got a lot of nerve wasting my time this way when I could be out golfing with a real customer. In your anger, you blurt out, "All right, just forget it. We'll just continue doing the same things we have always done here, which is nothing new!" As Nick bolts out of your office, he shouts back, "All right, I'll think about it and give you my final decision Monday morning." Monday comes and goes. When you approach Nick and ask him what he has decided, he just tells you he's still thinking about it.

Motivating Type 1s

Always remember that Type 1s have a very narrow focus on what they perceive their business is all about. In Nick's case, he sees himself involved in running a manufacturing company and cannot relate to how a newsletter fits into the manufacturing process. Clearly you're not suggesting that your company branch out into the newsletter business. What you are suggesting is a low-cost mechanism to communicate with your customers. If you can show Nick why that is important to the company, before you suggest the use of a newsletter as the communication mechanism, you should get a more favorable reaction.

Motivating Type 2s

The way Nick perceives matters, he's saddled with a subordinate who is long on imagination and short on common sense. Contrary to the way in which Nick reacted to your newsletter idea, he cares about you or he would not have canceled his golf game. At this juncture, you would be well-advised to play on Nick's sense of commitment, another Type 2 attribute. For example, if you can point out a growing need that the customers have for being kept abreast of technological changes in the industry that you discovered perhaps as a result of a survey you ran, he should be more inclined to listen to you. The new letter simply offers the company a way to communicate with its customers.

Motivating Type 3s

Type 3s tend to be lazy and often act without direction. Nick is insulted that you caused him to miss his golf game to listen to an idea he perceived as frivolous. Appeal to the tolerant behavior of his Type 3 personality. During the course of your short-lived presentation on the newsletter, you allowed yourself to get pulled into a confrontation with Nick, which will turn off any Type 3, particularly if he or she is your boss. In the interest of damage control, apologize for your abrupt behavior and request a second meeting to present your idea in a more favorable atmosphere. Type 3s will almost always give you a second chance.

Motivating Type 4s

Type 4s are always looking for a way to be popular with everyone. Your newsletter idea offers Nick that opportunity, if only he could see that. In your initial presentation, you missed the mark. Perhaps if you had approached the subject from a different slant, you would have sparked a more favorable response. For example, if you had pointed out that it is the company's mission to propagate goodwill within its customer base, it goes without saying that the CEO would look favorably on those who can improve customer satisfaction. Let Nick make the suggestion for the newsletter by offering him a "what if we did this" scenario that includes a newsletter. That way, you get your newsletter, Nick gets the credit for the idea from the CEO, and hopefully recognizes the important role you played in making it all happen.

Wimps

Wimps are managers who are afraid to do anything, and they will often act like jerks if it suits their purpose. They are those managers who refuse to take any risk whatsoever. Wimps are also classic compromisers who do things strictly by the book and will ponder ad infinitum even the most trivial decision. They'll always maintain a stockpile of alibis and fall guys whom they can use to cover their tracks. Wimps love to call meetings, form committees, participate on fact-finding studies, and hire outside consultants. They'll use whatever diversion tactics that are available to them until they find the safest way to proceed. Over time, most wimps fizzle out in the power game because of their inaction. It's not uncommon for them to step out of management and back into the line organization if they are given the opportunity.

The Situation

In the race for top jobs, outstanding job performance is a necessity. It's your ticket to enter the race and it will help set you apart from your competitors. However, if your personnel jacket is missing outstanding job performance reviews, you'll never get that promotion you're looking for. Your boss, Scarlett, has just given you an outstanding performance review and endorsed your request to apply for the new vice president position that was announced last week. You ask Scarlett if she would insert a memo into your personnel file officially stating her high opinion of you to help you win the vice president slot. She readily agrees, but two weeks pass and there is still no memo in your file. When you confront her about the issue, she tells you she's not sure that her memo would be acceptable to the personnel manager. When you tell her that the personnel manager said he has no problem with your request, Scarlett gives you another one of her favorite wimpy excuses.

Motivating Type 1s

No Type 1 boss would ever want to be referred to as a wimp because Type 1s are supposed to be powerful and aggressive. The fact of the matter is you are dealing with a manager whose promises to follow through on a simple request don't happen. You need to find out why she is procrastinating.

Scarlett perceives that she has nothing to gain and everything to lose if you transfer out of her organization and become the new vice president. To get her to follow through with her promise, you need to offer her something that will motivate her to accommodate your simple request. For example, tell her that if you get the new position, everyone will know that you worked for her, which will make her look good.

Motivating Type 2s

Type 2s are typically loyal to anybody who works for them. The fact that Scarlett has not complied with your request is probably because she doesn't think it's important. If you stress the importance that you are placing on her recommendation, she will comply with your request, post haste.

Motivating Type 3s

Scarlett hasn't complied with your request because, like many Type 3s, she's lazy. The quickest way for you to solve the problem is to make all of your requests easy for her to comply with. Type up the memorandum the way you want it, hand it to Scarlett, and ask her to sign it. She will, and you'll probably end up with a better endorsement of your qualifications than you would have if she had done it herself. The point is, whatever you want out of a Type 3 wimp manager, do it yourself!

Motivating Type 4s

The irresponsible nature of Type 4 wimps is the primary reason why Scarlett hasn't completed, or even started for that matter, the memorandum you requested. The same approach that we recommended for motivating Type 3s will also work for motivating Type 4s.

(?) *Help:* Wimp managers act in a very similar manner to unmotivated mules. Review the section on page 145 for motivational techniques that may further assist you in dealing with wimp managers.

Bureaucrats

Bureaucrats love to say they agree with you, but that rules and regulations prevent them from acting in your favor. Incapable of independent thought, bureaucrats are often found in the roots of the management world. They thrive in old, established companies that are riddled with volumes of policies and procedures. Whenever bureaucrats feel threatened or endangered, they'll take refuge behind policies, official directives, a memorandum from a higher level, or any other document that allows them to stop an action. Although there is nothing wrong with well-thought-out policies, bureaucrats go out of their way to interpret policies in support of their points of view.

The Situation

It had been a great day for getting caught up at work. As the pleasant summer breeze drifts through the window in your office, you decide to give your status report one more admiring review before you hit the e-mail button to send it over to Ray, your bureaucratic boss. He should at least be pleased when he finds out you have completed the design of the company's Web site three weeks ahead of schedule. As you raise your finger to press the enter button on your keyboard, the ring of your phone breaks your action.

It's Ray who starts blurting out demands before you can even acknowledge that you are on the line. "Listen, it's about our Web site. I know you got approval to proceed with the project at the design review meeting last week, but I don't want to take any chances. Hold another meeting and ask for their approval again. Check with the Interstate Commerce Commission to see if we need anything else from them. Al says he's got some ideas that may improve the design you've come up with. Get together with him and see what he's talking about. That's it for now." In a fit of rage, you bang the delete key and send your status report into the electronic graveyard. This bureaucratic boss is driving you crazy!

Motivating Type 1s

Type 1 bureaucrats like to control people and events by throwing bureaucratic nails into the path of anything they control. It's their way of showing people how important they are. In our scenario, Ray actually thinks he is helping by insisting that duplicate steps be taken to ensure the success of the company's Web site.

You have to change Ray's self-righteous attitude so he can become less bureaucratic. Try to get him to focus on the added cost the project will incur if you add the duplicate work that he is demanding. Show

Ray how the added costs could be better deployed to support some other aspect of his organization.

Motivating Type 2s

Quality is of paramount importance to Type 2 bureaucrats. Unfortunately, they have a misguided perception that duplicating activities on a project is the best way to ensure that the highest quality standards are met. If you challenge Ray's approach in this instance, he will become suspicious that you are not interested in quality. You don't want that to happen.

Assure Ray that quality is most important in everything you do. Suggest to him that his dollars may be better spent monitoring the quality features of the Web site after it is up and running rather than duplicating quality control checks now.

Motivating Type 3s

Type 3s are often uninvolved in the work that gets done in their organizations and will subsequently resort to implementing bureaucratic procedures as a mechanism to validate what has been done. If Ray does not trust you, he will continue to raise bureaucratic barriers to the point where it will become almost impossible for you to complete any assignment.

Type 3 bureaucrats will begin removing bureaucratic barriers the moment they begin to trust you. Work on developing Ray's trust if you want to eliminate the bureaucratic obstacles that he is placing in your way.

Motivating Type 4s

Bureaucrats with Type 4 personalities respond well to the "lesser of two evil" management ploys. Find a rule, regulation, or procedure that is at least as important as the one Ray is trying to force down your throat. Convince him that both his concerns and yours must be dealt with and that you are willing to do whatever has to be done to head off the potential problem of doing nothing.

Bureaucrats cause more work to be performed. Because Type 4s do not like to work any more than they have to, you can leverage this trait to convince Ray to modify his bureaucratic behavior.

⑦ *Help:* Bureaucratic managers act in a very similar manner to wimp managers. Review that section for motivational techniques that may further assist you in dealing with a bureaucratic manager.

Con Artists

Con artist bosses are the politicians of the corporate world. What power mongers attempt to achieve with brute force, con artists accomplish with finesse and lies. These are the bosses who promise you everything and deliver nothing but tidbits of information and more promises. A good con artist will put his arm around you, tell you how far you'll get by following his instructions and pick your pocket with the other hand and your brain with conversation. No matter how much he says he likes your work, if it suits his needs, he'll tell his boss your mistakes are the cause of his problems.

The Situation

You had never worked harder than when you prepared this presentation for your boss, Sue. Three days ago she gave you the assignment of presenting to the CEO the rationale behind her organization's expansion into the northwest market. It's a real opportunity for you, and if you impress the CEO with your knowledge of the market, you could possibly be rewarded with a promotion and an opportunity to transfer to Seattle, the planned location for the region's main office. At 10 a.m. sharp, you walk into Sue's office for your planned dry run of the presentation. For some reason, you find your co-worker John sitting in one of the chairs in front of Sue's desk. Your surprised look catches Sue's attention, and when she asks you to have a seat, you know that something is wrong. As soon as you are seated, she makes a statement that almost sends you to the floor: "After a great deal of consideration, I have decided to have John make the presentation rather than you. This should not be considered as a negative reflection on you. I just think that John has a more in-depth knowledge of what's going on in the market than you do." Sue invites you to stick around while John makes a practice presentation using your charts, but you ask if you can be excused. As you quickly exit Sue's office, you can't help but think that this is the second time this con artist has pulled a stunt like this.

Motivating Type 1s

One of the inherent weaknesses of Type 1 bosses is that they can be very insensitive to the feelings of their employees. When insensitivity is combined with the conniving traits of a con artist, you have all of the makings for what amounts to an impossible situation. If you attempt to motivate Sue to change her behavior by calling her attention to how she has treated you, you could worsen your situation. The only thing we can suggest for you to do is to grin and bear it until you can either transfer out of Sue's organization, find another job outside the company, or wait until Sue moves on to another position.

Motivating Type 2s

Con artist behavior is contrary to Type 2 personalities, who are usually loyal. Before you approach Sue on this issue, first determine if she trusts you. If you are new on the job, she may not have had time to develop confidence in your capabilities. If this is the case, then she may not have had any other recourse but to call on John to make the presentation.

If you approach Sue with a positive attitude, she should be willing to honestly tell you if she is confident in your abilities. Listen carefully to her answer, and if you conclude that Sue is, in fact, a first-rate con artist, you have no other choice but to leave her organization.

Motivating Type 3s

Type 3s can demonstrate dishonesty traits that complement their con artist behavior. If you believe that Sue is a dishonest and deceitful con artist, there is nothing you can do to motivate her to change. You may talk to her about your dilemma and she will give you all of the appearances that she understands and wants to cooperate with you. Watch out because you're being conned again, and if she feels threatened by possible exposure, she'll find a way to get you fired.

Motivating Type 4s

You will seldom find a con artist boss with a Type 4 personality. It's not inherent in their friendly nature, but if Sue is a Type 4, watch out. She'll come across as the most friendly and trusting con artist you have ever met. Because Type 4s are so good at covering their deceitful nature, you may find yourself apologizing to Sue when she pulls the presentation assignment out from under you. Be careful not to let that happen. It you threaten to indicate her con artist behavior to her boss, she'll back off for fear of exposure. This may be your only recourse.

? *Help:* Con artist managers have a style that is similar to chameleon managers. Review the section beginning on page 223 for situations and motivational techniques that will further assist you in dealing with con artist managers.

Real Jerks

Any manager is capable of making mistakes on occasion, but real jerks make screwing up a way of life. They have neither the guts nor the brains to do anything right and have a difficult time managing their own careers or any assignment given to them, let alone helping you progress on your career path. Unfortunately, in spite of their gross incompetence, they do creep into upper management positions.

The Situation

You realize you may have to transfer to another organization or get another job if you can't figure out how to get along with your boss. You don't want to do what you have to do to get along with Jim, one of the biggest jerks you have ever worked for. If you decide to stay in your current position, you'll have to surrender most of your principles to avoid jeopardizing your job security.

However, if you take the other approach and refuse to bend to Jim's authority, you can be proud of your individualism even though it will probably cost you your job. Rather than going to the extreme, you decide to see if you can motivate Jim to accept a compromise, which you would consider a win. Although compromising with a jerk may be repugnant to a lot of people, you have decided to treat the exercise as a management learning experience.

Motivating Type 1s

If you want to get along with a Type 1 jerk boss, take the time to know what Jim's objectives are. Then go out of your way to make him think your efforts are essential to helping him achieve his objectives. What you do for Jim may not be earth-shaking, but as long as he believes your persistence and enthusiastic support are crucial to meeting his goals, he'll find you indispensable and will work on ways to reward your good performance.

Motivating Type 2s

The biggest compromise you have to make with a Type 2 jerk boss is to refrain from perceiving him as a jerk just because he disagrees with you. Type 2s typically want all of the answers before they make a decision. Maybe Jim is being stubborn or narrow-minded, but that doesn't mean he's wrong or a jerk boss. Go out of your way to provide Jim with everything he asks for and qualify the results. If he is still not satisfied, ask him what else he needs.

Motivating Type 3s

If you believe that Jim has a Type 3 personality, then you have a chance to present your compromise to him in a manner that will appeal to his desire to cooperate. Intelligent compromising does not mean giving up a lot and getting little in return. It means striking a balance that you and Jim can both live with.

Motivating Type 4s

Most Type 4 jerks are intelligent people who have obnoxious tendencies. Keep in mind that Type 4s are trusting individuals who, on the surface, want you to always be truthful with them. Since it would not be prudent to tell Jim that he is a jerk, start by telling him what he wants to hear. As you gain his confidence, use a variety of tactics to outsmart him into allowing you to have your own way.

(?) *Help:* Real jerk managers have a style similar to con artist managers. Review that section for motivational techniques that will further assist you in dealing with con artist managers.

Lone Rangers

Lone rangers want to be left alone to do things on their own and at their own pace. If you work for a lone ranger, find out what they like to do and volunteer to take on any work they hate to do that involves interaction with other people. If they know that you are the one who handles all of those interpersonal matters that they hate, they'll support you in achieving your career objective.

The Situation

If your boss had anything to say about anything, even the slightest hint of an opinion, you'd never know what it was. His uncanny ability to sit and stare into space is unnerving to say the least. Even the movement of his eyes upward when you asked him a question is unbelievable. Looking into his eyes is like looking into a vacant house. Once again, you repeat your question to see if you can get a perceptible answer. "Joe Caulfield has an opening in his organization and I would like to apply for the job. Is that all right with you, Gary?" After what seems to be an eternity, you finally get a response. "I don't know. Why don't you leave me alone and I'll think about it!" At least you managed to get a response out of the lone ranger, but you're concerned that if you leave him alone, you'll never hear from him again.

Motivating Type 1s

If you are attempting to motivate a Type 1 lone ranger who has a difficult time communicating with you, take the initiative and communicate with him. To spare Gary the burden of interacting with you, write him a memo. Don't ask for his permission, just tell him what you plan to do and ask for his authorization to apply for the open management position. Your memo should not contain any pleading tones, but rather it should be very businesslike and to the point. When Gary reads your memo, it may force him to talk to you, or at the very least, sit down and write you a response.

Motivating Type 2s

If Gary has a Type 2 personality, there is something bothering him that goes beyond anything you have done, so don't take the situation personally. There's a good chance that he is facing personal problems that are causing him to lose his focus on anything you may have requested from him. If you can, give him a couple of days to recover from whatever is bothering him, and approach him again.

Motivating Type 3s

There is a tendency for Type 3 lone ranger bosses to be uncommitted when asked to make basic management decisions. If you are dealing with a lone ranger who is uncomfortable dealing with people in the first place, you may never get him to give you an answer to your transfer request. If, after several attempts, you are unsuccessful at getting Gary to give you the commitment you want, take the request to his boss.

Motivating Type 4s

Type 4s are normally not quiet antisocial individuals. They definitely do not fit the lone ranger personality presented in this section. It is highly possible that he is demonstrating this behavior to be obnoxious. In this particular situation, it is appropriate to let Gary know how serious you are about getting an answer to your transfer request. Tell him that if he cannot give you an answer within a reasonable period of time, you will escalate your request to his boss. To avoid the confrontation, Type 4 bosses will quickly accommodate your request.

(?) *Help:* Lone rangers have a style that is similar to no-action managers because neither is comfortable with face-to-face confrontations. Review the section on page 204 for motivational techniques that will further assist you in dealing with a lone ranger manager.

Firefighters

Managers who consider themselves firefighters thrive on solving crises. They are never content to have things under control and are always on the lookout for a new catastrophe to take care of. If none exists, they'll find an assortment of insignificant matters and blow each up to colossal proportions. This way they can marshal their forces to prevent whatever disaster they predict will happen.

Firefighters have no sense of business politics and do not know how to set priorities. As a result, they prove to be very demanding of their people and expect them to be as driven by crisis as they are. They drive the people who work for them crazy by perpetually changing what they want and are constantly dreaming up new crisis projects. Firefighter managers are disasters at administrating or planning anything. They'll stop at nothing to meet a crisis objective and because they do everything in extremes, if they make a mistake, it can be a whopper!

The Situation

Valerie comes rushing into your office and slams the door. "You won't believe what I just discovered." As it turns out, the crisis that Valerie has discovered is, as you see it, an opportunity. One of the company's major competitors in Seattle has just declared bankruptcy, opening up the entire northwest market to your company. The crisis Valerie sees is that there is nobody capable of taking over that region. Maybe you are the one!

Motivating Type 1s

Unfortunately, Valerie is a highly opinionated Type 1 who truly believes that every crisis she identifies is a very serious situation. There is nothing you are going to be able to do to change this trait in her personality. You have an opportunity to get out of her organization by taking over the northwest market. Tell Valerie that you think this is a huge crisis and volunteer to take charge of its resolution. Then go for the job opportunity.

Motivating Type 2s

Type 2s are emotional people who are prone to feed their emotions with crisis situations, real or perceived. They also have good analytical minds. If you can convince Valerie that she needs to work on techniques that will help her prioritize the crisis she has identified, you will go a long way toward earning her respect and hopefully a promotion out of her organization.

Motivating Type 3s

The stubborn nature of Type 3s will make it next to impossible to convince Valerie that many of the crises she identifies are nothing more than routine problems. In her mind, every crisis is a priority, making it difficult for you to manage your schedule. If you can convince her to prioritize each and establish a reasonable schedule to conquer each crisis, you have a chance of returning to a normal work schedule.

Motivating Type 4s

One of the best ways to motivate Type 4 firefighters is to volunteer to do the work that they don't like or want to do. By enabling them to concentrate on fighting their fires without interruption, you can make yourself indispensable to them. Volunteer to look into what it would take to move into the northwest market, an assignment that will place you in an excellent position to take over that territory.

(?) *Help:* If you want to learn more about firefighting techniques, be sure to read Tom Peters' book *Thriving in Chaos*.

Degraders

It's difficult to try to excel at work if you're convinced that the deck is stacked against you because your boss constantly degrades you. In theory, how well you do your work should matter more than who you know. So much for theory. In practice, if your boss isn't excited about your performance, the advancement of your career comes to a screeching halt until the situation is either rectified to your satisfaction or you move on to another job. If you find yourself in this situation, cheer up; all is not lost if your degrader is willing to meet with you to explain why he believes your performance is negative. There is a chance that your boss cares about you or he wouldn't meet with you at all! You have a unique opportunity to exercise the motivational skills you've learned in this book to turn the situation around.

The Situation

"You screw up like this one more time and you're history!" Your boss, Jill, bangs the desk for emphasis, then turns and stalks out of the room. The two other managers in the room look at each other and follow her out without saying a word. One of them looks back at you and shrugs his shoulders. This isn't the first time Jill has chewed you out, but it's the first time it has been done in front of your peers. To make matters worse, she's accusing you of doing something on a project that isn't even one of your assignments.

Motivating Type 1s

Type 1s can get so angry that they'll pay no attention to the fact that you aren't alone when they chew you out. This was the case with Jill, who also gave you no chance to explain when she abruptly left the room. Jill was obviously in the wrong, but she may have a difficult time admitting it because as you know, Type 1s always think they are right. Privately approach her from a logical position by asking her how she could chew you out for something that was not your responsibility. Let her do the explaining and she will probably realize that she made a mistake. She probably won't admit it publicly, but you should at least get an apology from her.

Motivating Type 2s

Moody Type 2s think that degrading you in public is the only way to communicate. This is a primary concern if you are dealing with a Type 2. For whatever reason, Jill perceives that she has a real communication problem with you. She doesn't believe that you will listen to her unless she yells at you in a threatening tone in front of your peers. If you can convince her that you are loyal to her, she will talk with you privately on any future problems she has with you.

Motivating Type 3s

Jill lacks the self-discipline to wait to talk with you alone. She just lets go without considering the impact it will have on you. She chewed you out for a project you were not responsible for because she was probably dissatisfied with others in her organization and wanted to make an example out of you. She expects the others to learn what might happen to them if they fail. Her entire position and outburst were wrong and you need to point that out to her. Type 3s are usually considerate people, but approach Jill when she is in a good mood and not under any pressure just to be on the safe side.

Motivating Type 4s

It will be unusual for Type 4s to chew you out in public. If they do, they are in an extreme state of irritation at something that you have done. Although it may be the project that Jill referenced in our situation, most likely it is something else. She either feels threatened by you, doesn't trust you, doesn't like you, or a combination of things that you must resolve if you want to continue working for her. Discuss with her what you can do to correct the situation or ask for a transfer to another organization.

Warning: No matter what Jill's reason was, being degraded in public is a significant blow to anyone's ego. Make sure you take whatever time is necessary to resolve your anger before you approach Jill to work out a solution.

A Boss Who Doesn't Like You

Having a boss who doesn't like you reduces your effectiveness and productivity. They block initiatives, thwart ambition, and in extreme cases, threaten their subordinates so that they are unwilling to take on any risks. How do you keep your head above water and motivate your boss to lessen the pressure?

The Situation

You just completed another trying session with your boss, Helen. She has taken every good idea that you have had and thrown it back in your face. Your raise for next year has already been denied and when you request a transfer, she tells you there is no way she would risk her reputation by transferring a "company incompetent" to another department. It's clear to you that she doesn't like you and wants you to voluntarily resign. But you vow not to accommodate her.

Motivating Type 1s

If you are working for a hard-core Type 1 boss who wants everything done her own way, you have the most serious personality conflicts to face in this section. You're probably tired of being pushed around, fed up with not being allowed to do what is right, and watching helplessly at the incompetent results of your boss. To make matters worse, Helen has been with the company forever and her boss supports her. So much for the thought that if you hang in there, you'll outlast her. What are your options?

You could get another job in the same company, assuming that Helen will allow you to transfer, or you could simply quit. In order to facilitate this option, you must be prepared to bite your lip and play up to the inexhaustible ego of your Type 1 boss. Tell Helen whatever you believe she wants to hear and do whatever she asks you to do. It's imperative that you make her think you are her most trusted and loyal employee.

Motivating Type 2s

As much as you may think that your boss is a miserable person, take a moment and evaluate where you may fit into Helen's professional life. Perhaps her attitude toward you would change abruptly if you did something to make her happy. Type 2s want their feelings to be understood and they'll support anybody they believe understands that concept. If Helen believes that you are committed to her, she will begin to respect you and, more important, like you over time.

Motivating Type 3s

When Helen is in a good mood, suggest to her that you need her help. The need for help appeals to the ego of Type 3s, so you'll be on track to win her favor and support. When she asks you what kind of help you need, tell her you like working for her, but you're getting bored with your current position. Ask her if she will assist you in transferring to Department B, where they have just opened up a position that is of interest to you. If she agrees to help you with your transfer request, you're on your way out of a bad situation. If Helen rejects your request, update your resume and find another job.

Motivating Type 4s

The trick to working for a Type 4 boss who doesn't like you is to make yourself absolutely indispensable to her. In the process, Helen will think of you as being more useful whenever she asks for your help. Play the role to the point where she believes that she couldn't meet her goals without your support. Once you've accomplished that feat, you are ready to have a healthy conversation with Helen to diplomatically show her how to get off your back. Remember, Type 4s like to have fun more than they like to work, so appeal to her sense of humor.

Power Addicts

Power addicts feed off of power. The more power they can get, the more they want. Single-minded and egomaniacal, they don't care about the growth of anything other than their own personal empires. Driven to control everything and everyone in sight, they must have the last word and be the final authority on any subject, no matter how minor. They are more interested in bossing people around than they are in getting anything done. If you stand in their way, power addicts will use all of their energies to get rid of you, even if you are right.

The Situation

When you first met your boss, Bill, it was obvious that he had mixed feelings about you. Over a relatively short period of time, Bill's feelings quickly changed from mixed to negative. It became obvious to you that the man did not like you personally or professionally for reasons that were beyond your comprehension. You always went out of your way to be polite, accepted with enthusiasm every assignment he gave you, and always completed your projects on time. Your relationship with Bill deteriorated to the point where he refused to meet with you to discuss anything because, as he put it, "I've got more pressing matters to attend to right now." It became apparent that the man was a power addict and you were nothing more than a pawn in Bill's game.

Motivating Type 1s

Most power addicts have Type 1 personalities. They savor the fight more than the victory, and acquiring power over you is more important to them than merely having the power. They want the pleasure of transforming you from someone who is assertive into someone who squirms in their presence.

The way to handle a Type 1 power addict is to walk a fine line by selectively challenging Bill's authority to exercise power over you. On a daily basis, play up to Bill's ego by telling him what he wants to hear, letting him think he's in charge. Over time, you may be able to manipulate him to do whatever you want him to do.

Motivating Type 2s

Power addicts love to exercise control over you and want you to act as though you couldn't get anything done without their help. To survive, you must be willing to continually bow to Bill's authority by telling him how great he is and constantly praising his ideas. That will buy you the time you need to find another job.

Motivating Type 3s

Type 3 power addicts want to at least pretend that they are understanding of any given situation. You can catch Bill totally off guard if you tell him that you agree with his power-oriented decisions. However, also tell him that he wouldn't be making this decision if he was fully aware of what he's doing to the organization. Be prepared to explain to him how his power style is stifling the productivity of the department and that you know how to reconcile the situation. Give it your best shot!

Motivating Type 4s

Type 4 power addicts are very insensitive people. To them, you are nothing more than a pawn whom they can use to get whatever they want—usually favorable recognition for themselves with a minimum amount of work on their part. If you approach Bill with an idea, be prepared to tell him what he gets out of it. Tell Bill what he wants to hear and you will eventually earn his trust. Unless he's paranoid, most of the time he will leave you alone to do what you want to do, as long as he believes that whatever you are doing will ultimately benefit him.

(?) *Help:* For additional ideas on how to motivate power addict bosses, see the section beginning on page 195 that discusses motivating power monger peer managers.

Chameleons

In the classic movie *Best Little Whorehouse in Texas*, the governor of Texas was closely following the polls to measure public opinion, and as he would dance around the mood of the electorate, he'd sing, "Now you see me, now you don't!" He was a perfect human chameleon—agreeing with one popular opinion one day and another the next day. You never know what a chameleon is going to do until he does it. Experts at sleight-of-mouth techniques, chameleon managers cannot be trusted, are manipulative, and extremely deceptive.

The Situation

"No woman is going to be hired as a sales rep for this company as long as I'm in charge." If only Sam, your boss, had remained a high school football coach. Unfortunately, he's smart enough to know that his outdated attitude could get him into some serious trouble with the affirmative action people. Whenever the question comes up as to why his entire sales force is male, he always uses his carefully prepared canned answer: "We had a meeting on the subject just the other day. I don't know what is causing the problem, but you can rest assured I'm going to get at the bottom of this thing soon!" Like a chameleon, Sam can change his colors quicker than any executive you have ever seen. You have just interviewed an outstanding female candidate to take over one of your sales regions that desperately needs help. You have to get Sam to sign the new-hire paperwork. How do you motivate Sam to accept the first female on your sales team?

Motivating Type 1s

Calculating Type 1 execs are fully cognizant of the affirmative action laws and regulations. You do not even need to mention the subject to Sam when you deliver the forms to him for his signature. In his true chameleon fashion, he will tell you to leave them on his desk so that he can look at them later. Pin him down. Tell him that you will bring the forms back to him at a specific time for his signature. If he insists that you leave the documents with him, ask him when you can pick them up.

Motivating Type 2s

Type 2 chameleons tend to be unrealistic individuals who, for whatever reason, believe they can forestall the inevitable forever. If you remind Sam of the key affirmative action points of law, emphasizing the personal liability side, you'll quickly get his attention and he'll sign your forms.

Motivating Type 3s

Type 3 chameleons are reluctant and unsure people who have developed traits that allow them to hide from the inevitable. Use the same legal awareness tactics recommended for Type 2s to motivate Type 3s to sign your forms.

Motivating Type 4s

To Type 4s, playing the role of chameleon is nothing more than one of the many immature games that they enjoy playing. Take the fun out of the game by informing them of the legal consequences of their actions. They will quickly stop playing the game and will ask you where to sign.

Procrastinators

The word "manager" did not appear in the English language until around the year 1800. It took another 50 years before social scientists undertook serious study of the phenomenon of leadership. But in the last hundred years, researchers have been hard at work making up for lost time, inquiring how people become managers, what styles they use, how they affect group performance, and what makes them effective. A recent survey contains a bibliography of more than 5,000 comprehensive studies that have been made about the art of management. A disproportionate number of those studies address procrastination, the management art of doing nothing. The problem existed more than 100 years ago and it is still with us today.

The Situation

Your confrontation with your boss, Jeremy, starts out on shaky grounds with your opening remark. "Everybody in the firm knows that you are strongly opposed to switching over to Internet-capable computers. They can appreciate your concerns and so can I, but the time has come to make the change if we want to stay even with, let alone beat, our competition." There. You've finally said what has been on your mind for a long time. However, the look on Jeremy's face expresses his contempt for the idea. You think to yourself, "If this man continues to procrastinate on this fundamental decision, we're all out

of a job. How can I get him motivated to join the 20th century technical revolution?"

Motivating Type 1s

Jeremy doesn't have a clue as to what the Internet is all about, let
alone why your organization needs it to remain competitive. As a
Type 1, he's not about to admit to his ignorance on the subject, so the
safest approach for him to take is to procrastinate. You will have to
show him a demonstration of the Internet, in terms that he'll understand, before he will endorse the project.

Motivating Type 2s

Type 2s are analytical to a fault and subsequently make excellent
procrastinators. Jeremy will drop his analytical guard if you can show
him how cost-effective and risk-free it is to access and use the information that's provided on the Internet.

Motivating Type 3s

The indecisive nature of Type 3s makes them excellent procrastinators. They have a difficult time establishing direction in long-term
time frames. If you can show Jeremy how other companies similar to
yours are using the Internet to establish direction within their organizations, he may come to his senses and endorse the project.

Motivating Type 4s

Type 4s have a difficult time establishing any kind of planning direction. The depth and breadth of the Internet exceed their capacity to
even establish a short-term direction for their organization. You need
to eliminate the direction issue if you want Jeremy to endorse your
Internet project. Convince him that the Internet is nothing more than
a tool you plan to use to gain a competitive edge on your competition.

Summary

Motivating your boss to look at you in a favorable light is one of
the most basic of all methods you need to employ to get ahead. After
all, you're not going to get promoted to that job you've always wanted

if your boss doesn't like you or believe you are the best person qualified for the position. All of that is relatively easy if you are working for
a boss whom you get along with in the first place. But what happens
if you are working for someone with whom you don't get along? How
do you motivate him? This same thought process applies to upper
management. We'll show you how to use similar tactics to motivate
upper management in Chapter 9.

Chapter 9

Motivating Upper Management

A leader is the one who climbs the tallest tree, surveys the entire situation, and yells out to his team, "There are too many alligators in the swamp; let's get out of here." The harried managers below respond by saying, "Don't worry boss, we're making progress by draining the swamp." As managers, we're often so busy draining swamps that we don't realize there may be too many alligators to contend with in a given situation. The fact of the matter is, upper management wants us to get out of the swamp, a priority that we're ignoring. Our effectiveness as managers does not depend solely on how much effort we expend, but on whether we're expending it in the right direction.

Good proactive managers are constantly monitoring the dynamic changes that are occurring in their business environments—from consumer buying patterns to the strategic maneuvers of their competitors. They listen very carefully to what upper management is telling them and respond with the motivational drive necessary to get done whatever job upper management requires. It's not just a way to get ahead, it's the only way to get ahead.

In this chapter. You will learn how to use strategic motivational techniques on upper management to help move your career onto the fast track. You'll learn how to quickly recognize the often difficult-to-read personality types of upper executive managers so that you can adjust your motivational approach accordingly.

One-on-One Encounters

It is not uncommon for an executive to ask for an informal presentation on a subject that they think you know something about. In most instances, they will have first informed your boss of their request. The bottom line is that you have an opportunity to demonstrate how well-versed you are in a subject that is of interest to an executive. Even if you are the world's foremost expert on the subject, if you are not able to present the desired information in a format that motivates the executive, you will not accumulate any career points. In fact, you could even lose points if you fail to apply the appropriate motivational techniques in your one-on-one presentation.

The Situation

As you drive to work, you wonder what you're going to say in your one-on-one meeting with Rita, the company's chief financial officer. You've completed your strategic plan and are in the process of implementing it, but the word you're hearing in the halls is not good. Managers at all levels are calling it another one of those "here today, gone tomorrow" operational exercises. Somehow Rita heard about the dissension and wants to meet with you at 10 a.m. to find out what's going on. As you search for an answer, somewhere in the back of your mind, the word "paradigm" comes to mind.

You remember your college professor showing you how to use paradigms to create a model or pattern for improvement when he showed you how old and new paradigms work. New paradigms replace old paradigms by establishing a clear, result-oriented vision and a model showing how it can be applied. If paradigms are properly used, they can effectively motivate anybody, including the executive you'll be pitching to this morning.

Motivating Type 1s

The fortune cookie was right when it said you'll never get a second chance to make a good first impression, especially when dealing with a Type 1 executive. Typically, Type 1 executives are the most difficult of all the personalities to motivate. They have limited attention spans and about as much patience as a piranha about to attack a floating piece of prime rib.

Assuming that you made a good first 30-second impression, a lode of data well-presented in meaningful charts addressing exactly what Rita wants to know should solidify your presentation of meaningful material. If you blow this part of the presentation, even if you made a good first impression, you will not be given an opportunity to recover. The following comment demonstrates our point: "I've invited you into my office to discuss the company's strategic plan. While I'm impressed with the way you've handled yourself, you still haven't answered my basic question. Is our plan too optimistic?"

If you fail to make a favorable first impression with a Type 1 exec, you probably won't get a second chance. If Rita tells you politely that she will digest what you have said and will get back to you later, you can rest assured that you have not made a favorable impression. Your chances of getting on the fast track through this particular executive are slim to none.

Motivating Type 2s

Appearance is a critical component if you're trying to motivate quality-conscious Type 2 execs. More than anything, appearance influences their perception of you and may even determine their attitude toward you at the outset of your meeting. That's why people whose appearance suggests high status are treated measurably better than those whose appearance suggests low status. Like it or not, that is a fact of life and most executives think of themselves as being in the high-status echelon.

The first 30-second impressions of a Type 2 executive will be based on your appearance, facial expression, movement, and the tone of your voice. If that picture is positive, you have a chance to make a favorable impression on Rita. If the impression is negative, your odds are significantly reduced.

Motivating Type 3s

If you are dealing with a Type 3 executive, nonverbal appearance and your facial expressions are the single most important attribute to them. They also must believe that you are a person who is committed to the company and loyal to the cause before they will believe anything you tell them.

Nonverbal communication, from appearance to facial expression to movement is the primary factor Type 3 executives will use to judge your initial net worth. It tends to be even more heavily relied upon if your words give a contradictory message because it is one of the most revealing differences between people with power and those with little power. You want to come across as a powerful person, which Type 3 executives respect.

Motivating Type 4s

Facial expressions are extremely important to Type 4 execs. What might your face say to Rita at your first meeting? You're angry because of your perpetual frown or you are not interested because of the blank look on your face. You're nervous and anxious because you have a tight smile. Always keep in mind that your smile is the most important facial expression you have for communicating. It is your chief component for attracting the attention of the exec you're trying to motivate and it radiates a level of confidence that Type 4 execs want.

(?) *Help:* What do you look like? If you walk into a meeting where you are the only one dressed in casuals, you're not going to measure up to their presentation standards. What do you sound like? Your voice tells a lot about your personality, attitude, and level of confidence. What do you say? To enhance the image of what you look and sound like, lock it all down by communicating your message in a clear and concise manner that executives understand.

Group Encounters

First impressions begin with what others see in you. If you are standing in front of a group of executives about to make a presentation, it is absolutely critical that the first minute of your presentation be viewed as positive rather than negative. The more you know about the culture and personality types of each executive in the group, the more accurately you can predict their expectations and tailor your presentation to leverage a favorable first and lasting impression. While we recognize that it is highly unlikely that all the execs in the group will have the same personality type, prototyping their person-alities in advance of the meeting to gauge how you will want to struc-ture your presentation is absolutely critical to your success.

The Situation

As you are walking down the hallway past the boardroom, you're startled when the door suddenly opens and your boss, Jerry, appears in front of you. "Quick, get in here and tell the board of directors eve-rything you know about the Peabody Project. They think we are out of control and my backside is on the line if you don't convince them oth-erwise." Before you can utter a response, Jerry grabs you by the arm and you're suddenly standing at the head of the conference table fac-ing the 12 board members. As Jerry introduces you to the board, you quickly survey the group to determine how you will approach your presentation. If you believe that two thirds of the audience is made up of Types 1 and 2, then slant your presentation with an approach that appeals to these types. Appeal to the optimistic needs of the Type 3s who are in the meeting. If the ranking exec in the group happens to have a Type 4 personality, use exciting words to tell your story.

Motivating Type 1s

To grab the attention of and to motivate the Type 1 board mem-bers, show them the big picture of the project at the very outset of your presentation. Because you haven't had time to prepare any briefing charts, make use of the white board to quickly recap key proj-ect status points. For example, you may want to compare projected cost to actual cost, noting the reasons for any over- or underruns.

Motivating Type 2s

Remember, the more consistent you can make what you say with how you say it, the more favorable your first impression will be with the Type 2 board members. Consistency covers all three channels of communication that you will be using—body language, your voice, and words. If you are presenting some serious numbers on one of your charts and smiling at the same time, you're not consistent in the mes-sage you're trying to convey. A more serious look is in order. Always know what your face is saying. It is your most controllable nonverbal clue and the one the execs will be relying on to gauge your attitude.

Motivating Type 3s

Gesture with purpose and always toward your Type 3 viewers. Don't make cramped gestures or quick hand movements and never fiddle with coins, bracelets, pens, ties, or other objects that will distract the Type 3 board members.

Motivating Type 4s

Smiling and head-nodding are the most powerful nonverbal clues you can use when addressing Type 4s. Start your presentation off with direct eye contact as your point of reference and adjust from there. If you are uncomfortable about making eye contact, look at the person's forehead. Unless they are very close to you, they will not be able to tell if you are avoiding direct eye contact. Type 4s like colorful, artistic graphs and charts instead of bland tables and charts.

Social Encounters

The pen is mightier than the sword, but neither is mightier than the mouth, especially when it come to creating first impressions in social settings with people who count. Voice communication is second only to body language as a means of communicating in social settings. In face-to-face interactions, it isn't enough to be physically attractive. The moment you open your mouth, you either confirm or deny an initial impression that a person has about you. Abraham Lincoln once said, "It's better to keep your mouth shut and let others think you're a fool than to open it and confirm that you are, in fact, a fool." If you sound harsh and abrasive, you will be viewed as harsh and abrasive. If you sound timid and insecure, you will be considered as such. And if you sound strong and confident, chances are others will be motivated to think of you in a preferable way.

The Situation

The annual chamber of commerce Christmas party is an event to which you have been going for years. It offers you a great opportunity to rub elbows with community business leaders and have a great time as well. As you glance over at the bar, there's Ed, the senior vice president of your company, sitting all by himself. Boy, would you like to get to know him a little better. Word has it that he's about to become the new CEO when Harrison retires next month. As you walk over to Ed, you size up his personality type as you wonder what you're going to say.

Motivating Type 1s

When you walk up to Ed and introduce yourself, he asks you what you want. You are not surprised because you believe he's a Type 1 who likes to intimidate people. The best way to stop him from intimidating you is to tell him something like, "Oh, I'm sorry if I bothered you." He'll quickly apologize for his abrupt behavior and will allow you to enter into a healthy social conversation with him.

Motivating Type 2s

When you walk up to Ed and introduce yourself, you note that he at first has a suspicious look in his eye as if he's wondering what you are after, which is a Type 2 characteristic. To neutralize the situation, avoid getting into any discussion about company business. Talk about subjects of mutual interest like sports or the upcoming seasonal activities.

Motivating Type 3s

When you begin your conversation with Ed, you can't help but think he is one of the most unenthusiastic people you've ever talked to. Type 3s can be unenthusiastic individuals unless you can discover one of the few subjects they like to talk about. Ask Ed what he likes to do when he's not working, and then talk about what he likes to do to spark his enthusiasm.

Motivating Type 4s

Your voice is a remarkable tool that can be used to reduce tension and anxiety and convey calmness and control, all of which are attributes that mean a lot to Type 4 execs. This is particularly true in a social setting where Ed's first priority is to relax and enjoy the party setting. His last priority is to get trapped into a conversation about some work-related subject. When you address Type 4s in a social setting, keep your conversation light and friendly. Avoid talking about any work-related subject and address topics that you know are of interest to your Type 4 exec, such as golf, tennis, or barbecuing.

Illicit Encounters

William Hazlitt wrote, "There is nothing that helps a manager's conduct through life more than their knowledge of their own characteristic weaknesses." While this is certainty true, you must also be capable of recognizing other people's weaknesses so that you are in a better position to handle bizarre situations when they occur. For example, if a manager with power tells you to do something that is wrong, what will you do? The quickest way out of the illicit encounter is to simply do what you are told. In the short run, that approach will get you to first base. But you'll never make it to home plate—that promotion that you want—with a boss who now expects you to be the implementor of all of her illicit demands.

The Situation

"You want to see me, Sally?" you ask as you walk into her executive office. "You know that shredder that we have in the mail room? I want you to run this through it, and don't tell anybody what you are doing, not even your boss. I haven't shown him the report, so that should not be a problem." When she hands you the papers, you abruptly realize it deals with the severe safety hazards that the company's independent auditor discovered. Sally stares at you with an intent look. "I have to have your complete trust to permanently dispose of this report. If I can count on you, you can count on me to be quite helpful to your career later on."

Motivating Type 1s

Sally is trying to intimidate you to do something with a report that points out deficiencies in one of her areas of responsibility. For some reason, she is not willing to fix the problem. You can assume that it's a cost issue or the fear of bad press if the problems are publicized. You need to find out why she wants to destroy the reports so that you can present her with an alternative solution. If she insists that you destroy the report, see the warning message at the end of the section.

Motivating Type 2s

Type 2s are suspicious people. Sally may feel that the report is inaccurate and not worth taking the time to address. If this is the case, suggest to her that she conduct a study with another consultant so you can compare the findings of the studies before you destroy the report. If she insists that you destroy the report, see the warning at the end of the section.

Motivating Type 3s

Type 3s can be lazy individuals who will become very inventive at figuring out ways to avoid work and stress. In her naive frame of mind, Sally has asked you to destroy a report without considering the personal consequences of her request. When you point out the legal liabilities, she will withdraw her request. If she insists that you destroy the report, see the warning message below.

Motivating Type 4s

The impulsive nature of Sally's Type 4 personality tells her to destroy the safety report so that the problem will go away for the time being. She plans to address the problem in the future, when she has more time. You know intuitively that will never happen. Simply tell Sally that you cannot comply with her request because of the risk of personal liability you would bear. When you explain to her what the consequences are, she will tell you she had not considered that issue and will withdraw her request to destroy the document. If she insists that you destroy the report, see the warning below.

Warning: You are being asked to do something that is not only immoral but illegal. Think of the worst case and the personal consequences that it holds for you. If you destroy the report and someone on the factory floor dies because one of the identified safety hazards was not corrected, both you and the company are liable. Is it worth it?

Strategic Encounters

A strategic encounter is one of the most powerful political weapons an astute manager has in his or her arsenal. Here is how it works. You have a brilliant idea that, when implemented, will catapult your company into Fortune 500 heaven. You know you're the best person to successfully carry this thing off and there is only one person standing in your way. It's one executive who has the authority to approve your idea. How do you strategically meet with this person and motivate her to approve your idea?

The Situation

The party that is planned for Friday to celebrate the company's closure of its fiscal year with record high sales and earnings presents a perfect opportunity for you to rub elbows with Haley, the division's new president. You've heard through a reliable grapevine that she has already started to scout for a senior vice president. Why not see if you can't get a chance to step up to the plate and hit a home run! To take advantage of the situation, you plan to simply walk up to Haley, introduce yourself, and enter into a conversation with her that will leave a lasting favorable impression.

Motivating Type 1s

Type 1 execs love adventure and action-oriented ideas. When you enter into a conversation with Haley, briefly describe to her the action side of your idea and conclude with a hook that will pique her interest. For example, you might say, "Haley, I have an idea for a new product line that is years ahead of our competition. If it is properly introduced, our company will be a Fortune 500 company in six months. Can I meet with you on Monday to discuss the specifics of my idea?" She will meet with you.

Motivating Type 2s

Creative ideas are important to Type 2 execs. When you meet with Haley, discuss the creative aspects of your idea, what makes it unique, and why it is better than anything your competition has to offer. In a social setting, you will want to keep your conversation with

Haley short and to the point. Conclude by saying you are prepared to show, at her earliest convenience, examples of what you are talking about. If you have done your job, she will set up a meeting with you on the spot.

Motivating Type 3s

Type 3 execs are good listeners but they are reluctant to entertain new ideas unless they are absolutely sure they will fly. When you introduce your idea to Haley, briefly describe what your idea is and then tell her why your idea will succeed. If you have facts and data that support your claim, point that out to her and ask her for a time when you can show her your complete plan.

Motivating Type 4s

On the surface, Type 4s can get excited about anything. If you ask Haley what she thinks about this or that, she'll tell you they are great ideas. However, if you pursue your idea with her, she'll eventually tell you that good ideas are a dime a dozen. You won't get her attention until you can convince her that you have solid dates, then she will agree to meet with you to hear the details of your plan.

Heading Down the Fast Track

The expression "fast track" has different connotations to different companies. But basically, when you extract all of the hype that is typically associated with the term, it still only means one thing—fast-trackers will get a significant promotion if they can meet an important company goal. The specific objectives of the goal are usually well-defined, the tasks that must be completed already identified, and most important, a completion date has been established. The only missing component is somebody who the company execs can trust to head up the effort. In the scenario that follows, you have an opportunity to head a fast-track team assigned to open a major new market for the company. You have been asked to make a presentation to a selection committee that is made up of four company executives. Your presentation must show them why you are the right person for this assignment.

The Situation

As the four execs enter the small conference room and take their seats, Latin music plays softly in the background. A notebook holding an information packet has been carefully placed on the meeting table in front of each chair. You are pitching to four execs, each with a different personality. Your Type 1 and 2 execs won't care what kind of paper you used in the notebook, but you chose a good quality stock with a rough linen-like texture that you knew would appeal to the aesthetic nature of your Type 3 and 4 execs. You have carefully planned this presentation to motivate each personality type with a blend of techniques that won't offend one personality type while trying to motivate another.

Motivating Type 1s

Tom is a focused Type 1 who will want to see the facts first without wasting any time. For this reason, you begin your presentation with a slide that shows the size of the market you're going after. You conclude with a strong statement and the qualifying remark, "As you can see, we have a substantial market opportunity here. How does that sound to you, Tom?" When he responds with "Great. What's next?" you know you're heading down the right Type 1 track.

Motivating Type 2s

Gary is your Type 2 exec, and although he likes to see the numbers like his Type 1 counterpart, he's more guarded. He'll want to know what source you used to extract the data you're presenting before he'll give you his nod of approval. When you say during your introduction of the first slide that all of your data came from the U.S. Census Bureau, you lock in your credibility with Gary.

Motivating Type 3s

Type 3s appreciate meetings where there is a relaxed atmosphere. When Elizabeth compliments you on the music, you inform her that the music is by Caballero. She tells you that Caballero is one of her favorite musicians. Of course, you already knew that. You got her secretary to confide in you and tell you what her favorite music was.

During the course of your presentation, appeal to the inventive side of Elizabeth's personality by pointing out what your unique qualifications are for this assignment.

Motivating Type 4s

Be extra careful not to ignore Dale, your Type 4 exec. Type 4s tend not to say much and will give you the appearance that they are on your side—until you're done with the presentation. Then you'll find out that they are not about to support you. Find out what Dale's hot button is and leverage it early in the presentation. For example, if you know that Dale is infatuated with the Internet, present a well-designed slide that shows how you plan to create a Web site to support your project. When you complete this part of your presentation, stop and ask him what he thinks. Hopefully, you'll get a favorable response.

Idea: For future reference, set up a file for each of the personality types and record motivational techniques that you have applied that work. Make a special note of items that work particularly well on mixed personality types.

Can't Get Them to Commit

Everybody responds to different situations with different levels of assertiveness. During times of management challenge, difficulty, or stress, managers tend to move out of their comfort zone, and either become more passive or more aggressive than their normal mode of operation. When challenged, a highly assertive manager might make his presence known by speaking louder or taking faster action. Conversely, a manager with low assertiveness might become increasingly reluctant to say or do anything. These commitless managers are relatively easy to spot from the way they look (nervous), how they sound (mumbling to silent), and what they say (awkward phrasing). In this section, you'll learn how to motivate commitless managers to make a decision that is in your best interest.

The Situation

You're in the conference room Friday morning a full half-hour before your presentation, giving yourself plenty of time to check every detail and to practice key portions of your presentation. The layout of every page has been done professionally, with just the right amount of white space, no crowding of words, and crisp type, with just the right amount of color to set off each chart.

At the assigned hour, Ben, the senior vice president of operations, and his staff arrives. As soon as everybody is seated, you begin what you believe is your best presentation on what has to be one of the hottest products ever introduced. You conclude with an outstanding summary of everything you have talked about. When the lights come back on, you find yourself standing with a bold smile on your face that radiates your confidence. You conclude, "As you can see, it is imperative that we move on the introduction of this product as soon as possible. Are their any questions before I turn this over to my product introduction team?"

The response you get back from Ben floors you. "There's plenty of time to implement this product. No reason to push things along too fast and make mistakes. I'll let you know what I want to do as soon as I have had time to think it over." You're stunned and bewildered. You wonder what you did wrong.

Motivating Type 1s

If Ben has a Type 1 personality, pull him aside after the room clears and ask him to give you an honest appraisal of your presentation. He'll probably tell you, "I just didn't hear anything that convinced me. Sure, there were lots of pretty pictures, but it all sounded superficial. It didn't sound to me like you knew what you were talking about. I think your problem was that you were relying too much on the pizzazz of your presentation rather than what's required to get this project off the ground."

This reaction is typical of Type 1 commitless managers. You should have concentrated on the importance of timing so that it would have been difficult for Ben to delay his decision.

Motivating Type 2s

Type 2 execs are analytical, and although they may admire you for the good work you put in on the slides, that by itself won't win their approval. If Ben doesn't get the feeling that you have a firm grasp on what you are proposing and feels you can't justify all of the numbers, you will not earn his trust. You were offering a completely visual presentation of a case to a personality who relies on his ears for information processing. He doesn't care about the aesthetic appearance of your charts. Modify your charts so that they are full of the information Ben is looking for and needs to make a decision. Conduct a follow-up presentation with him to win his approval.

Motivating Type 3s

Different personalities have different sensory preferences that they rely on to process information. Any presentation strategy that fails to take those preferences into account risks failure, no matter how good the presentation may appear to be. Type 3s respond well in a relaxed atmosphere. The fact that you had to turn the lights out so that you could show your foils on a screen changed the presentation from light to dark, or from relaxed to tense. If Ben becomes tense, he will not commit to anything.

Motivating Type 4s

Talking alone without any visual aides to a Type 4 exec is a waste of time. If you want Ben to understand what he's supposed to do, you have to give him something to look at, which you did through your elegantly prepared charts. Wrap your presentation up with a final set of charts that clearly ask for Ben's decision immediately. Ben may tell you, "I'm sorry, but I don't really see how this product is very promising. At the risk of sounding negative, I can't picture our division doing it."

(?) *Help:* Commitless managers act in a very similar manner to wimps. Review the section beginning on page 206 for motivational techniques that may further assist you in dealing with commitless managers.

(?) *Help:* Suzette Elgin offers some excellent advice on how to use the gentle art of verbal persuasion in her book *BusinessSpeak*.

Chapter 10

Motivating People Outside the Company

Take yourself out of your management role for a moment and let's assume you own a farm—a natural system—that is the sole source of your livelihood. Consider how ridiculous it would be if you did not follow the farming system—you forget to plant in the spring, and instead, play golf. Then you try to get all of the planting done in the summer so you can have a fall harvest. A consistent process must be followed over time if you want to reap the rewards of what you sow. No shortcuts are allowed on the farm or any other natural system, for that matter.

This same principle applies to human relationships, which are also natural systems subject to the laws of the harvest. In the short-term, you can get by and make a favorable impression by exercising your charm and pretending to be interested in other people. Eventually, the challenges of life will cause your true motives to surface and your short-term relationship will disappear because you didn't take the time to understand the person's personality, learn what turns him on and off, and what motivates him.

If you take the time to sow motivation into your relationships outside the company, they will have long-term staying power. How many times have you thought of someone whom you haven't seen for months or even years? What makes you think of them? It is probably because they had a way of motivating you—you were always up when you were with this person. In this chapter, we'll show you how to use motivational techniques to get people who are outside your company to help you achieve your career objectives, even in adverse situations.

Angry Subcontractors

It's hard enough keeping your employees motivated, much less your vast network of subcontractors and suppliers. However, Harold Plumley, founder of Plumley Company, found a way to do it. Every May, Plumley invites his top 50 suppliers to a two-day weekend getaway that's paid for by his company. In addition to a banquet and golf tournament, there is an awards ceremony. Prizes are given to the outstanding suppliers and subcontractors in quality, cost control, technology, and market support. The company executives explain exactly why they have chosen the winners, hoping that the other vendors will shoot for those goals next year. Plumley tells all of his vendors that his door is always open if they need to discuss any problem with him.

The Situation

"Charlie, I can't believe Arthur would do that to you. He told you that you had the contract with us, you went out and hired the people you needed, and then he told you he changed his mind? Why would he pull a dumb stunt like that? Can we get together over lunch to discuss this further?" Charlie runs Titanium, Inc., a key supplier and fabricator of titanium products for your company. You don't want to lose him because he is the only subcontractor in the state who is qualified to do this work. Charlie is angry and you've got to figure out a way to neutralize the situation.

Motivating Type 1s

Type 1s demand action, so be prepared to tell Charlie the action you have taken to neutralize the damage that has been done. Tell him Arthur has been reprimanded for making a false statement to him and has been instructed to place all future Titanium, Inc., orders through you.

Motivating Type 2s

Type 2s are hard to please, so when you meet with Charlie for lunch, make sure you have a concrete solution to the problem. Review the sample solution that we presented for a Type 1 and assure Charlie that the problem has been resolved.

Motivating Type 3s

Most people with Type 3 personalities are easygoing, so you really have to push them to get them irritated. Do not underestimate Charlie's loss of confidence as a result of the action taken by Arthur. Assure him that the situation will never occur again and back your statement up with proof. For example, if you have brought the problem to the attention of the senior vice president, invite Charlie to confirm what you have said by calling the vice president.

Motivating Type 4s

If Charlie has a Type 4 personality, review the suggestions that were presented for Type 3s. Type 4s tend to be somewhat naive in their business dealings. Ask Charlie if he got anything in writing from Arthur before he proceeded to hire people for the job. Chances are he did not, which places some of the burden of the problem on him. Let him know this. If he did, then your company may be responsible for reimbursing Charlie for his costs.

When You Need Support from Competitors

How much should you know about your competitors? A lot, according to Federal Express. The company's monthly newsletter includes a "Competitive Corner" section that is packed full of information about what Federal Express's competitors are doing. Things like United Parcel's test of a radio dispatch system are covered, along with financial highlights of major competitors. Insight, an aggressive direct marketer of computer hardware and software, routinely e-mails all of its employees with stock updates in which the vice president compares the company's stock prices with its competitors' prices and provides comments as to why different stocks went up or down. A lot of this information would not be available if competitors could not be motivated to share information.

The Situation

Computech is one of your major competitors and you know they are facing the same dilemma your company is facing. You both make hard drives at a price that, until recently, nobody else in the industry could touch. That was before Tosho entered the market last month with disk drive prices that substantially undercut you and Computech's prices by as much as 25 percent. If you could convince Ed over at Computech to compare his product cost with yours, you could determine if Tosho is selling disk drives below their cost to capture the market—a violation of U.S. antitrust laws.

Motivating Type 1s

Before Ed will agree to share competitive cost information with you, you must show him how your cost comparison analysis will help you discover if Tosho is selling their products below cost. Task-oriented Type 1s need all of your answers before they will give you their answer.

Motivating Type 2s

When you approach Ed about the Tosho problem, find out if he is concerned about the cost issues. Chances are, he is very concerned because Type 2s are easily upset by competitive events. Suggest to him that your two companies form a cooperative effort to share sensitive cost information in the interest of determining if Tosho is undercutting cost.

Motivating Type 3s

When you approach Ed about the Tosho cost problem, don't be surprised if he demonstrates a passive attitude. He probably thinks it will go away in time. You must convince him that the problem is serious before he will share confidential cost information with you.

Motivating Type 4s

Like their Type 3 counterparts, Type 4s will not take the Tosho problem seriously because of their optimistic nature. Ed believes that Tosho is selling its product below cost to capture market share, but feels that it is just a short-term event. Tosho will eventually have to raise their prices to stay in business. He may be right, but if you can quantify the short-term risks that both of you face, Ed will be inclined to provide you with the information you need.

Headhunters

"Headhunter" is the title we've given to executive recruiters who try to steal your most valuable employees. In reality, nobody ever gets stolen away from a company unless she wants it to happen! The fact of the matter is that executive recruiters are responsible for placing more than 35 percent of the top executive positions in the country. You may not need a headhunter today, but it would be beneficial for you to keep a couple of them motivated just in case you need one tomorrow.

The Situation

Susan is the senior executive recruiter retained by a Fortune 100 company to find them a new vice president to replace Forest, who was forced to resign last month. As she studies the stack of resumes for the hundredth time, she can find nothing she dislikes about you. You have the brains, ambition, energy, and motivation to be anybody's vice president. You certainly look good on paper and you talked a good story during countless interview sessions. You're her client's top prospect for the job.

Weary of the long hours and months that have been spent on the recruiting process, Susan calls her associate recruiters into her office for a hastily held meeting. "Let's get this show on the road and extend an offer to our top candidate. The company's president has authorized the offer. Do you all agree on our first choice?" They all agree that you are the best person for the job. Susan picks up the phone and calls you at home. When you answer the telephone and hear her offer, you are caught off guard. For several personal reasons, you're no longer interested in either the position or the company. However, you want to motivate Susan to keep you in mind for future executive positions that may interest you. That will not be an easy task in view of the fact that she will lose a $25,000 recruiting fee when you decline her offer.

Motivating Type 1s

To survive in their profession, Type 1 headhunters have to be action-oriented individuals. By turning down the job offer that Susan presented to you, you have disrupted her action-oriented style of work.

Explain to her why the job offer was not a good fit for you and she will respond favorably.

Motivating Type 2s

Type 2s are moody, and by turning Susan's job offer down, you have not done anything to improve her mood. Assure her that your decision was strictly personal and that it had nothing to do with her. You might reinforce your statement by telling her that you plan to use her services in the future.

Motivating Type 3s

Susan probably thinks that you turned down the job offer because of something she did. Because she is unsure of what happened, take the time to explain to her why you turned down her offer and assure her that it had nothing to do with her.

Motivating Type 4s

Fun-loving Type 4s don't have any fun when they lose big orders. To help Susan get back on track, compliment her about the quality of her professional services and assure her that you intend to use her services in the future.

Unscrupulous Vendors

Motivation, self-esteem, and integrity. They are all part of the same package that we try to put into our respective organizations. When someone steps onto our turf and displays unscrupulous behavior, it's like waving a red flag in front of a raging bull. Our first reaction is to eliminate the intruder with whatever means are at your disposal. However, understanding why some people act the way they do and initiating constructive action to correct the problem may be in order and will make you a much stronger manager.

The Situation

"Are you sure that your numbers are right? Twenty-five percent of Ace Printing's invoices that we have received over the past two months overcharged us for their services?" You hang up the phone, reflect on what your accounts payable supervisor has just told you, and decide to take a stroll outside to cool off. Ace has been a vendor with your company for more than 22 years and you have never encountered a problem like this before. It would be easy to find another printer, but you decide to rise to the challenge and find out what's going on. You call Ace's general manager, Sharon.

Motivating Type 1s

When you mention the problem to Sharon, she becomes very argumentative. This is a Type 1 trait, so exercise patience and try to get her to address the problem, rather than arguing with her. If she refuses to address the problem, you will have to tell her you will be forced to terminate your relationship with her company. That tactic will motivate her to address the problem and work out an acceptable solution with you.

Motivating Type 2s

Types 2s will be overly sensitive to the fact that you have discovered Ace's significant billing error. After Sharon apologizes to you for the 10th time, ask her what she intends to do to correct the problem. Listen carefully to her answer to determine if you want to continue doing business with her company. If Sharon offers constructive ideas to eliminate the problem, continue working with her to ensure a favorable ongoing relationship.

Motivating Type 3s

Sharon will quickly accept your billing error accusation. This may lead you to believe that she knew about the problem all along. If she did, you should terminate your relationship with Ace Printing. However, because of her Type 3 impatience for detail, Sharon may honestly not be aware of the problem and may deserve a second chance to correct it. Openly discuss with her steps that she can take to become more cognizant of what's going on in her organization.

Motivating Type 4s

Type 4s are afraid of facts. When you approach Sharon about the problem, she'll tell you that it's impossible. If you invite her over to see your records, she'll make up whatever excuse is necessary to avoid facing the facts. As a last resort, tell her that if she does not take the time to review your records to confirm the problem, then your relationship with Ace Printing is over. The use of this extreme measure will motivate Sharon to review the records and acknowledge the problem. Mutually agree on the steps your organizations must take to resolve the problem.

(?) *Help:* Unscrupulous vendors act similarly to con artist managers. Review the section on page 211 for motivational techniques that may further assist you in dealing with unscrupulous vendors.

Angry Customers

Lots of managers chatter away about the importance of keeping customers satisfied. But Frank Meeks, owner of a 42-store Domino's Pizza chain, thinks that employees have difficulty committing to abstractions. So he spells it out for them. Employees are taught the dollar consequences of losing a customer. He explains, "Our customers do business with us at least once a week, spending close to $500 annually, not including your tips. That's $2,500 over five years, which is what it costs us if they leave us because they are unhappy. And the unhappy customer tells about a dozen people about their negative experience, multiplying the damage even further." Not all problems disappear by educating people, but it sure beats doing nothing, as you will see in this section.

The Situation

When Susan calls you and tells you she is disgusted with the way she has been treated by your customer service department in her attempt to return a defective computer you sold her, you decide to look into the situation. Susan is the CEO at a company that orders more than $750,000 of computer hardware from you annually.

Motivating Type 1s

Type 1s respect immediate action. When you call Susan, tell her that the customer service person she contacted has been reprimanded and that her defective computer will be replaced. Type 1s expect immediate satisfaction and that statement should neutralize Susan's anger over this instance.

Motivating Type 2s

Type 2s can be very arrogant and chances are that 100 percent of the problem did not belong to your customer services department. Under the best of circumstances, Susan is difficult to handle. Nevertheless, if you are sincere with her when you tell her you have taken corrective action to prevent the problem from occurring again, she'll be pacified when you give her a Return of Merchandise Authorization (RMA) number.

Motivating Type 3s

When you approached your customer service people about Susan's complaint, they will tell you they had no idea that there was a problem with Susan. As far as they were concerned, they issued her an RMA to return the defective computer per her request and met each of her demands. Their documentation backs up their statements. Type 3s can become overtly judgmental. In this instance, Susan perceived that she was not getting the attention that she deserved, when in fact she was. Tell her that!

Motivating Type 4s

If you have an angry Type 4 customer on your hands, then chances are that someone in your customer service department had to go out of their way to irritate her. Type 4s do not get angry easily. Susan will accept whatever apology you offer her. Find out who in your organization irritated her and correct the problem.

Attorneys

It may be expensive to hire attorneys to convert agreements into legally binding contracts, but there are several compelling reasons to do it anyway. Vague contracts can come back to haunt you by plunging your company into major legal battles down the road. Randall Wise, legal counsel for IBM's Lotus Development Corporation, says that, in his experience, deals have been killed or prices lowered because of vague contracts or informal agreements. It costs money to clean things up after the fact and that cost could come right out of your organization's bottom line. If you can't afford the legal expense of drafting every agreement, have your lawyer develop boilerplate contracts that will help you to at least get by. How do you motivate your attorney to do what needs to be done without costing you a fortune?

The Situation

It has been a tough year on your organization as you approach the last month of your fiscal year. Somehow through all of the ups and downs, you've managed to keep your expenditures in balance with your budget. To cap everything off in style, you have negotiated a contract with one of your most prestigious customers who sent over the final draft of the contract for your signature. His company is six times the size of yours and you know his legal beagles pore over every word of the document, which you cannot afford to do. You've got $1,000 left in your legal fund. When you call your corporate attorney, Gavin, he enthusiastically invites you over to his office to review the contract. How will you motivate him to give you the maximum amount of legal support for the minimum amount of dollars you have to spend?

Motivating Type 1s

Challenge the aggressive side of Gavin's Type 1 personality by telling him up front that your customer has spent several thousand dollars in legal fees to review the contract. You only have a thousand. Can he help you? Stand back and watch Gavin accelerate into action.

Motivating Type 2s

Type 2 attorneys tend to be perfectionists. You don't have the funds to make sure every "i" in the contract is dotted. Tell Gavin to concentrate on the big picture because that is all that you can afford.

Motivating Type 3s

Type 3s are very adaptable individuals. You should have no problem getting Gavin to focus on your immediate needs, once you explain your budget constraints to him.

Motivating Type 4s

If Gavin has a Type 4 personality, be on guard when you meet with him. Type 4s are very outgoing and talkative individuals, and if he has the clock running when you meet with him, you're the one who's paying for all of that talk. Restrict the conversation to the business at hand if you want to get the most out of your legal funds.

Consultants

Ray McCormick, CEO of American Sports Inc., has weathered three different consulting firms during his company's 15-year history. The experience has taught him a valuable lesson. "Anyone who is thinking about establishing a lasting relationship with a consulting firm should be prepared to commit at least 10 percent of their time to the consultants if they want to benefit from the relationship. Otherwise, they won't get the right people involved in helping to run their business." McCormick followed his own advice when he set up his latest consulting team. Although the team formally meets four times a year, McCormick meets with each consultant privately between sessions.

One of his most time-consuming functions in the process is deciding on what issues should be placed on the quarterly agendas, and then compiling the background information the consultants need to be responsive. Does McCormick's time with his consultants take away from the time he needs to run the company? No, because his consultants have become an active part of his company's operations.

The Situation

If a board of directors pays off in consulting advice when you're planning your company's future, then why not assemble one that's temporary, like a consulting team to help you with the growth of your organization? The more you think about it, the more sense the idea makes. You want to create a five-year strategic plan for your organization; one that is dynamic and can be quickly modified as events dictate. Although your management team will be intricately involved in creating the plan, you want outside consultants to provide an independent and unbiased review of it on an on-going basis. To round out the team, you decide to select one consultant from each of the four personality types. The contributions that you can expect from each of the personality types are summarized below.

Motivating Type 1s

Your Type 1 consultant will add force and purpose to your team. Her positive and assertive personality traits will require little coaching on your part to make sure that she is on the right track. Business teams are always enhanced by a well-balanced Type 1.

Motivating Type 2s

Type 2 consultants are highly motivated when they are allowed to commit to a relationship. Because you want to establish a long-term commitment with a consulting team, your Type 2 member will be your strongest advocate. Type 2s enjoy team working environments and will give freely of themselves to ensure the success of the team.

Motivating Type 3s

The gentle nature of your Type 3 consultant will shine through when the other team members are at odds with each other. Your Type 3 member will be the stabilizing force on your team.

Motivating Type 4s

Your Type 4 consultant will prove to be a spirited and excited member of your team who has an innate ability to be happy. His attitude will allow him to appreciate what he has rather than what he lacks. He'll constantly bolster the spirit of your team.

Auditors

Most managers view auditors as annoying headaches. However, the truly astute manager realizes the valuable function the auditor performs. You can't solve a problem until you know you have one, which is the precise function of an auditor—looking for and identifying hidden problems that deserve management attention. In most cases, you have no control over selecting the audit firm or individual auditor. The decision is usually made by the accounting department or an executive committee. Your mission then is to motivate the auditor to provide you with a briefing on her findings before the audit report is submitted to upper management.

The Situation

Ever since your company went public three years ago, you've been forced to submit to annual audits, where someone you don't know comes into your organization and rummages through every piece of paper she can get her hands on in her neverending search for something you did wrong. This year they brought in Rachel. When she was introduced to you, all she said was, "When can I get started?" The first day of the audit did not go well as Rachel proceeded to alienate everyone in your organization. You don't need that, and worse yet, if the situation continues to degenerate, you know that Rachel will do everything she can to slam your organization. What can you do to motivate her to work with you rather than against you?

Motivating Type 1s

When you meet with Rachel after her first day on the job to discuss her relationship with your organization, she starts ridiculing everything that she believes is wrong with your organization. You guessed that she was a tactless Type 1, and you were right. If you want to take immediate control over the situation, remind her that auditors are paid by your company to provide a service, and if you are unhappy with that service, it will be discontinued.

Motivating Type 2s

Type 2s can be very difficult, if not impossible, to please. Rachel is no exception. She has been given whatever she wants but she never seems to be satisfied. She is always asking for more. To neutralize the negative impact that this is having on your people, tell Rachel that all of her requests must first be approved by you. She won't like it, but it will reinforce your authority within the organization.

Motivating Type 3s

Rachel continues to demonstrate the stubborn traits of a Type 3 and is driving the people in your organization crazy. If she can't find a problem in a particular area, she'll refuse to move on to the next audit issue until she finds something. A purchase order for $35 did not have a second signature on it. She wrote up a three-page violation report on the mishap. Your best approach to motivate Rachel is to diplomatically point out to her how insignificant the $35 purchase was in comparison to the thousands of purchase orders your organization processes each week.

Motivating Type 4s

When you try to pin Rachel down as to what areas in your organization she wants to review, she won't tell you because she is an uncommitted Type 4. This is not acceptable. As the manager of the organization, you have every right to know what areas she will be auditing. Tell her that she cannot begin the audit until you have that information. She'll quickly provide you with the information you need.

Stockholders

As a company grows, it becomes harder and harder to keep track of who is responsible for what. You have people constantly crossing functional lines and external investors demanding to know what is going on. In the past few years, stockholders have become a very savvy group. Armed with the Internet, they have the capability to monitor, on a daily basis, the financial progress of their investment. They'll even tap into their company's Web site to learn about new product and service releases, find out who's been promoted, and what's going on from the inside! Today's average stockholder is a very informed person!

The Situation

Although you're getting tough, it's time to get tougher. In spite of all that you have accomplished in your organization, the board of directors and the stockholders are still dissatisfied with your company's lackluster financial performance. In an era of endless restructuring, downsizing, and rightsizing, the company's dismal financial picture hasn't changed. You finally take the time to listen to what your marketing department has been trying to tell you ever since you joined this company and you abruptly realize that your customers have changed enormously in the past few years. Their product demands are changing, and the shift in the global economy has given them unbelievable power to command exactly what they want. You've been asked to address an angry group at tomorrow's stockholders meeting. Your mission is to convince them that the current rightsizing plan will restore the company's profits once it is implemented. Before the meeting, you want to determine how you will strategically address each of the four personality types that will be present.

Motivating Type 1s

Task-oriented Type 1 stockholders will want to know what specific steps will be implemented to resolve the company's profitability problem, when the steps will be implemented, and when they can expect to see the results. Concentrate your comments on short-term tasks where results can be seen at the end of the next full quarter.

Motivating Type 2s

Your analytical Type 2 stockholders will like what you tell the Type 1s about the action-oriented plan you are about to implement. But they will register their concern over whether it's the right plan. If you explain to them how the plan was selected, you will eliminate their concerns.

Motivating Type 3s

Your Type 3 stockholders will not demonstrate the impatience that you will witness from the Type 1 and 2 stockholders. Type 3s are patient individuals if they are given a viable reason for their patience. If you tell them that the tasks you are about to implement took time to develop after you had considered several alternatives, you'll satisfy their reason to be patient while you implement your tasks.

Motivating Type 4s

Type 4 stockholders are normally trusting individuals whose trust in your company has been shaken by its recent profit problems. To restore their trust, you need to give them something that they can latch on to. Show them how the actions that you are taking will favorably impact the bottom line of the company.

Summary

Your success as a manager depends as much on the relationships you develop outside your organization as it does on those within your organization. If you are not adept at effectively handling situations that are outside of your immediate organization, such as angry subcontractors and customers, your value as a manager will be significantly reduced. In this chapter, we provided you with a variety of situations to consider and offered several solutions that you could employ to bolster your worth as a manager. In the final analysis, always be cognizant of good outside relationships. They are like insurance policies in the career world—you never know when you may need to call one for a reference or a job!

Chapter 11

Staying Totally Motivated

There are several premises on motivation that underlie the theme of this book. We started with the basic premise that people generally fall into one of four personality types, as we choose to call them. And depending on what their respective personality types are, different motivational techniques can be employed to more effectively motivate one personality type over another. However, despite their personality differences, all people share three common motivational drives:

1. People have reasons for everything they do. They do not act blindly and, in fact, will set up goals in one fashion or another in their attempt to get what they want.

2. People are generally selfish. They'll choose to do something because they believe it is good for them. Although their behavior is directed toward goals, each goal must offer something that's good for them or the goals will quickly be discarded.

3. Whatever goals people choose to pursue, they must be attainable. People do not simply choose a course because it has value to them. If they discover that their goal is not attainable, they'll stop pursuing it.

You as a manager have the unique ability to offer goals that will motivate your employees. You have the opportunity and responsibility to increase your employees' expectations of reaching their goals and enhancing their personal situations, which is the essence of good management. It's the fun part of management that should drive your enthusiasm and personal motivation every day. There are numerous roles you can play to motivate everybody around you. Good managers recognize that their success is directly dependent upon the success of the people who work for them, which is influenced largely on how effectively they apply motivational techniques.

Let's review some of the principles that are behind staying totally motivated. To begin, managers have the assigned responsibility of motivating everybody who has an influence on the success of their organization, internally or externally. As the principle motivator, you can only accomplish this task if you are totally motivated yourself. We learned that every person's motivation is influenced by three primary factors:

1. Her personality type.
2. Her perception of the person who is trying to motivate her.
3. Her desire to achieve goals that are personally meaningful.

We also know that a manager's success as a motivator depends on three primary factors:

1. His understanding and recognition of the person's personality characteristics.
2. His accurate perception of the situation that demands the use of the right motivational techniques.
3. His follow-up to ensure that the motivational techniques employed are working.

And finally, we know that a person's reaction toward your attempt to motivate her depends on three factors:

1. Her orientation toward change, which depends on her personality type.
2. Her values and understanding of what she needs to do to become motivated.
3. Her perception of what others will think if she does or does not change.

To maintain motivation throughout an organization, the totally motivated manager doesn't just talk the talk, but walks the walk, through the hallways and into every crevice of his organization where he is always demonstrating by example. As a manager, you should constantly be setting examples that others can see and touch. Your constant level of enthusiasm, your drive, and your relentless pursuit of your goals all set the tone for motivation throughout your organization.

Your day-to-day management job revolves around a series of human interactions that require the use of different motivational techniques and strategies. Your motivational strategies are dependent upon your understanding of how people think, what turns them on, and what turns them off. You must constantly increase your awareness of everyone who touches your organization. How are the people you work with feeling? Learn all you can about these people by asking them questions, listening to what they have to say, and observing their nonverbal behavior. Determine what type of personality they have so that you can begin to apply motivation techniques that are tailor-made for their particular personality.

As you apply the motivational techniques that we discussed in this book, observe more than what people have to say. Observe their voice inflections, speaking manner, eye contact, facial expressions, posture, and self-confidence. When you are confident that you understand the person you want to motivate and know their personality type, seize the opportunity to motivate them. Don't wait until tomorrow or allow distractions to get in your way. A totally motivated manager motivates everyone who can help improve the overall performance of the organization. When you instill this practice into your management style, you'll be amazed at how productive your people will become, how easy it will be to get others to help, and how totally motivated you'll become in the process.

About the Author

David Rye is the author of a number of books, including *The Corporate Game, The Entrepreneurial Game, Two for the Money, Starting-Up,* and *The Vest Pocket Entrepreneur.* After receiving his MBA in 1970 with honors from Seattle University, David formed Computech Corporation, a company that specialized in the development of computer hardware and software. By the end of its third year, Computech was a $40-million-dollar-a-year company.

David accepted an acquisition offer from Seattle First National Bank in 1971 and remained with the company as general manager until 1975, when the company achieved annual sales of more than $175 million. For the next 10 years, David was the general manager for two NYSE companies: Damon Corporation and Ventura Corporation.

In 1985, he formed Western Publications, an outdoors book publishing company. He conducts motivational management seminars and runs an active management consulting business out of his Scottsdale, Arizona, office. If you would like to contact him, you can reach him at: 602-905-3023.

Index

D

Degrader managers, 218-220
Derringer, Harold, 85
Diplomatic players, 11, 18, 33-38
Divorce, 133-135
Domino's Pizza, 252
Downsizing, corporate, 155-158
Drug addicts, 139-142

E

Emotionally threatening
  behavior, 189-191
Employees
  motivating, 75-131
  needing a peer's, 185-187
Ethos, 199
Executives, motivating, 229-243

F

Fallout, bottom-line, 160-161
Fast track, heading down
  the, 239-241
Fear, 172
Federal Express, 247
Fighters, 95-98
Financially challenged
  employees, 143-145
Firefighter managers, 216-218
Forbes, 179

G

Gates, Bill, 50
Getty, J. Paul, 103
Goals, 19-20, 46
  failing to meet, 50-55
Grieving employees, 149-150

Group encounters, with
  executives, 232-234

H

Habits, employees' bad, 110-111
Haggar, 167
Hallway talkers, 103-106
Hazlitt, William, 236
Headhunters, 249-250
Helpless souls, 117-119

I

IBM, 253
Illicit encounters, with
  executives, 236-237
Improving character, 42-44
Inflation, 166-167
Insight, 247
Intimacy, 44

J

Jokers, 194-195

K

Kids, problems with, 70-72

L

Layoffs, 163-165
Learning to Manage Conflict, 191
Levi Strauss, 167, 173
Liars, 150-153
Lincoln, Abraham, 234
Logos, 199
Lone ranger managers, 214-216
Lost market share, 167-168

V

Vendors, unscrupulous, 250-252
Verbal attacks, 95-98

W

Weaknesses
  Type 1, 22, 24-25
  Type 2, 31-32
  Type 3, 36-37
  Type 4, 40-41

Wimp managers, 206-208
Wise, Randall, 253-254
Wriston, Walter, 117

Z

*Zapp the Lightning of
  Empowerment,* 128